ONION

ONION

The **essential cook's guide** to onions, garlic,
leeks, spring onions, shallots and chives

BRIAN GLOVER

southwater

This edition is published by Southwater, an imprint of
Anness Publishing Ltd, Blaby Road, Wigston, Leicestershire LE18 4SE
Email: info@anness.com Web: www.southwaterbooks.com; www.annesspublishing.com

Publisher: Joanna Lorenz
Executive Editor: Linda Fraser
Editor: Susannah Blake
Copy Editors: Bridget Jones (recipes) and Gwen Rigby (reference)
Indexer: Hilary Bird
Designer: Isobel Gillan
Photographer: William Lingwood
Food for Photography: Sunil Vijayakar (recipes) and Tonia Hedley (reference)
Stylist: Helen Trent

ETHICAL TRADING POLICY

At Anness Publishing we believe that business should be conducted in an ethical and ecologically sustainable way, with respect for the environment and a proper regard to the replacement of the natural resources we employ.As a publisher, we use a lot of wood pulp in high-quality paper for printing, and that wood commonly comes from spruce trees. We are therefore currently growing more than 750,000 trees in three Scottish forest plantations: Berrymoss (130 hectares/320 acres), West Touxhill (125 hectares/305 acres) and Deveron Forest (75 hectares/185 acres). The forests we manage contain more than 3.5 times the number of trees employed each year in making paper for the books we manufacture.Because of this ongoing ecological investment programme, you, as our customer, can have the pleasure and reassurance of knowing that a tree is being cultivated on your behalf to naturally replace the materials used to make the book you are holding.Our forestry programme is run in accordance with the UK Woodland Assurance Scheme (UKWAS) and will be certified by the internationally recognized Forest Stewardship Council (FSC). The FSC is a non-government organization dedicated to promoting responsible management of the world's forests. Certification ensures forests are managed in an environmentally sustainable and socially responsible way. For further information about this scheme, go to www.annesspublishing.com/trees

For all recipes, quantities are given in both metric and imperial measures and, where appropriate, in standard cups and spoons. Follow one set of measures, but not a mixture, because they are not interchangeable.
Standard spoon and cup measures are level. 1 tsp = 5ml, 1 tbsp = 15ml, 1 cup = 250ml/8fl oz.
Australian standard tablespoons are 20ml. Australian readers should use 3 tsp in place of 1 tbsp for measuring small quantities.
American pints are 16fl oz/2 cups. American readers should use 20fl oz/2.5 cups in place of 1 pint when measuring liquids.
Electric oven temperatures in this book are for conventional ovens. When using a fan oven, the temperature will probably need to be reduced by about 10–20°C/20–40°F. Since ovens vary, you should check with your manufacturer's instruction book for guidance. Medium (US large) eggs are used unless otherwise stated.

PUBLISHER'S NOTE

Although the advice and information in this book are believed to be accurate and true at the time of going to press, neither the authors nor the publisher can accept any legal responsibility or liability for any errors or omissions that may have been made nor for any inaccuracies nor for any loss, harm or injury that comes about from following instructions or advice in this book.

CONTENTS

INTRODUCTION

Members of the onion family have been cultivated ever since people started to form communities and grow their own food. Wild onions were gathered and eaten even before that. With a few exceptions, onions are now used in the cooking of almost every culture across the world. There is no country where this indispensable vegetable, in one form or another, is not now grown.

The evolution of the first, wild onions into the cultivated plants that we know today is not entirely clear. Many varieties, such as the common or garden onion, only seem to exist in their cultivated form and are not known to grow wild at all. There is a "missing link" in the development between the wild species of the plant and today's cultivated onions.

The mystery surrounding this transition suggests that the cultivation of onions occurred a very long time ago. People would seem to have perceived onions as good things to eat very early on in history, and onions are among the first plants to have been grown to add flavour to the human diet.

Onions belong to the allium family, which contains more than 300 species. Many of these different varieties are grown in gardens, some as ornamentals in flower borders, others as herbs and edible plants in vegetable patches. For a long time, botanists disagreed about whether the alliums belonged to the larger plant group of lilies (*Liliaceae*) or amaryllis (*Amaryllidaceae*), but now most place them in an order all of their own – the *Alliaceae*.

From the grower's point of view, alliums are very easy to identify. They form bulbs, or fleshy leaf bases; they have long, narrow, flat or tubular leaves, usually blue-green in colour; they have round, globular heads of flowers made up of many individual flowers; and all, to one degree or another, have the same unmistakably characteristic onion smell, especially when the bulb or leaves are damaged or broken.

pejorative associations have been made. They are forbidden to certain social groups, and are sometimes considered taboo or to have evil powers. The effect of their odour on the breath and sweat has led them to be labelled as vulgar, and unacceptable in polite society.

The relationship of the onion family to people throughout history is marked by these contradictory attitudes. While onions and other alliums are revered and praised and popular in dishes around the world, they are also frowned upon and rejected by many cultures and social groups.

Left: Alliums are an important crop in France as its traditional cookery has always made very good use of these vegetables, especially onions and garlic.

The pungent onion smell is caused by the presence of allicins – chemicals that include volatile sulphur compounds – which are released by the action of enzymes when any part of the plant is cut or bruised. It is these compounds that make the eyes water when an allium is chopped and which give onions that are used in cooking their characteristic flavour and bite.

The alliums' inescapable chemical signature has brought them to people's attention from the earliest times. Their smell and taste have made them into plants with an ancient and special place in the evolution of human culture.

From the earliest records, it appears that onions have always been regarded as important foodstuffs, and imbued with symbolic and religious meaning: they were grown in the best fields and can be found in important tombs and paintings. However, along with this reverence and value, a number of

Opposite: Onions have been cultivated for thousands of years. Their distinctive blue-green leaves and round flower heads make them easy to recognize.

Right: Delicately flavoured bunching onions and green onions are popular in Vietnamese cooking, and can always be found in their food markets.

ONIONS AND OTHER ALLIUMS
THROUGHOUT HISTORY

Whether praised or criticized, the onion family has attracted attention from the very earliest times. In different societies and at different periods in history, these vegetables have been bestowed with symbolic and spiritual meanings and have been considered vital in herbalistic and shamanistic medicine. The onion figures prominently in folklore, literature and even painting: few other vegetable families have such a value-laden history.

The actual origins of the onion are not known. However, they do seem to have been among the first families of plants to have been cultivated and selected. The recorded evidence suggests that onions were first cultivated over 5,000 years ago, around 3000 BC, in Asia Minor – the area of central Asia that now includes modern-day countries such as Iran, Pakistan and Afghanistan. These onions

would have been close relatives of the cultivated varieties that we are familiar with today.

Garlic probably began in this area too, and was then taken to Greece and on to Egypt. A type of garlic (*Allium sativum*) still grows wild in some parts of the Mediterranean, particularly on the island of Sicily. Shallots are also likely to have originated in central Asia and, according to food historian Alan Davidson, were known and used in India before they travelled to the Middle East.

Onions were also being cultivated in parts of China around 3000 BC. These would have been bunching onions (varieties of *Allium fistulosum*), rather than bulb onions. The Chinese also grew leeks, although these were a different variety from European leeks and derived from *Allium ramosum*.

At some point in the Han dynasty, dating 206 BC–AD 221, bulb onions (*Allium cepa*) and true garlic (*Allium sativa*) were introduced into China, probably from India. The bulb onion is still known as *hu-t'sung* or "foreign onion" in Chinese.

The cultivation of onions and garlic is mentioned in some of the early Vedic writings of ancient India. They are also noted in scribal records from Sumer (*c*.2400 BC), which record that the city governor's onions and cucumbers were grown in "the gods' best fields". The mentioning of the various alliums in these early texts shows that they were considered to be a most important crop.

Below: Onions and garlic have been an essential cooking ingredient in many countries, such as Brazil, for centuries.

ALLIUMS IN ANCIENT EGYPT

By the time of the ancient Egyptians, there is evidence that onions, garlic and leeks were being grown and consumed in huge quantities. Onions figure prominently in the decoration and hieroglyphics of one of the Egyptians' best-known legacies – the pyramids. They appear on the walls of the pyramids of Unas (*c.*2423 BC) and Pepi II (*c.*2200 BC) and onions were found in the eye sockets of the mummy of Rameses IV, who died in 1160 BC.

The Greek historian Herodotus, in 450 BC, reporting on his travels in Egypt, writes of inscriptions on the walls of the pyramids that show a breakdown of the cost of building these great monuments. Among the items listed is an entry showing how much was spent on "black radish, red onions and garlic" for the labourers on the pyramid at Giza.

Centuries later, the 17th-century diarist John Evelyn remarks in his *Acetaria* (1699) on "How this noble bulb was deified in Egypt ... and that whilst they were building the pyramids, there was spent on this root ninety tun of gold among the workmen". When the labourers' onion and garlic ration was cut, they are believed to have gone on strike.

Below: Egyptian labourers working on the pyramids received rations of onions, garlic, leeks and beer. It was believed that all the alliums provided physical strength and prevented disease.

Right: Onions have been found in eye sockets, armpits and body cavities of ancient Egyptian mummies, which were stored in decorative cases. This may have been because onions acted as antiseptics or because they were believed to have supernatural powers.

Above and above right: Onions are commonly depicted in the wall paintings in Egyptian tombs. It is thought they acted both as symbols of eternal life and as food and medicine for the journey into the afterlife.

The significance of alliums to the ancient Egyptians seems to have been very complex. Onions were placed in tombs as food for the journey into the next life and as symbols of eternity because of the circle-within-a-circle structure of the bulb. Many paintings show onions as part of religious symbolism. They were also known as powerful antibiotics and antiseptics. Labourers were fed on onions, leeks and garlic as these vegetables were believed to keep them fit and well for their manual work.

There is evidence also that the lingering smell of the onion in the body had great significance for the ancient Egyptians. The passage of the onion smell through the body was considered a sign of good health and fertility in women; though it was taboo for certain priests to eat or smell of onions.

The onion family was also popular with the Egyptians' neighbours, the Hebrews. In the Bible in Numbers XI:5, the Israelites led out into the desert by Moses complain about how hungry they are, and remember "the cucumbers, and the melons, and the leeks, and the onions and the garlic", which they used to enjoy in their captivity in Egypt.

The association of alliums with this part of the eastern Mediterranean remained strong for many centuries. For instance, in many European countries, the name for shallots (*Allium cepa*, Aggregatum Group) is derived from the ancient Palestinian port of Ascalon. This was reflected in their old Latin name (*Allium ascalonicum*) given by the Romans. No doubt Ascalon was the place from which shallots were first imported to Rome, and the name stuck.

Centuries later, the tree onion (*Allium cepa*, Proliferum Group), and the shallot-related potato onion, were still both called Egyptian onions by the English and French.

Below: Onions and other alliums are mentioned several times in the Bible. The most famous occasion is when the Israelites recall the pleasures of eating onions, leeks and garlic before their flight from Egypt (Numbers XI:5).

ALLIUMS IN GREEK AND ROMAN TIMES

The classical Greeks used alliums too. Hippocrates (*c.*400 BC), who is credited with founding modern medicine, notes that onions, garlic and leeks were grown in kitchen gardens or harvested from the wild. The food historian Alan Davidson points out that a section of market in Athens was called simply *ta skoroda*, meaning "the garlic", suggesting that the trade in alliums was an important feature of everyday Athenian life. The alliums even merit mention in Homer's great epic poem, the *Odyssey*.

Like the Egyptian pyramid builders, the Greeks believed in the onion's ability to promote health, virility and potency. Onions were used to prepare athletes for games, and competitors not only ate onions but also rubbed onion juice over their bodies. Greek soldiers were fed on onions to develop a martial vigour, and it was said that the enemy always knew when the Greek army was advancing by the powerful smell of onions that preceded the arrival of the troops.

In Rome, bread and onions were the standard diet of the poor. Archaeologists excavating Pompeii have found onion-shaped cavities where onions were growing in gardens, just as the writer Pliny the Elder (AD 23–79) described in his *Historia Naturalis*.

Because onions played such a vital role in the diet of the poor in Rome, they were held in some contempt by sections of the wealthy élite. The priestesses of Cybele, for instance, refused entrance to their temple in Rome to anyone who smelt of garlic. The poet Horace considered the smell of garlic a mark of real vulgarity and called it "more poisonous than hemlock", and Juvenal mockingly writes of onions as "kitchen gods".

Leeks seem to have been universally popular at all levels of Roman society, which may well have been because they were milder and tainted the breath less. There are many leek recipes in Apicius' 1st-century *De Re Coquinaria*, a cookery book intended for the literate middle classes. Apicius was a shadowy figure, and there may have been more than one person known as Apicius involved in the book over a considerable period of time. The recipes show a great love of leeks, and to a lesser extent onions, in a range of sophisticated dishes that include Beets with Leeks in Raisin Sauce,

Below: As with the Greeks, the Roman army was fed on onions and garlic, and took them on their invasions. They are credited with introducing garlic, onions and leeks to Britain, Germany and Gaul.

Above: The Roman emperor Nero was nicknamed porrophagus *or "leek eater" because he ate so many of them in his belief that they helped his singing voice and oratory.*

Peppercorn Leek Sauce, and Quinces Stewed with Leeks. *De Re Coquinaria* contains few recipes for garlic, however, which suggests garlic was less popular with middle-class Romans.

The Romans not only cultivated and cooked with alliums, but are thought to have been instrumental in taking these vegetables into all parts of Europe.

While Romans enjoyed eating onions and other alliums, they did not imbue them with the same significance as the ancient Egyptians and the Roman satirist Juvenal (*c.*AD 60–140) mocks the Egyptians' contradictory beliefs:

*How Egypt has grown mad
   with superstition
She makes gods of demons as
   is well known
It is a deadly sin to eat an onion
But every clove of garlic has a
   holy power.
A pious country, and with fine
   houses
But every garden is overrun
   with gods.*

ALLIUMS IN THE MIDDLE AGES

After the Romans' introduction of edible alliums to other parts of Europe, these vegetables soon became established as an important part of the European diet. They were popular in the Middle Ages, especially among the poor. Even before the introduction of cultivated varieties, it is certain that wild alliums, such as rocambole (*Allium scordoprasum*) and ramsons (*Allium ursinum*), would have been gathered and eaten. The English words leek and garlic come from the Anglo-Saxon word *leac,* meaning plant, and *garleac,* meaning spear-shaped plant. In Anglo-Saxon, the leek was known as *porleac* and the onion *ynioleac.* Onions get their name from the Latin *unio* via the French *oignon* and Anglo-Norman *union.*

Alliums became an important crop in medieval Britain, particularly leeks, which were one of the few vegetables to withstand a normal winter unprotected. In the *Forme of Cury* (*c.*1390), a cookery book written for Richard II, a *salat* was made from *persel, sawge, grene garlec, chibolles* [Welsh onions], *oynouns and leek* all dressed with oil and vinegar. And *porray* (from *porrum,* the Latin for leek) was a white soup made from leeks, almonds and rice.

The trade in alliums was important in medieval Europe. Onions from Brittany and garlic from Picardy are recorded as having been sold in London food markets as early as the 13th century.

By Chaucer's time, in the late 14th century, it is obvious that leeks were considered commonplace, everyday fare. He often uses the phrase "Not worth a leke" to suggest something that is entirely worthless.

Because they were so hardy, leeks could be grown in the coldest places and are associated particularly with Scotland and Wales, becoming, in Wales, a symbol for Celtic doughtiness and survival. Legend has it that the Welsh wore leeks, like feathers, in their caps, as a badge of identification during their victory over the Saxons in AD 640. It is probable that these would have been wild alliums – ramsons or rocamboles maybe – rather than the familiar modern-day leeks. But by Shakespeare's time, the Welsh wearing of leeks on their national day – St David's Day, March 1 – had clearly become well established. In the play *Henry V*, Pistol taunts Fluellen about his Welshness by promising to knock "his leek about his pate upon Saint Davy's day".

To this day, leeks still figure as a part of Welsh identity. They are an essential ingredient in cawl, a comforting soup or stew of lamb and leeks, which may be considered traditional Welsh soul food. Championship leek growing is still a major competitive hobby in many areas

Alea.

G. namte c. m. s. f. i. 3'. melins er co. modice acuitatis. lunamentum, tossicis. nocumentum, expulsiue 7 cerebro. remono nocumentum. cum accetoso et oleo.

Left: In medieval herbals and medicinal manuscripts, many members of the onion family were recognized to have curative and therapeutic properties.

Left: In Chaucer's Canterbury Tales *the Summoner's vulgar character is shown by his love of garlic, onions and leeks.*

The ribald and lewd associations of onions and leeks started early in Britain. This Anglo-Saxon riddle dates from before the Norman conquest of 1066:

I stand erect and tall, well-rooted
I stand proud in bed
I am hairy below. Sometimes the
fair peasant's daughter ...
... grips my body and holds me
hard ...
I will bring tears to her eyes.

Above: An illustration of garlic from Pierre Jean Francois Turpin's Flore Médicale *showing the bulb structure.*

of south Wales. Most people, however, have taken to wearing the less odorous daffodil on St David's Day.

Although onions were important in dietary and medicinal terms in medieval Europe, the Roman inhibitions and prejudices about how onions smell and the effect they have on an individual's moral character also prevailed.

Throughout the Middle Ages, alliums were associated with vulgarity. For the Egyptians and Greeks, the alliums were thought to promote strength, fertility and vigour, and it was only a short step until onions became associated, in ribald terms, with licentiousness and sexual prowess. In the 14th century, Chaucer's lecherous Summoner in *The Canterbury Tales* is described thus:

Wel loved he garleek, onions, and
eek lekes,
And for to drinken strong wyun, reed
as blood.

Similarly, in William Langland's *Piers Plowman*, an allegorical poem dating from the 14th century, Gluttony is offered "a pound of garleek" as an inducement to step into the ale-house rather than go to church.

In France, the various members of the onion family were also associated with sexual potency. King Henry IV, for instance, was commonly reputed to have been baptised with garlic water, so prodigious was his sexual potency and so strong his breath.

Within late-medieval philosophy, edible bulbs such as garlic and onions were considered among the least noble of food plants. Existence was structured into a Great Chain of Being, a hierarchy which placed God at the top and inanimate objects, such as plants, at the bottom. All creation was ascribed a level in this hierarchical way of seeing the world and bulbs were placed at the very bottom.

THE ALLIUMS' FALL FROM GRACE

Despite their associations with the poor, vulgar and lecherous, onions, garlic and leeks continued to be popular in British cooking until the 17th century. Eating them uncooked, however, began to be frowned upon and was seen as a distinct social taboo, particularly for women and those who held social pretensions or aspirations.

Towards the end of the 17th century, there was a noticeable rise in the social prohibition against garlic, the most odourous of the alliums. The diarist John Evelyn, a great grower and eater of vegetables, wrote a treatise on salads as a preface to his *Acetaria* in 1699. Regarding "garlick" he writes: "we absolutely forbid it entrance into our salleting, by reason of its intolerable rankness, and that made it so detested of old … to be sure it is not for ladies' palates, nor those who court them".

Below: In some sections of society onions were considered as only fit for poor people as in this scene of humble living called 'Preparations for Lunch' by Bernard Lepicie.

Above: Towards the end of the 17th century, alliums became unpopular in genteel society and tended to be associated with the poor and vulgar. Although onions were still used in cooking, they were rarely used as a main ingredient in their own right.

Throughout the following centuries, garlic features little in British cookery books, and although onions continue to appear in countless dishes, they rarely figure as a main ingredient in their own right. In Hannah Glasse's *The Art of Cookery Made Plain & Easy* (1747) onions are pickled, stewed, "ragoo'd with cucumbers" and made into a pie. Garlic, however, is not included. Leeks are not mentioned at all by Glasse. As with onions and garlic, they had become associated purely with peasant food and thought unsuitable for the middle classes (at which audience most 18th- and 19th-century cookbooks were aimed). Isabella Beeton, the great

bastion of the 19th-century middle-class kitchen, sums up the doubtful regard in which leeks were held when she advocates boiling them really well or else "they will taint the breath".

Throughout Anglo-Saxon Europe and much of the United States, the social taboo surrounding the effect of onions and garlic on human breath and sweat lasted for almost three hundred years. Undoubtedly, onions, leeks and, to a lesser extent, garlic were still eaten, but to smell of them was considered socially impolite and a mark of low breeding. In countries outside Europe and the United States, similar social taboos were attached to the eating of onions and other alliums. For example, in Japan, to smell of onions or garlic has traditionally been perceived as being discourteous and has a great social stigma attached to it. Japan is still the one country in Asia that makes very little use of garlic in its cooking.

From the time of the earliest records, onions, and in particular garlic, have been accused of exciting sexual and libidinous desires: Egyptian priests were denied garlic precisely because they had to remain celibate. To this day Kashmiri Brahmans and Jains are forbidden from eating strong-tasting foods, in particular onions and garlic, because they are thought to heat the blood and have the ability to inflame carnal desire. Some Chinese Buddhists avoid the prohibited "five strong-smelling vegetables" for the same reasons.

The Hindu sacred texts place great emphasis on the idea that a man is what he eats and rules are given for the right foods. The three upper castes, Brahmans, Kshatryas and Vaisyas, should avoid onions and garlic in their diet. The Sanskrit poem, *Mahabharata*, suggests that onions and garlic should not be eaten by "honourable people".

Left: Garlic became very unpopular in countries such as Britain towards the end of the 17th century, but garlic and bay sellers such as this one were still able to eke out a living in France where garlic was not frowned upon to such a great extent.

THE REHABILITATION OF ALLIUMS

Some countries in northern Europe maintained their antipathy towards onions and garlic but much depended on the general food culture of a society. In the 1580s, when the German ambassador of the Holy Roman Emperor visited the court of the Byzantine emperor Nicephoros II, his entourage was appalled by the food and the smell of garlic on the emperor's breath. For the northern Europeans, the great consumption of large quantities of vegetables, including onions and garlic, was little short of scandalous. In large parts of northern Europe, especially in comparatively rich countries such as Britain, Germany and the Netherlands, good food was synonymous with meat.

However, many cultures, typically those around the Mediterranean, never fell out of love with the onion family. It was for this reason that the vegetable-loving cultures of the Mediterranean region were for centuries looked down upon as gastronomically uncivilized.

In France, in particular, onions, garlic, leeks and shallots – in fact the whole allium tribe – remained extremely popular at almost every level of society. Brittany, a region well known in the 20th century for its bicycling onion sellers, and the west of France were particularly linked with cooking with onions and garlic.

The French trade in onions and garlic began early; onions from Brittany were imported to London as early as the 13th century. The trade continued until well into the 20th century, with onion sellers cycling around southern English towns selling their familiar strings of onions and garlic from their bicycles. Food writer Lindsay Bareham notes that the last of these onion sellers was still working in the mid-1990s.

Onions and garlic were, and still are, an intrinsic part of much French provincial and peasant cooking. Garlic festivals, such as the garlic and basil fair at Tours on St Anne's Day, 26th July, occur throughout France, usually when the new season crop has been harvested. Even when the alliums were at their most unpopular in Britain, in the 18th–19th centuries, onions were still celebrated in France. As food historian John Ayto points out, the classic sauce, *sauce soubise*, was named after an 18th-century French general and courtier Charles de Rohan, Prince de Soubise, showing that aristocracy did not see any shame in being associated with onions.

In sophisticated Paris, onions had their ups and downs but by the early 19th century they were actually thought quite *de rigueur* in polite society. The poet Shelley, writing of a trip to Paris, seems quite delightedly shocked at the

Above: In the early 19th century, Parisian society considered onions and garlic positively fashionable.

thought of the onions' fashionable status: "What do you think? Young women of rank eat – you will never guess what – garlick!"

In Spain, too, onions were consumed with gusto despite the fact that certain elements of society frowned upon the practice. An old Andalusian saying states that "*Olla sin cebolla, es baile sin tamborin* [a stew without onion is like a dance without music]". In Cataluña they celebrate the new crop of their local, large green spring onions – *calçots* –

Onions in the United States
Columbus, and then the first pilgrims, took onions and garlic to North America, while the Spanish introduced them to Central and South America. But many varieties of wild onion, leek and garlic grew indigenously in North America and were used by native Americans in cooking and, especially, in medicine. Chicago was named after the Illinois Indian name for "the place which smells of onions". *Chicagoua* – the plant that gave Chicago its name – was probably a form of wild garlic or ramps (*Allium tricoccum*). This species and other wild onions, such as *Allium cernuum* and *Allium canadense*, still grow profusely throughout North America. Père Marquette, the French Jesuit explorer and missionary, who camped on the shores of Lake Michigan in 1670, wrote of being saved from starvation by eating the various kinds of wild onion and garlic that grew there. Later generations of Americans took these plants to their heart, and much onion breeding took place in the first decades of the 20th century. The emphasis was on producing sweet, early-summer-cropping onions, which have a high water and sugar content. There was also a move towards producing low-sulphur and hence less smelly onions.

with a special feast called *la calçotada*. *La calçotada* consists of masses of green onions, grilled over charcoal and then served with salsa romesco, made from chillies, nuts and garlic.

Despite the popularity of alliums in such countries, these odorous vegetables were slow to return to favour in England. Onions, shallots, even leeks, but most especially garlic, remained fairly unpopular and became associated with "foreign food". Writing in 1861, in her hugely influential *Book of Household Management*, Isabella Beeton observes rather sniffily of garlic: "It was in greater repute with our ancestors than it is with ourselves ... on the Continent, especially in Italy, it is much used, and the French consider it is an essential in many made dishes". Mrs Beeton gives only one dish that includes garlic – a Bengali recipe for hot mango chutney – highlighting the influence of Indian cooking on the English kitchen.

Why did the alliums stay so popular in some cultures but attract such great opprobrium in others? One answer may lie in the nature of cooking in different cultures. In northern Europe, especially England, and in North America, regional, peasant and rural cooking lost ground

Above: During World War II when onions were in short supply in Britain, leeks became even more important.

in the face of a growing move towards industrialization as people moved to big cities in search of work. Alliums have always been associated with regional, peasant cooking. These traditions remained strong in all the Mediterranean countries and had a great influence on the middle-class cooking of the day. In Britain, cooking was effectively cut off from its rural and peasant roots and a "genteel" style of middle-class cooking – ironically influenced by notions of French *haute cuisine* – was adopted in its place.

By the late 20th century, the vegetable-based Mediterranean diet, including lots of onions and other alliums, was vaunted in Britain and the United States as a much healthier way of eating. This had always been the case in poorer areas of Europe, where onions have always remained a vital and much celebrated way of injecting flavour into the diet.

Left: French onion sellers, like this one depicted by Stanhope Alexander Forbes, were once a common sight in many English towns.

ALLIUMS OVER THE LAST HUNDRED YEARS

Apart from long-standing religious and social taboos, the history of the onion family over the last century or so has been one of gradual rehabilitation. In the United States and Australia, the massive influx of immigrants from garlic-loving cultures (Greek, Italian, Hispanic), has had an effect. In Britain, the growing love affair with Indian "curries", especially after World War II, was important, too.

Italian and Greek food, both heavily garlic- and onion-reliant, came into great vogue in the 1960s. Food writer Elizabeth David, whose books on Mediterranean and French cooking were published in the 1950s and '60s, had a huge impact on breaking down the social taboo against garlic.

There had been a few earlier voices. *The Gentle Art of Cookery* (1925), written by Miss Olga Hartley and Mrs C. F. Leyel, included a whole section solely on onions, including soups, stuffed onions and a recipe for an Alsatian *gâteau aux oignons*. Mrs Leyel was the founder of Culpepper's herbalist shops, head of the Society of Herbalists, and was obviously an adventurous cook and traveller. She includes garlic as one of the essential ingredients in her "Alchemist's Storecupboard". In 1933, the cookery writer Ambrose Heath wrote his *Book of the Onion*: a whole book (albeit small) devoted to recipes containing onions as a major ingredient. But these were lonely voices.

As the century progressed, the old middle-class sanction against using (and hence smelling of) onions and garlic started to falter. By the 1960s

Below: Onions and bicycles have long been associated with each other because of the traditional French onion and garlic sellers who, even today, can be seen selling their produce.

onion-smelling breath or body odour became less of a problem than it may have been in previous centuries.

Nowadays, onions, garlic and leeks are celebrated as never before. Garlic and onion festivals are held in places as distant as the Isle of Wight in England, and Gilroy, California in the United States. New varieties of onion are constantly being developed and bred, providing a year-round supply. Some restaurants devote themselves to wholly garlic-based menus, introducing such unusual dishes as garlic ice cream. Thousands of websites on all members of the onion family have been launched.

Exciting discoveries are being made about the medicinal qualities of the alliums. Today, the onion family is perhaps more popular and considered more indispensable than at any other time in its long and complex history.

Above: Specialist growers selling many different kinds of garlic, shallots and onions are a familiar feature of French and Italian markets.

Right: These enormously long strings of garlic for sale at Korla market in the Kinjiang Province in China demonstrate the popularity and importance of this allium in Chinese cooking.

and '70s, using garlic in food became a mark of culinary sophistication and trendiness. The famous "garlic dinner", cooked by American chef Alice Waters in 1976 in her Berkeley restaurant Chez Panisse, launched a huge garlic revival in mainstream American food culture and was extremely influential in establishing the important Californian garlic-growing industry.

Whereas the taboo started in the 18th century as a middle-class attempt to mark themselves out from the lower classes, it was to be the middle classes themselves in the 20th century who started using garlic as a mark of their sophistication and extensive travel. No doubt, as the food writer Jane Grigson noted, standards of hygiene improved in the 20th century, and diets and digestion with them, so the issue of

MYTHS, FOLKLORE AND MEDICINE

Throughout their long history, all manner of special powers have been attributed to the onion family, especially to garlic, and many myths and taboos have built up around them. To some extent these have grown out of the alliums' potent medicinal properties.

ALLIUMS IN MYTH AND FOLKLORE

Priests, shamans and healers have used alliums throughout the ages, and it is inevitable that the onion family has been attributed mystical powers. The ancient Egyptians considered that the layered structure of the onion made it a symbol of eternity, and they were certainly aware of the onion's curative powers. For the Egyptians, the onion not only cured disease and gave vitality, it also replicated the cycle of life itself. As such, it was also a fertility symbol: used in tombs to grant souls a fertile afterlife; used to ascertain female fertility; and denied to priests who might be incited to lustful acts of procreation if they ate onions.

For the Greeks, too, alliums were bestowed with sacred significance and linked to the afterlife. Theophrastus records that garlic should be placed on the side of the road at crossroads as a gift to placate Hecate, goddess of the Underworld, and this practice was continued well into the 11th century AD when the Christian Church put a stop to it. In Homer's *Odyssey*, the power of an onion (probably *Allium moly*) allows Odysseus to enter the lair of Circe. A well-known creation myth of Turkish Muslims records that, when the devil was expelled from Paradise and fell to earth, garlic sprung up where his left foot landed and onions from where his right foot came to rest. An Indian legend concerning the origins of garlic tells that when King Rahu, lord of the demons, stole the elixir of life and was punished by the god Vishnu by being decapitated, garlic sprang from where his blood fell. To this day, the followers of Vishnu refuse to eat any alliums.

From ancient times, onions have always had something of a diabolic, other-worldly connection, but they also suggest the triumph of life over death.

Above: The many different members of the onion family, including garlic, leeks, shallots and chives, all contain allicins – compounds which are believed to have natural antibacterial and antifungal properties.

The devil in onions, present in their fiery bite and effect on the palate, was also thought to incite men to lust and carnal desires. Again and again during the Middle Ages, a connection is made between eating onions, drinking alcohol and sexual incontinence. Or, as Thomas Nashe put it in his book *The Unfortunate Traveller* (1594) "Garlic ... makes a man winke, drinke and stinke". This attitude towards the alliums persisted beyond the Middle Ages in cultures as disparate as Imperial China, caste-structured India and 19th-century Britain.

All these beliefs come into play in one of the best-known myths that surround the allium family – that of the vampire. This myth began in the 16th century in central and eastern Europe but culminates in Bram Stoker's late 19th-century classic, *Dracula*.

Above: In country districts, strings of garlic, such as these sold by a French garlic seller, were often hung on thresholds or on children's cradles to ward off evil spirits.

In the vampire myths, garlic wards off evil and protects potential victims against the undead. Traditionally, in Romania, garlic was used in amulets to protect against the evil eye. In Stoker's *Dracula*, the threshold, windows and hearth are all rubbed and strewn with garlic flowers to prevent Dracula from entering his victim's bed chamber. The hero is also offered garlic as a protective talisman by the peasants on his way to visit Dracula's castle.

In the 19th and 20th centuries, the story becomes a sexual allegory: virgins may protect themselves against male desire by using garlic – men do not like the objects of their desire to smell of garlic. Garlic's part in the Dracula myths brings together all the various qualities ascribed to the "stinking rose" through history. In this story we find garlic's other-worldly, dark associations; garlic's connection with sexuality and desire; garlic's quality as a life force in the face of death; and even its ability to fight off infection as a natural antibiotic.

THE ALLIUMS IN MEDICINE

Alliins, the chemical compounds that create allicins, which give all onions their characteristic smell, are also the source of their remarkable medicinal and curative qualities. Alliins are the thioallyl or sulphur compounds present in all alliums. These compounds are volatile, which means that they break down when any part of the plant is cut or bruised. When the cell walls are damaged and exposed to the air, the compounds are converted by enzyme action to diallydisulphides or allicins – which work as effective antibacterial and antifungal agents. Of the everyday culinary alliums, garlic, with its naturally low water content, has the highest concentration of alliins (1–2 per cent) and hence the greatest medicinal value.

Throughout history the health-giving properties of all the alliums, especially garlic, have been recognized by many writers and many cultures, especially in folk-medicine and herbalism. Garlic was thought of so highly as a medicinal herb that Galen, the Greek medical codifier of the 2nd century AD, labelled it the

Above: The ancient Egyptian Eber Codex, The Book of the Dead, *suggests garlic as a remedy for a wide variety of medical problems.*

poor man's theriac, or cure-all. This passed into medieval English as the "poor man's treacle" (or treat-all), and for many centuries garlic was used to treat a great variety of complaints. As John Trevisa, the 13th-century writer, says, "it [garlic] is cleped tryacle of cherles among auctours in olde tyme".

Early medicinal uses

The earliest texts to mention the use of onions as medicine are the 5,000-year-old Ayurvedic texts from India. Garlic is mentioned as a useful treatment for digestive disorders, throat and bronchial complaints and even for typhoid. The Egyptian *Eber Codex, The Book of the Dead*, is a medical work of therapies and cures from around 1550 BC. Garlic is again mentioned here as useful for treating many complaints, as diverse as headaches and the pains of childbirth. Throughout the classical and medieval period, writers again and again extol the curative properties of the alliums. The most common complaints mentioned include chest and bronchial problems

(Nero was not alone in thinking alliums improved the voice), worms, intestinal problems, bladder problems and lack of libido. They were also used to treat open wounds, to guard against infection from animal bites and to treat colds, headaches, haemorrhoids, sunburn and even leprosy.

The Greek Hippocrates (*c.*400 BC), the father of modern medicine, thought garlic good for wounds and toothache. Dioscorides, the Greek doctor who travelled with the Roman army (which was largely fed on onions, leeks and garlic) in the 1st century AD, notes its use against tapeworms and snake bites. He was also convinced that garlic could help clear the arteries and cure coughs. Pliny the Elder (AD 23–79) in his *Historia Naturalis* gives over 60 garlic remedies, including cures for bites by wild animals and low libido. This latter is a common theme in the use of garlic, and links in with the idea that all the onions excite the carnal appetites.

*Right: An early illustration of garlic (*Allium sativum) *showing the flowers and the mature bulb.*

Below: Hippocrates, the father of modern medicine, praised the healing powers of garlic and posited it as a cure for a great number of diverse ailments.

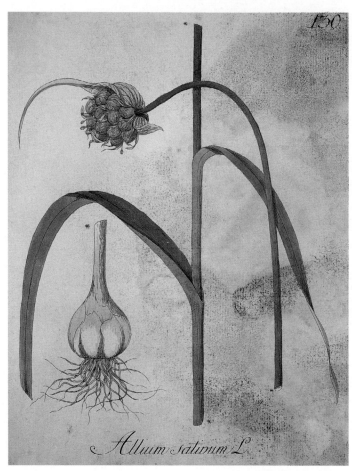

Allium sativum L.

Medieval medicine and beyond

These notions held by the Greeks survived well into the Middle Ages. The 14th-century French herbal *The Four Seasons of the House of Cerruti* claims that white onions help to bring forth milk in nursing mothers and promote virile semen in men, and the herbal also considers garlic to be an undoubted aphrodisiac. Food historian John Ayto quotes an observation from *Andrew Boorde's Dietary of Helthe* (1542), which claims that "onions do promote a man to veneryous [sexual] actes", much as the Roman writer Pliny had done centuries earlier.

Medical thought and practice was governed throughout the Middle Ages by the doctrine of the humours, which explained how humans interacted with the natural world. The humours were the four bodily fluids: blood, choler, melancholy and phlegm, which were thought to determine character and physical health. The four elements of fire, water, air and earth also had characteristic qualities: hot, moist, cold and dry respectively. All living things – plants, animals, human beings – were governed by one or more elements and displayed one, or a combination of, these qualities.

Onions were considered hot and moist and were thought to govern the blood, the humour of the sanguine personality. Garlic was considered hotter and drier and thought to be good for treating the cold and wet phlegmatic personality. In John Trevisa's 13th-century translation of *De Proprietatibus Rerum*, he says of garlic "if colerik men ete to moche therof it maketh the body to hoot … and is cause of madnesse and of frenesye", but later he admits its use: "and garlek abateth the ache of guttes aboute the reynes [period pains] also". John Evelyn, in his *Acetaria* (1699), observed that garlic was "dry toward excess … and more proper for our northern rustics, especially [those] living in uliginous and moist places. Whereas leeks are hot, and of vertue

prolifick … the Welch, who eat them much, are observ'd to be very fruitful". In the doctrine of humours, a plant's fecundity is thought to reflect its good effect on human fertility.

Other cultures also developed systems of categorizing the natural world and hence food. In China, the alliums are yang in the yin-yang balance of properties. Yang foods are male, dry and hot so, during the T'ang Dynasty (AD 618–907), garlic was endorsed as good for heating the blood and as a tonic. The Iranian "Araqi" classification ranks garlic as one of the hottest foods.

The alliums, especially garlic, have repeatedly been mentioned for use as treatments for open wounds, bites by venomous snakes and wild animals and cleansing the blood. Trevisa writes in

Above: Nicholas Culpepper, the 17th-century apothecary, extolled the curative virtues of onions and other alliums in his popular herbal, The English Physician.

the 13th century that garlic has "many maner vertu yfounde … to putte out venym and all venemous thinges". Thomas Tusser, the 16th-century writer of agricultural doggerel, says that "now leeks are in season, for pottage full good and spareth the milch-cow, and purgeth the blood". Nicholas Culpepper in his well-known 17th-century herbal remarks that onions "Provoke urine and women's courses, helps the biting of mad dogs and other venonmous creatures … [it] kills the worms".

There is also evidence that, in pre-Colonial America, native Americans used roasted wild onions and honey to neutralize snakebites and to help heal open wounds. Even as late as World War I (1914–18) garlic was used by the British as an antiseptic on a large scale, as noted by Mrs Grieve in her *Modern Herbal* (1931). The garlic was pounded to express the juice, which was then applied on swabs to open wounds to help staunch bleeding and prevent the wound from becoming infected.

Left: This medieval illustration shows the harvesting and bunching of garlic, which was believed to be good for treating a phlegmatic personality.

Alliums as preventives

In general, onions and garlic have been considered to be preventives and act as a general tonic against both infection and infestation. They are mentioned as preventives in outbreaks of the plague, for instance, both in France and England. The alliums' prophylactic properties were often linked with their use as talismans to ward off disease, rather than as remedies to be imbibed or rubbed on the body.

The Egyptian *Eber Codex* advocates wearing garlic around the neck as a way of driving out tapeworms. Greek and Macedonian mothers hung garlic around their babies' necks or cradles to ward off disease. In ancient China, onions, garlic and bunching onions were considered part of the "five strong-smelling foods" (*wu han*) and were hung on red cords at the threshold to protect the household against disease. John Evelyn (1699) considered garlic "a charm against all infection and poyson", even though he despised it in salads. Pre-colonial native Americans considered that wild onions worn around the neck protected the wearer from colds and bronchitis. Most famously, of course, a garland of garlic was supposed to guard the wearer against being attacked by a vampire. Even in garlic-phobic Japan, in the northern town of Tsukuba-Khinoya, there is an annual festival, which dates from the Heian period of more than 1,000 years ago, when garlic is hung at the entrance to the house to prevent disease crossing the threshold during the coming year.

Alliums in the modern diet

Many contemporary writers consider that the onion family, particularly garlic, should be an essential part of our diet. Alliums aid good digestion, maintain a balanced blood pressure and work as a general tonic to help stave off infection. Recent research seems to confirm most of the herbalist lore that has built up through the ages.

Left: With the growing interest in the healing potential of food, organically grown food, such as these leeks, is becoming more popular.

Below: Of all the members of the onion family, garlic in particular is renowned for its healing properties.

Above: Links have been made between garlic and cancer prevention, and experts agree that even a small amount every day will help strengthen the immune system.

There is evidence that garlic reduces blood pressure, helps lower LDL (low-density lipo-protein) cholesterol and may prevent the build-up of cholesterol within the arteries. Raw garlic has always been considered an effective antibiotic. There is evidence that although garlic is not as strong as modern antibiotics, the way in which it works is so different that it can kill strains of bacteria that have become antibiotic-resistant. Garlic and onions generally have great antifungal and antiviral properties, and they play their part in maintaining a healthy intestinal flora and fauna.

Research is also progressing to examine the link between garlic and cancer. Garlic certainly has antioxidant properties and contains selenium, which is known to strengthen the body's ability to resist cancer. Clinical tests have also shown that garlic reduces the size of certain tumours in animals or prevents them from growing. Most experts agree that even a small amount of garlic every day – say one clove – will help maintain good health and strengthen the immune system. Garlic can also help thin the blood and prevent blood clotting.

Lore, remedies and old wives' tales
• As a remedy for corns, bandage a cut slice of garlic over the corn and replace it every day until the corn drops off.
• A syrup made from garlic steeped in vinegar and honey is good for asthma, coughs and general bronchial problems.
• To soothe a dry and painful cough, take a spoonful of honey mixed with a little crushed raw onion or garlic.
• It was once recommended that a roasted onion be applied to the affected ear as a cure for earache; it was also said to be good for boils.
• All onions are good for getting rid of moles in the garden. Drop peeled garlic or cut onions into their holes.
• Chopped garlic, bandaged to the soles of the feet and renewed daily, was thought a remedy for smallpox and even leprosy.
• Cut garlic rubbed over the lips will prevent them being burned by the sun.
• Mixed with lard and applied to the chest or back as a poultice, garlic is thought good for whooping cough and other chest conditions.
• A cut onion will rid a room of other strong smells, such as paint.
• An Irish folk-belief is that garlic planted on a Good Friday will protect people from fever during the whole year.
• A cut onion is said to attract all infection from the air into it and will kill air-borne infection.
• To cure baldness, rub the cap of a cut onion mixed with honey on the bald patch until the skin reddens – then wait.
• According to Brewer's *Dictionary of Phrase & Fable*, the phrase "to know your onions" is probably derived from Cockney rhyming slang, as in "onion rings" – "things". However, some have suggested that it refers to the man who edited the *Oxford English Dictionary* – C. T. Onions.

The World of Onions

While we tend to think of onions as being more or less the same, there are many different
varieties, colours and sizes. Some are better suited to roasting, others to frying; some are
delicious cooked whole, others are better for chopping, slicing and eating raw. The same is
true of the other members of the onion family — especially shallots, garlic and leeks.
This fully illustrated reference section will help you to identify all the main varieties
of edible alliums and give guidance on how best to use them in the kitchen.

The Allium Family

There are more than 300 distinct species in the allium family, many of which have been used as food plants. For culinary purposes the best-known species are the onion (*Allium cepa*), the shallot (*Allium cepa*, Aggregatum Group), the leek (*Allium ampeloprasum* var. *porrum*), bunching onions (*Allium fistulosum* and *Allium cepa*, Proliferum Group), garlic (*Allium sativum*) and, finally, the various chives (*Allium schoenoprasum* and *Allium tuberosum*).

Onions, shallots, leeks and garlic are commonly known only in their cultivated forms. Although we do not know the wild forms of many of these plants, we can make informed guesses as to their origins. Many wild forms of edible alliums still exist around the world, as well as many varieties of allium that are purely ornamental.

The one thing that connects all the members of the allium family is their characteristic smell. Alliums contain chemical compounds known as alliins. When a plant is bruised or damaged, the alliins immediately begin to break down into the sulphur compounds known as allicins, which produce the instantly recognizable smell and flavour. The release of these volatile compounds can make us cry when we chop onions. If you wander through a woodland carpeted with wild garlic (*Allium ursinum*) in the late spring, the acrid,

pungent smell is almost overpowering. Place a bunch of unwrapped garlic chives in the fridge, and you will find that within a few hours the eggs, milk and butter will be tainted with their strong smell. Onions are some of the most potent flavouring ingredients available for use in the kitchen, so it is no wonder they have been used by cooks for countless generations.

Wild Alliums

Ramsons (*Allium ursinum*) are one of the commonest wild alliums in Britain and they grow in damp, shady areas throughout Europe. They form broad, fresh green leaves and have lacy heads of white flowers in late spring. The whole plant is very odorous and will affect the milk of any goats or cattle that graze on it. Ramsons used to be fed to chickens before they started laying, as a spring tonic and to "kick-start" them into productivity. The leaves are good wrapped around fish before grilling over charcoal. The flowers may be added to salads, and young leaves may be shredded into omelettes or rice dishes; they were commonly used in place of scarce onions during World War II. Ramsons have left their mark in a number of English place names, such as Ramsbottom in Lancashire and Ramsey on the Isle of Man.

Rocambole *Allium scorodoprasum* and *Allium sativum* var. *ophioscorodon* have both been called rocambole. The first is commonly called the sand leek, for it likes to grow in sandy soils; the second is a form of garlic. Both have coiled or twisted stems and grow widely across Europe. They have a good, mild flavour and were once exceedingly popular in salads and for flavouring cheese. John Evelyn, the 17th-century diarist and gardener who was quite against garlic, thought rocambole far more socially acceptable: "a clove or two of roccombo, of a yet milder and delicate nature, which by rubbing the [salad] dish only, imparts its vertue agreeably enough" (*Acetaria*, 1699).

Above: The pink-flowered wild sand leek has a mild, garlicky flavour, which has been popular with cooks for centuries.

Babbington leek or kurrat (*Allium ampeloprasum* var. *babbingtonii* or *Allium ampeloprasum* var. *kurrat*) is probably related to the elephant garlic (*Allium ampeloprasum*). It is grown in the Near East for its narrow leaves. The sectioned bulb may be used as a mild version of garlic.
Other wild onions that have been used in the kitchen are crow garlic (*Allium vineale*) in Europe; *A. canadense*, *A. tricconum* and *A. cernum* in America.

Left: The flowers of ramsons can be found in European woodlands in spring.

Left: Spanish, or yellow, onions are usually large and have a mild flavour.

ONIONS

These are all varieties of *Allium cepa*. Onions are grown for the bulb, formed by layers of fleshy, swollen leaf bases; the actual stem of an onion is the small layer of hard tissue at the top of the roots. The onion probably originated in western and central Asia, in an area stretching from modern-day Israel to India, and has been cultivated since the earliest times. It is likely that various kinds of onion were first cultivated around the Middle and Near East.

The uses of onions in the kitchen are myriad. They are used in the savoury cooking of almost every country and culture. They are fried, boiled, roasted, baked, stuffed and grilled.

There are many different kinds of onion and they are classified for kitchen use according to size, shape and colour.

Yellow onions

These are the most usual type of onion and are characterized by a light brown skin and a greenish white to pale yellow flesh. There are different varieties within this basic type but they are commonly known as Spanish onions, regardless of their place of origin; Bermuda is the similar generic title for this kind of large, mild onion in the United States. For culinary purposes, Spanish onions are usually large, round and mild. Other types of yellow onions include brown onions, which have thick brown skins, and French onions, which have a

stronger flavour. Generally, the younger and greener the onion, the more pungent the flesh. Several varieties of yellow onion have been favoured for the mild sweetness of their flesh, such as the Vidalia from the north-western states of America and the Maui from Hawaii. The Walla Walla, named after the town in Washington State where it was first grown, was brought to the United States by Corsican immigrants in the early 20th century. Most onions in the northern hemisphere are autumn-cropping from a spring sowing, but some varieties have been bred to overwinter from an autumn sowing and crop in summer. Of these, the Japanese varieties are best known in Europe. The Vidalia is a summer-cropping onion in America.

Below: Brown onions have a thick, brown skin.

Above: French onions tend to have a stronger, more pungent flavour than Spanish onions.

Uses in the kitchen Yellow onions are suitable for most kitchen purposes. Choose large round onions for baking, stuffing or cutting into rings. Longer or squatter onions are better for slicing or roasting whole. Some people consider them too strong to eat raw, although a mild yellow onion is good in potato salad or in marinated fish dishes, such as ceviche and soused herrings.

Uses in the kitchen
Red onions usually
have a much milder,
sweeter flavour than
yellow onions and they
are popular in salads; this
is, no doubt, also because of
their attractive pink-tinged flesh.
They are frequently used raw in
salsas, relishes, antipasti and
marinated dishes. Red onions
are also good roasted, either
whole or cut into wedges, which
concentrates the sweetness of
their flesh. They are less useful
for basic frying, when they have less
flavour than other varieties
and their lovely pink
colour tends to turn
to a murky mauve
or dull brown.

*Above: Red onions have beautiful
purple-red skins and pink-tinged,
mild flavoured flesh that is excellent
in salads and salsas.*

Red onions

As with yellow onions, there is a
great variety of size and shape
among red onions, but all are
characterized by shiny, papery
skins of a glorious purple-red. The
flesh is basically white, stained red
at the edges of each layer. The colour
is released by contact with acids, such
as vinegar or citrus juice, and red onion
slices tossed in vinegar will soon turn a
beautiful, uniform deep pink.

White onions

These are usually medium to large
onions with a papery, white outer skin
and white flesh. They tend not to vary
as much in size, shape and flavour as
yellow and red onions. They are usually
fairly strong in taste.
Uses in the kitchen White onions may
be used for all general cookery purposes,
although many people consider them
too strong for eating raw. Their even
size and shape make them good for
baking whole or stuffing.

Cipolla or borettane onions

These are quite small, flattish or squat
onions with a pale golden skin and pale
yellow flesh, while some varieties are
tinged with pink. Cipolla or
borettane onions are popular in
Italy and some varieties are
grown in France, too. They have
an excellent, sweet
flavour combined
with an agreeable
strength of taste.

*Left: Evenly
shaped white
onions have a
stronger flavour than
red onions and are
good for stuffing.*

*Right: A string of mixed
onions makes an attractive
sight hanging in a cool spot,
and will cover all
your onion needs
in the kitchen.*

Left: Cipolla onions are common in Italian markets and are excellent for braising, pickling and in salads.

Uses in the kitchen

Because they are generally small and have such a characteristic shape it would be a shame to use these onions for slicing or chopping so, generally, they are peeled and cooked whole. They are excellent caramelized or cooked à la grecque in a mixture of olive oil, wine and spices. They are also excellent for roasting whole, bottling and pickling.

Below: Tiny silverskin onions have a strong flavour and crisp texture.

Pickling onions

This is a general term for many different varieties of small onion. Some varieties may simply be immature yellow or red onions; others have been specially bred to produce small onions.

White silverskin pickling onions These strong-flavoured tiny "pearl" onions are nearly always used for pickling. When a small, pickled silverskin onion is added to a martini, the drink is called a Gibson.

Yellow and red pickling onions These are usually larger and milder than the silverskin varieties. They also keep much better than silverskins. Store them as you would normal onions.

Uses in the kitchen These onions are excellent for pickling whole in spiced vinegar and for roasting whole, or for caramelizing. Small onions are good added whole to casseroles and stews. Typically, the bourguignonne garnish, characteristic of the cooking of Burgundy in France, uses fried onions and button mushrooms to finish stews.

Grelots

This is the French term for small, flattish onions with a green skin and very white flesh. They are very like a bulbous spring onion. Various types of this kind of fresh onion (they must be eaten fresh as they will not store well) are often labelled salad onions in supermarkets and food stores. They have a generally mild-flavoured flesh with a crisp bite.

Above: Small yellow pickling onions are good for adding whole to stews and casseroles.

Uses in the kitchen Grelots are used extensively sliced raw in salads, but are good in many quick-cooked dishes, such as omelettes and frittatas, or sliced into stir-fries. They are less useful for general frying or long-cooked recipes, when they tend to disintegrate.

Below: Pickling onions are favourites for traditional English pickled onions.

Left: Banana shallots (or frog's leg shallots) are large and mild, and may be used in the same way as small onions in most recipes.

SHALLOTS

These are a distinct sub-species of *Allium cepa*, and are grouped botanically under the umbrella term Aggregatum Group, from the Latin meaning "a whole formed from several units". This is what distinguishes shallots from onions: they form clusters of several bulbs at the leaf bases. Their name comes from the ancient Palestinian port of Ascalon (now the port of Ashkelon in southern Israel), where it is thought they were first grown, but it is more likely to have been the port from where they were first exported to Rome. There is quite a variety of different shallots, but most are smaller than onions, composed of finer layers and they contain less water. As a result, they have a more concentrated flavour than onions, which makes them useful in the kitchen.

Banana shallots are the largest variety and get their name from their elongated shape. They have a smooth tan skin and a slightly milder flavour than other shallots.

Pink shallots and *échalote grise* are perhaps the most strongly flavoured shallots and are the most popular varieties in France. Pink shallots have a reddish skin and pink-tinged flesh; *échalote grise* are paler but still have a pinkish cast to the flesh. They have a crisp texture and pungent, but not harsh, flavour, which is good raw and cooked.

Brown, English or Dutch shallots are probably the most common shallots found in food stores. These small, tan-skinned shallots often separate into subsidiary bulbs when they are peeled. They are good general-purpose shallots with good-flavoured but reasonably mild flesh.

Asian or Thai red shallots are small, round red bulbs, which are used extensively in the cookery of many South-east Asian countries. They vary from the strong to exceptionally strong in taste and are used most commonly in spice pastes, when they are pounded with other ingredients. Because of their low water content they are also excellent for slicing and frying to make crisp-fried shallots, which are common as a garnish on Thai salads and curries.

Chinese "shallots" are actually a different species (*Allium chinense*) and not a shallot at all. It is a wild species that is cultivated in China (*jiao tou* in Cantonese or *rakkyo* in Japanese).

Below: French shallots generally have a good, strong flavour and separate into several small sections when peeled. They are excellent in raw and cooked sauces and in salad dressings.

Left: Pink Thai shallots are used extensively in Thai curry pastes and are also used as salad garnishes. They are exceptionally pretty pickled in rice vinegar with herbs and spices.

Uses in the kitchen Shallots are excellent roasted whole, caramelized or pickled. Raw, they are essential in salad dressings and a wide range of French dishes. Chopped raw shallot is often sprinkled over a seared, rare steak *à la bordelaise*. Cooked, shallots are an essential ingredient in many sauces that need the flavour of onion but not its bulk. Shallots have a low water content, which means that they can burn and toughen easily, so care should be taken when frying. Potato onions may be used like ordinary onions.

They are grown mainly for pickling, and that is the form in which they are usually seen in the West.

Potato onions are related to shallots and belong to the Aggregatum Group of *Allium cepa*. The species is peculiar among the onions in that it develops entirely underground, in the same way as garlic. Because of this, it is a little hardier than other onions and shallots and, in the past, it was often planted in autumn. It forms clumps of small, yellow-skinned onions that store well. As many as eight small onions may form per clump.

Potato onions were once far more popular than they are now, especially in the mild west of England and Ireland, from where they were taken to the United States. They filled a gap between the end of the stored autumn-cropping onions and the new crop of shallots in late summer. Today, the potato onion is regarded as a bit of an oddity, mainly restricted to the herb patch, but the bulbs are of good flavour and are just as useful as ordinary onions in the kitchen. It is an interesting rarity that keen gardener-cooks might like to consider growing.

Right: English or Dutch shallots are generally brown skinned and have a mild flavour.

LEEKS

As a cultivated vegetable, the leek has even more ancient origins than the onion. It is probably derived from the wild *Allium ampeloprasum*, although some botanists call it a species in its own right (*Allium porrum*). The wild leek is a native of the Mediterranean and islands such as the Azores, Madeira and the Canaries. This wild leek has been traced back as far as Jericho 7,000 years ago. "Leeks" of a different species – *Allium ramosum* – have also been cultivated in China for thousands of years. Although there are many hundreds of varieties of cultivated leek, in fact, they vary only in size and winter hardiness. Some leeks have been bred to grow to vast dimensions and others to withstand quite severe winter frosts.

In the kitchen, the cook is mainly concerned with size. Traditionally in the northern hemisphere, leeks have been seen as a winter vegetable. These large leeks are one of the few vegetables to survive outdoors without protection. In recent years, baby leeks have increased in popularity, and while these may simply be immature, miniature versions of ordinary leeks, there are now special

Below: Baby leeks are good for serving whole. Steam, then brown in a hot griddle pan to bring out their flavour.

varieties that are grown to mature quickly and provide slender, tender leeks throughout the summer.

In leeks, the "bulb" or layers of leaf base are elongated to form what is commonly regarded as a stem, although botanically the stem is strictly the sometimes slightly bulbous base of the leek just above the roots. The leek divides into the white, fleshy basal portion and the green leaves or "flags". All the fleshy part of the leek may be used, but the green part is tougher and requires more cooking. Leeks have an almost universally popular flavour that is both milder and more rounded than that of onions. It lacks the pungency of onions but makes up for it in the gentle depth of its flavour.

Uses in the kitchen Young, fresh leeks may be used raw, shredded in salads (a favourite with the Romans), but their chief use in the kitchen is when they are cooked. They are superlative in soups. Leeks cook more quickly than onions, so they should be added to stews towards the end of cooking. Whole, they are good braised or blanched then grilled. Baby leeks are almost always cooked whole. They are excellent if briefly boiled or steamed, then dressed in oil and vinegar.

Below: Large leeks, with their sweet, mild flavour, are among the most popular of alliums in the modern kitchen. They are excellent in soups and cooked salads.

SPRING ONIONS

Most of what are sold as spring or salad onions (scallions in the United States) are simply early-maturing varieties of onion (*Allium cepa*). However, the need for a year-round supply and recent breeding, especially by the Japanese, means that some spring onion varieties now have genes from Welsh onions (*Allium fistulosum*) in their makeup. If the cross-section of the leaf is circular, then the onion is a variety based on *Allium fistulosum*; if the cross-section of the leaf is crescent-shaped, then it is derived from *Allium cepa*.

As the English name suggests, these onions probably started out as the spring thinnings from ordinary onions. In culinary terms, the distinction between the different types of spring onion is purely one of size – they vary from the really tiny (thinner than a pencil) to those that are as large as, if not larger than, a baby leek. Some varieties of spring onion have a markedly bulbous base, and show a relation to the type of salad onions the French call *grelotes*; others are more leek-like, with no particular basal swelling.

Spring onions have a mild, sweet flavour with a fresh green snap, which makes them good in salads. Use thinner spring onions for salads and thicker ones for cooking. Red spring onions have been developed: these look pretty in salads, but do not differ significantly in flavour from white spring onions.

Left: Bulb spring onions are the best ones to use for grilling whole or for cooking in dishes such as Chinese stir-fries, or deep-frying whole in batter.

Uses in the kitchen In Britain, spring onions have traditionally been served whole (trimmed) in salads. They are good as crudités with a black olive tapenade and are excellent chopped or sliced into mixed or composite salads; they are widely used like this in the Middle East. They are a good addition to Mexican salsas. Spring onions are also excellent cooked, and are an essential ingredient in Asian stir-fries, because they cook quickly. They grill well, taking only a few minutes to cook. In Cataluña, in north-east Spain, they are widely used in this way: known as *calçots*, they are grilled over hot coals and served with all sorts of grilled meats and a nut/chilli sauce called *salsa romesco*. The tops of young spring onions may be used as a garnish in the same way as chives, and spring onions curls and brushes are popular garnishes in Chinese food.

Below: Thin spring onions are excellent in salads, whether left whole or chopped small.

BUNCHING, WELSH AND TREE ONIONS

Bunching or Welsh onions (*Allium fistulosum*) are very popular in China and Japan. They are called Welsh as a corruption of the Germanic *welsche*, meaning foreign. This label was probably given when they were first introduced into Europe from Asia. In Wales itself they used to be known as "holtzers" and they were once a popular flavouring because they grew in early spring when few other vegetables were available. They are also known as *chiboules* or *cibols*. In Chinese cooking, bunching onions are used in stir-fries in place of spring onions. The onion grows in clusters of bulbs, so individual onions may be removed, leaving the plant growing. The flavour is mild.

Right: Tree onions, or Egyptian onions, are vigorous, clumping onions that grow well in the herb patch.

Below: Bunching onions are the most popular type of onion in China and Japan, and are used like spring onions.

Tree onions (*Allium cepa*, Proliferum Group) are true perennials for the herb patch. As with bunching onions, individual onions may be removed from the plant for use in the kitchen. Tree onions also form little bulblets at the tips of the stem, which may also be used in the kitchen or may be planted to form new plants. A particularly vigorous and tall form of the tree onion, known as the Catawissa onion, was a popular pot herb in America during the 19th and early 20th centuries.

Uses in the kitchen Both the basal stem and the green flags may be used in sauces, stir-fries and salads, but because tree onions are slightly tougher than spring onions, they do not grill well. The bulblets are good chopped in sauces and salad dressings.

Above: Chive flowers have a surprisingly oniony flavour and make a pretty addition to salads in early summer.

CHIVES

European chive (*Allium schoenoprasum*) is a common wild plant, occurring from northern Russia to the Mediterranean and as far east as the Himalayas. Various larger-growing varieties have been selected for domestication. Chives are one of the first herbs to start into growth in the early spring, and the first shoots are remarkably strong and pungent; later on, as the plants develop, they become milder. The flowers also have a mild oniony taste and are good in salads and as a garnish. Chives are usually eaten raw or very lightly cooked.

Chinese chives (*Allium tuberosum*) are also known as *kuchai* (*gow choy* in Cantonese) or, garlic chives. They have a much more pungent smell and taste than European chives and because of their strong flavour are usually cooked. They come in two forms: the leaf form has flat, slightly twisted leaves with a pronounced garlic smell; the flowering stalk with a round, hollow stem is normally sold with flower buds intact. A third kind, Chinese yellow chives (*gow wong*), are simply a version of Chinese chives that have been blanched by excluding all natural light. They are highly regarded by the Chinese as a vegetable in their own right for stir-

frying. Garlic shoots are also used in Chinese cookery and are sometimes known as garlic chives.

Uses in the kitchen European chives are widely used as a garnish, but they have a surprising amount of flavour, especially when picked young from the garden. They are excellent in egg and cheese dishes, but care should be taken that they are not left in contact with eggs or dairy products as they will taint them. Chives are useful for adding a mild oniony taste to salad dressings, soups and sauces, and are particularly good in potato dishes. Chinese chives are more robust and need brief cooking. They are excellent in stir-fries, in rice dishes and stirred into soups and stews.

Right: Chinese chives are often sold in tight bud and may be chopped and used in stir-fries.

Below: Chives (Allium schoenoprasum) are popular throughout Europe and North America, and give a mild, oniony flavour that is particularly good in cheese and egg dishes.

Left: Young, new-season or wet garlic that has not been dried has a particularly sweet and mild flavour.

There are many different varieties of garlic, most of them geographically specific and therefore adapted to local climate and conditions. Garlic stores well when it is dried, but has a different taste from when it is used green and freshly pulled. There are some garlics with very white skin, while others are stained or mottled deep pink. Some garlic varieties separate naturally into tiny cloves, while others are characterized by large, fat cloves. Generally, the larger and less dried the clove, the milder and less pungent it is, but this is not an unbroken rule.

Above: Solo garlic is a mild form of garlic in which each small bulb comprises a single clove.

Below: Garlic is often sold in strings and will keep for several months if hung in a cool, dry place.

GARLIC

At various times, garlic (*Allium sativum*) has been the most lauded and the most despised of all the onion tribe because it is the fieriest and most pungent. It is one of the few culinary alliums that forms its bulb underground rather than on the surface of the soil.

Typically, a garlic bulb, or head, is formed of several separate cloves, each wrapped in its own papery skin, and the whole head is enclosed in a further papery skin. Garlic is widely cultivated, but needs a long growing season and a period of cold weather to initiate proper bulb development.

Most cultures consider it a herb or flavouring rather than a vegetable in its own right, but many dishes exist that include several whole heads of garlic rather than the odd clove that more timid cooks employ. A whole head of garlic, gently roasted until it becomes sweet, mellow and purée soft, may easily be consumed by one person at a sitting. There are French recipes for chicken or lamb with forty cloves of garlic, which achieved an almost mythical status in garlic-phobic Britain of the 1950s. Some Asian dishes contain huge quantities of garlic by Western standards, such as southern Indian dishes of whole garlic cloves cooked with spices and coconut milk.

Middle East and in all Mediterranean countries. Crisp, fried garlic is a popular garnish to Burmese food, and in both Thailand and Korea pickled garlic is an accompaniment to many meals.

Garlic alters in flavour according to how it is prepared and for how long it is cooked. Crushed garlic, either raw or briefly cooked, is the most pungent and strongly flavoured; a whole head of garlic, slowly roasted, will have a mellow, nutty, toasty flavour. Garlic may be fried, baked, roasted or braised. It is a ubiquitous ingredient in most spice pastes, Spanish salsas, Italian pestos and Mexican moles. It is also widely used in all types of cuisine in dressings, marinades, soups and stews.

Left: Smoked garlic is infused over wood smoke. It is good in garlic mayonnaise, marinades and salad dressings.

Below: There are many different kinds of garlic, which are often geographically specific: white garlic is popular in California. California Late and Silverskin are well-known varieties.

Elephant garlic (*Allium ampeloprasm*) There is some confusion in food stores between this variety and large-growing varieties of true garlic. Elephant garlic is actually more closely related to the leek than to garlic proper. It has a mild, creamy, garlic flavour and the cloves are very large in comparison with ordinary garlic. Another variety of allium (*Allium gigantum*) has also been known as elephant garlic, but most gardeners grow this as an ornamental, for its very large, purple drumstick flowers, rather than as a food plant.

Solo is a variety of garlic that has been specially bred to develop just one, large clove, making it easy to peel and prepare. It is useful for dishes using a lot of garlic, but expensive to use in any quantity. The flavour is fairly mild.

Wet or new season garlic may simply be labelled "fresh" or "green" garlic. Typically, in the northern hemisphere, this is ready in late spring to early summer, when the papery skin has not fully developed and dried out. Usually the head is used whole: it is creamy white, streaked and flushed with green and pink, and has a delicious mild flavour that is ideal for European garlic soups and to roast whole.

Smoked garlic usually consists of large, whole heads of garlic that have been hot-smoked so that they are partly cooked and infused with wood smoke. They have a light, tan-brown exterior skin that should be peeled before the cloves are used for crushing into mayonnaise, for making garlic butter, or for tossing with pasta.

Garlic shoots – the first shoots of early spring – are considered a great delicacy in many areas of southern Europe (Italy, France and Spain) and are used in much the same way as chives or spring onions. They are also much used in Chinese stir-fries. Soup made from garlic shoots is a great favourite and is considered a splendid health tonic – a sort of "spring clean" for the blood and circulation. The shoots are also pickled for use later in the season in relishes, salads and sauces.

Uses in the kitchen Garlic is an almost universal favourite for flavouring in cuisines all around the world. It is widely used, both raw and cooked, to flavour all kinds of dishes. It is used raw in dressings, salsas, butters and salads. Cooked, it is used in huge quantities in most Asian countries (apart from Japan), Mexico and South America, the

ALLIUM FLAVOURINGS AND INGREDIENTS

There are a large number of allium flavourings and ingredients available. Some are made from onions, while others are not even related to the alliums but impart an oniony flavour.

Asafoetida

This is a pungent spice obtained from a resin from the root of a giant fennel (*Ferula asafoetida*). It is not related to the alliums but does give a distinct garlicky taste to the dishes in which it is used. It was favoured in Roman cookery and was used by the Roman epicurean Apicius in the 1st century AD. Today, asafoetida is used in Afghanistan, India and Pakistan. It is usually bought ground and should be kept well sealed, because the smell of the uncooked spice is disagreeable. It is used in Indian Brahman cooking in place of the forbidden onions and garlic.

Onion seed or kalonji

The name onion seed is a complete misnomer, because the Indian spice kalonji is not a relation of the alliums, but is related to the familiar, blue-flowered annual "love-in-the-mist" (*Nigella sativa*) of our flower borders. It is much used in India, especially in Bengali cooking. It is good stir-fried with green vegetables, and sprinkled on the top of Indian breads and pancakes.

Dried onion flakes

These are simply dehydrated thin slices of onion, but as onions are available all year round, they are rarely used today. They should be rehydrated in warm water for 15–20 minutes before using, or they may be gently fried, to form crisp fried onions, which are much used as a garnish for Thai salads and curries. Dried shallot flakes are also available.

Crisp fried onion flakes

These are ready-fried crisp scraps of onion, which are useful as a garnish in salads, soups and rice dishes, or may be added to egg dishes. Once the pack is opened, the flakes should be used quickly or they will go rancid.

Left: Pungent asafoetida is much used in Indian vegetarian cooking.

Above right: Dry-roasting kalonji seeds will bring out their nutty flavour.

Right: Fried onion flakes are good sprinkled over salads and rice dishes.

Below: Dried shallot flakes may be added directly to slow-cooked stews.

Garlic salt

This is a mix of dried garlic and salt. It can be used to add instant garlic flavour to dishes such as garlic bread, but the drying process alters garlic's flavour, and many cooks prefer to use fresh garlic.

Garlic pastes

Ready-prepared garlic pastes are widely available. However, as with dried garlic, some of the preservatives used in the preparation of commercial garlic pastes alter the flavour and can give a slightly metallic tang to the finished dish. It is better to make your own roasted garlic paste, which will keep for 1–2 weeks covered with olive oil in a screw-top jar in the fridge.

Above left: Garlic salt is used in Cajun cooking for their blackened dishes.

Above: Fried garlic and garlic granules

Below: Small onions, garlic and shallots are popular in pickles.

Right: Minced garlic

Bottled or pickled alliums

In many countries, onions, garlic and shallots are pickled or bottled in vinegar or oil. These preserved alliums make a delicious addition to mixed salads, egg and rice dishes. Bottled green shoots of sprouting garlic are a popular spring flavouring in Spain, Italy and China. They are occasionally available fresh from Oriental food stores.

CULTIVATION

The fact that the onion family has been cultivated since the earliest times and that it has spread far and wide across the globe suggests that onions are easy to grow. This is largely true: for the most part, onions are easily grown, hardy plants that are adaptable to a wide range of climates and soils. Certain varieties have been bred that are more suited to specific climatic conditions, and these different types vary in flavour and strength. Generally, the quicker an onion grows, the milder its flavour will be. Ideal quick-growing conditions, such as those found in large parts of Spain, the west-coast states of the USA and Hawaii, foster sweet, mild onions, such as the Vidalia from Washington State and the Maui from the Hawaiian island of the same name. Onions that grow more slowly, say in northern Europe, tend to be stronger and more pungent. Home-grown onions, which have had to survive the vicissitudes of

Below: Seedlings of the onion Vera Prima, ready for planting out.

the garden, possibly with periods of drought and neglect, tend to be stronger in flavour and odour than commercially grown onions, which have led a pampered and well-watered life.

Onions can be grown in almost any type of soil but most members of the onion family like a friable, open, slightly sandy soil. The best way is to plant in ground that has been manured in autumn before planting. All members of the onion family prefer an open, sunny position: they do not grow well under the shade of trees or buildings, nor do they like the competition of roots from trees or large shrubs. Onions like to be well fed, but not with a fertilizer with a high nitrogen content, as this will make them grow large leaves rather than foster the formation of the bulb or stem.They also need to be well watered, as this helps the bulb to swell, but they can stand short periods of drought.

Onions (*Allium cepa* vars.) are biennial plants, which means that they form a bulb or storage organ one year, in order to flower and set seed the next. If the climate is mild enough, onions left in the ground during winter will shoot, flower and set seed in late spring.

The gardener grows the onion for the bulb it produces in its first year of growth. If it is properly dried off and stored, this bulb will survive throughout the winter dormant period and will not attempt to grow again until the following spring. Onions that are kept in a place that is too warm or damp may well shoot while they are in storage. An onion that does this is still edible, but the winter dormancy has been broken and it will not keep.

Onions are grown by two methods: either from seed, or from small, infant onions called sets. Shallots and garlic are, effectively, grown only from sets, while leeks and spring onions are grown exclusively from seed. The bunching onions and chives are perennial plants (they live for several years and do not die upon flowering) and may be grown either from seed, division (when the plants are separated to make several new plants) or, sometimes, from little bulblets produced by the adult plant.

GROWING ONIONS FROM SEED

Onions are fairly hardy plants, and small seedlings, growing outdoors, will survive a mild frost. Therefore, seed may be sown outdoors in mid- to late spring, or, with some varieties in mild climates (zones 7–8), in the early autumn.

Sowing onions outside

1 Prepare the ground by removing all weeds, then fork it over and rake it to form a fine tilth and a level surface.

2 Make a drill about 5mm/¼in deep with a thin stick or the corner of the rake head.

3 If the soil is dry, water the bottom of the drill before sowing.

4 Sow the seeds thinly along the bottom. Cover with the soil and firm it lightly with a rake. If sowing on a heavy, clay soil, a thin layer of sharp sand trickled along the bottom of the seed drill will prevent the seed from rotting before it starts to shoot.

5 The seedlings should germinate in 10–15 days. When they are 5–7.5cm/ 2–3in high, thin them to 7.5–10cm/ 3–4in apart. Water if conditions are very dry and keep free from weeds.

6 When the seedlings are growing strongly and the leaves are beginning to meet, thin them again to 13–15cm/ 5–6in apart. The thinnings at this stage of growth may be used as salad or spring onions. Unless you are intending to grow very large onions, you will not need to thin the onions again.

7 If you prefer small onions, space them closer together or let them grow as clumps of seedlings – you will then get clumps of small bulbs that you can pull as they are required. Autumn-sown onions are often left to grow as clumps of seedlings, as these often overwinter better than the single seedlings.

Sowing onions indoors

In colder climates or on cold, heavy soils, sow onion seeds indoors under glass and then plant them outside in the garden in late spring. The seeds may be sown in early to mid-spring.

1 Fill a seed tray with sterilized seed compost, level the surface and firm it slightly by pressing down gently with your finger.

2 Sprinkle the seed thinly over the surface of the compost.

3 Cover with either a thin layer of sifted seed compost or sprinkle with a thin layer of fine vermiculite to a depth of about 5mm/¼in.

Above: North Holland Blood and Red Mate are both good growing varieties of onions.

4 Using a watering can with a fine rose on the spout, lightly water the seeds, label and cover with a propagator lid or a plastic bag. Gentle heat under the tray will aid germination, but is not essential. As soon as the seedlings begin to emerge, move the tray into full light, but protect the delicate leaves from scorching in strong sunlight.

5 When the seedlings are 5–6cm/ 2–2½in high, prick them out into trays of compost, spacing them 5–6cm/ 2–2½in apart.

6 Alternatively, sow the seeds in divided trays or seed modules, 3–4 seeds per module. When the seedlings are growing strongly, thin to one seedling.

Planting onion seedlings outside

Seedlings grown inside will need to be planted outside in late spring. Harden off the seedlings before planting out by standing the trays outside for about 12 days. Cover and protect from heavy rain or frosty weather in a cold frame or greenhouse. When the seedlings have been hardened off, plant out 15–18cm/6–7in apart, in rows 25cm/10in apart. The tiny bulb should be no deeper than it was in the seed tray. Water well and protect from birds.

Some varieties of onion have been specially bred (mainly in Japan) to overwinter in a mild, temperate climate. These should be sown in late summer/early autumn. The seedlings or young plants overwinter, then grow in the spring. These onions are ready for harvesting in the early summer of the year following sowing, and usefully fill the gap between the end of the stored onions and the new season's crop of spring-sown onions. The most famous of these onions are the Vidalia onions, grown in the town of the same name in Washington State, USA. The Vidalia onion is famous for being particularly sweet and mild.

GROWING ONIONS FROM SETS

Onions can also be grown from sets, which are small, immature bulbs. Sets have been grown and treated so that, once planted, they will continue to grow to form a full-size onion. Because onions are biennial there is a danger that the set will bolt, that is run to flower, rather than grow to make a fair-size bulb. However, some sets have been heat-treated to kill the flower and prevent bolting. Onion sets are planted in early to mid-spring and will stand a little light frost. They are best planted in open, well-dug soil which has been manured the autumn before planting.

If the soil is heavy, put a little sharp sand beneath each set. Push into the soil in rows, allowing 10cm/4in between sets and 25cm/10in between rows. The top of the set should be just visible. Apart from watering in extremely dry weather and weeding, they should need no more care.

Sometimes birds will work their way down a row pulling out the sets before they have time to root. If this happens, simply push them back into the soil, making sure that they are firm. If birds are proving to be a particular problem, try laying twigs over the soil, or covering the sets with netting. This may well be the best solution to the problem.

Good varieties of onion

Spring sowing: Buffalo, Giant Fen Globe, Ailsa Craig, Sturon, North Holland Blood, Long Red Florence, Red Baron, Southport Red Globe, Red Mate. Autumn sowing: Express Yellow, Imai Early Yellow, Vidalia, Senshyu Yellow. Pickling onions: Paris Silver Skin, Shakespeare.

Championship onions and leeks
Around the world, specialist and competitive growers prepare deep beds of special soil in which to grow mammoth onions and leeks. There is great competition between growers. Show leeks are blanched by growing them through drainpipes or wrapping them in thick, corrugated cardboard, and they are fed with "secret" compounds of liquid fertilizer to encourage growth. Some onions can grow to over 2.75kg/6lb, while leeks can grow up to 1m/1yd long, with a stem as thick as a person's arm. Good varieties for championship onions are Mammoth and Beacon.

GROWING LEEKS

Leeks are grown from seed in exactly the same way as onions. Sow outside in mid- to late spring or inside under glass in early spring. Sowing seeds indoors provides a longer growing season and produces bigger leeks. Leeks sown outside should be thinned to about 2.5cm/1in apart. Inside, prick out the seedlings into trays or modules about 2.5cm/1in apart. In early summer, plant the leeks outside. Indoor-sown leeks should be hardened off first.

1 If you want long, blanched leeks, dig a trench of prepared soil. The trench should be about 30cm/12in across and about 25cm/10in deep. Fork over the bottom of the trench thoroughly and dig in some well-rotted manure or fertilizer. Heap the removed soil alongside the trench for infilling later.

2 Half-fill the trench with removed soil, then make holes with a stick or dibber 20–25cm/8–10in apart. They should be about 2.5–4cm/1–1½in across and 13–15cm/5–6in deep.

3 Drop the seedlings into the holes so that the leaves poke out of the top.

4 Water the leeks well, by pouring water into the hole to wash soil over the roots.

5 As the leeks grow, gradually return the remaining soil to the trench. This blanches the stem, and forces the leeks to grow a longer, white stem.

6 For leeks for general cooking, holes may be made in well-prepared soil, rather than a trench. Drop in the leek seedlings and water in as above. Some gardeners on heavy clay soil find they get better results if they grow leeks in raised beds of deeply prepared soil.

Below: De Saint Victor leeks have distinctive blue-purple leaves; they are winter-hardy and have excellent flavour.

This aids drainage, whereas a trench may fill with water on badly draining land. Support the sides of the beds with planks of wood, bricks or old railway sleepers. The beds should be about 1.2m/4ft wide so that they can be cultivated without stepping on the soil.

Good varieties of leek

Bleu de Solaise: a handsome leek with blue-purple foliage; Autumn Giant: an early maturing leek that will last to late winter in the ground; Musselborough Improved: a good winter-hardy variety; King Richard: a quick-growing variety, good for harvesting as baby leeks; Jolant; De Saint Victor: winter-hardy.

> **Fertilizing onions and leeks**
> In ordinary conditions, onions need little or no feeding during the growing period, although they may be fed with a potash fertilizer when the bulb is well formed. This helps the bulb ripen and prevents it developing "thick neck". Leeks need no extra feeding during the growing season as long as the ground was manured to start with.

GROWING SHALLOTS

Shallots are generally grown from sets rather than from seed. They grow as clumps of bulbs, each one of which may be grown on as a set. They are grown in exactly the same way as onion sets but they grow much more quickly.

1 In late winter to early spring, plant shallot sets in open, well-dug soil that has been well manured the autumn before planting.

2 If the soil is very heavy, place a little sharp sand under every shallot to aid drainage and prevent the bulb from rotting in the wet earth.

3 If any of the sets are pulled up by birds, press them back into the soil. Alternatively, protect the sets with a layer of netting or by laying a few twigs over the soil.

4 The shallots will be ready to harvest by midsummer.

Good varieties of shallot

Atlantic: golden-skinned shallots with a high yield; Pikant: a pink-fleshed shallot of fine flavour; Giant Iona; Topper.

Pests and diseases

The potent chemicals that alliums produce generally give them an in-built defence against pests and diseases. Garlic, in particular, seems resistant to most garden pests.

Rabbits, rodents and deer give all alliums a wide berth because they find the smell and taste offensive. Moles, too, avoid making their runs near an onion or garlic bed. Despite this, mice or rats are known to eat onions in store, so, when storing alliums, they should be protected against these vermin.

In very wet summers, and on heavy, poorly drained land, onions can be susceptible to downy mildew, which can cause rotting. Affected onions should be pulled up and discarded, but not on the compost heap. Onions should not be grown on the same patch of ground for about 3 years.

The major pest of onions is onion fly. They lay their eggs in the bulb, which is then eaten by the maggots that hatch from the eggs. There are no chemical treatments that protect onions against this harmful pest, but companion planting is said to be effective in deterring them. Plant tagetes (French marigolds) and parsley in rows among the onions if the pest is known to be prevalent.

Leeks sometimes get a rust disease, which causes rust-coloured spots on the foliage. However, it does not affect the leek stem so there is no need to spray or discard the leek plants, but do not put affected leaves on the compost heap.

Above: Once harvested, shallots are best strung for storage and kept in a dry, frost-free place. They should keep throughout the winter if stored in this way.

GROWING GARLIC

Garlic is grown from individual cloves in a similar way to onion and shallot sets. There are many different varieties of garlic that have been specially bred to suit specific climates. It is better to order an appropriate variety from a seed firm, rather than using a head of garlic from the supermarket as it may have been imported. These will, however, often grow. Garlic needs a long growing season and also a period of 1–2 months of cold weather (0–10°C/32–50°F) to make a good-size head.

Garlic is different from other alliums (apart from the seldom-grown potato onion) in that the head, or bulb, grows underground rather than on the surface of the soil. Because of this, garlic is best planted in the autumn, to be harvested in mid- to late summer the following year. It will tolerate some frost. Little or no growth will be visible above ground until the following spring.

1 Plant individual cloves 10–15cm/ 4–6in apart in rows 25cm/10in apart just below the surface in well-dug soil. Place a little sand beneath each clove if gardening on heavy, clay soil to help drainage and prevent rotting.

Growing garlic shoots

Garlic shoots can easily be grown by planting cloves of garlic in pots of good, free-draining compost from early spring onwards. Keep well watered in a sunny, open position. Harvest the young shoots when they are about 15–20cm/6–8in high. More shoots will soon grow to replace them.

Good varieties of garlic

Moraluz: large white heads; Cristo; Mediterranean.

GROWING SPRING ONIONS

Spring onions are grown from seed. Sow as for bulb onions in rows about 20cm/8in apart. Spring onions mature quickly, so sow short rows in succession every 3–4 weeks during spring and early summer. If you sow the seed thinly, there is no need to thin out spring onions, simply pull the onions as you need them.

Good varieties of spring onion

Santa Claus: a Japanese variety with deep-red stems; White Lisbon: a traditional, white, quick-growing spring onion.

GROWING BUNCHING ONIONS

Asian varieties of bunching onions are grown in a similar way to spring onions, but you can keep on harvesting them over a longer period, so thin the plants to about 10cm/4in apart.

Good varieties of bunching onion

Summer Isle; White Evergreen; Ishikura, Kujo Green.

GROWING WELSH ONIONS AND TREE ONIONS

These perennial onions are best bought as small plants from a herb nursery, although it is possible to grow them from seed sown indoors in early spring. If growing from seed, prick out clumps of little seedlings in 7.5–cm/3–in pots. Harden off the seedlings and plant them out in early summer. If you have a mature plant, you can create more by simply digging the plant up and dividing it into smaller plants. Replant small

Above: Freshly harvested garlic ready for cleaning and stringing for storage.

sections from the healthy, outer edge of the clumps, rather than from the congested centre. Bulblets from the top of the stem of tree onions will also grow into new plants if pushed into a pot of good compost.

GROWING CHIVES

Chives are propagated by division. They prefer a good, moist soil, but will grow more or less anywhere. Divide the plant when it is actively growing in early or mid-spring and set the divisions about 25cm/10in apart. Chives should be harvested as you need them. During the growing season, they can be cut down to ground level 2–3 times and they will sprout again, with fresh, full-flavoured leaves. Water well after cutting back. In the autumn, pot up chive plants, cut them back and keep them in a cool, frost-free place indoors where there is plenty of good light. This is a good way to have fresh chives available for use throughout the winter.

HARVESTING AND STORAGE

The harvesting of alliums depends on the length of time that they can be stored. Onions, shallots and garlic, which, if stored correctly, can keep throughout the winter, should be harvested when they are fully grown. Leeks, spring onions and chives, which have a shorter shelf life, are better left in the ground until they are needed.

ONIONS, SHALLOTS AND GARLIC

It is obvious when onions, shallots and garlic are ready to be harvested. With onions and shallots, the leaf stem keels over at the top (neck) of the bulb. With garlic, the leaves start to die back, wither and keel over. When this happens, it is fairly certain that the bulb has finished its growth for the season and is as big as it is going to get.

Sometimes onions develop a "fat" or "thick" neck. This is not a disease, but a physiological condition. Some varieties are more susceptible than others; wet weather is an additional factor. The neck of the onion becomes thick and remains green, and the leaves do not keel over but stay upright and healthy. The onion still continues to grow, rather than to ripen and dry off. If left in the soil, the onion would eventually bolt, or run to flower. Such onions are perfectly good to eat, but they will not keep for a great length of time, so use them as quickly as possible.

When the onion leaves keel over, it is best to leave them in the soil for a week or so, especially if the weather is dry and sunny. After that, gently pull the onions up to expose the roots to the air and leave them on the ground to finish drying and for the root to wither. If the weather is cold and wet, remove the bulbs to a dry but well-ventilated place: lying on the greenhouse staging is ideal, or on a frame made of netting. Do not remove stems at this time. When the onions have thoroughly dried, the stems may be twisted off and the onions placed in trays with ventilation holes.

Above: Stringing garlic is an excellent way of ensuring that it stays dry and well ventilated.

Left: Lift onions with a fork, then let the bulbs dry off either on the ground, if dry, or on a rack under cover.

Stringing onions, shallots and garlic

If the stems are left intact, the onions may be strung together to form ropes or skeins, either by plaiting the stalks together or tying them together with string or raffia. Shallots and garlic should be treated in the same way. An alternative method of "stringing" garlic is simply to thread a stiff wire through the dry necks of the bulbs.

Strung onions, shallots and garlic may then be hung up for storage, which is an excellent way of keeping them well aired. All three should keep through to the following spring if stored in a dry, well-ventilated room or shed that is cool and just frost-free. Check your store of onions throughout winter and discard any that feel soft. Towards the end of winter, some onions may begin to sprout. Use these immediately. Do not try to store garlic ropes in the kitchen, however decorative, or they will sprout.

How to string onions, shallots and garlic

Onions, shallots and garlic can all be strung together in the same way. Either tie them into a skein with string or raffia, or plait together the dried stems.

1 Take the first bulb and tie a loop of string around the neck. Pull the string tight to allow for shrinkage later.

2 Add more bulbs, each one just above the last, forming a loop of string around the neck of each. Bind any surplus stem into the skein.

3 When you have reached the end of the skein – usually about 12–15 onions – tie all the stalks together firmly, folding over any surplus.

Above: Young leeks, like these 4-month-old De Saint Victors, may be harvested as soon as they begin to thicken.

LEEKS

These are best left in the ground rather than lifting them as they mature. Simply harvest as and when you need them in the kitchen. They will withstand quite hard frosts and can be left in the ground throughout the autumn. When dug, the leeks will keep for about a week in a dry, well-ventilated room. Washed and prepared, leeks should be stored in a plastic bag in the vegetable drawer of the fridge.

SPRING ONIONS AND CHIVES

If the spring onions have been sown thinly enough then, as they mature, you can simply pull them from the ground as and when you need them. Once pulled, they should be stored in the fridge, wrapped in a plastic bag.

CHIVES

These should not be pulled, but can be snipped near to the soil with a pair of kitchen scissors. Harvest chives as they are required in the kitchen. They will keep for a few days in the fridge, well-wrapped in a plastic bag or in a polythene tub.

PREPARING ONIONS AND OTHER ALLIUMS

This section looks at most of the basic techniques for preparing and cooking onions, leeks and other alliums. It is worthwhile spending a little of your time studying and mastering these techniques, since they ultimately help to save time and tears.

CHOOSING ONIONS AND OTHER ALLIUMS

When buying onions, choose firm, undamaged specimens with light skins. Reject any that feel soft when gently squeezed, show signs of dampness or with green shoots at the top. These rules apply to shallots and garlic too, except new season's garlic which should have moist, fresh skins.

Examine the leaves of spring onions and leeks – they should be fresh and not brown or slimy. Be careful when buying leeks in late spring and early summer, since they may well have a hard, central core. This core is the developing flower stalk and it will not soften on cooking.

When preparing onions, discard any that have brown patches or are brown or slimy at the centre. The onion will be tainted, and even if the bad portion is cut away and discarded, the onion will still taste nasty.

Green shoots at the centre of a garlic clove, and dried-out, old or withered garlic cloves should be discarded – they will give a bitter or musty taste to the finished dish.

PEELING ONIONS

1 The easiest way to peel an onion is first to cut off the top and bottom.

2 Slit the skin with a sharp knife and peel it off.

Peeling whole onions

Onions or shallots used for braising or for adding to a *boeuf bourguignonne*, for example, must be left whole. Some cooks even find it easier to slice onions, which can be quite slippery and tough, if the root end is temporarily left intact.

1 To peel an onion or shallot, when it is important that the onion stays whole, trim any root from the base, making sure you leave the base intact.

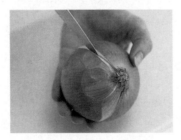

2 Then, working from the neck down, make a shallow slit in the skin from top to bottom with a small, sharp knife.

3 Pull the skin off the onion, working from the neck down.

Peeling small onions and shallots

If you are peeling a lot of small onions or shallots, it is easier if you first blanch them in boiling water. This is particularly helpful when peeling varieties that have tenaciously clinging, tight skins. This also works with garlic cloves.

1 Cut off the neck of the onions or shallots and cut a thin slice off the bottom, but leave the root base intact or the onions may fall apart in cooking.

2 Place in a bowl and add enough boiling water to cover.

3 Leave for about 3 minutes, drain, then slip the onions or shallots out of their skins.

TRIMMING AND CLEANING LEEKS

Particles of soil can easily become trapped in between the leaf layers of a leek. The tighter the layers, the less likelihood there is that soil will have managed to penetrate.

Baby leeks and tight, ready-trimmed leeks from the supermarket are unlikely to be very gritty, but it is still worth checking before cooking, since nothing ruins a leek dish more than the mere trace of grittiness from hidden soil. Leeks fresh from the garden are always the worst culprits and therefore need to be washed thoroughly.

Trimming and cleaning large leeks

1 When preparing large leeks, trim off most of the loose green leaves, or flags, cutting at the point where the layers begin to get tighter.

2 Discard any loose green leaves but, unless the recipe specifies the white part of the leek only, do not discard the green part of the bulb.

3 Trim off excess root. Discard one or two outer layers of the leek, which are tough, fibrous and quite likely to have been damaged.

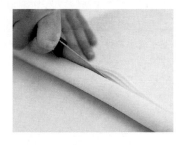

4 Make a slit starting about 2.5cm/1in from the base of the leek to the top, cutting through to the centre.

5 Carefully wash the leek under cold running water, fanning out the layers with your fingers to make sure you wash away all the dirt. Hold the leek so that the water runs from the base to the top, so dirt will not be washed back into the layers of leaves.

Trimming and cleaning baby leeks

1 Cut off as little of the green leaf as possible, as it is tender enough to eat.

2 Baby leeks are usually clean enough to cook whole, but check one by cutting a slit through to the centre.

3 Peel off the outer layer of the leek if it looks tough or damaged.

4 Wash the leeks by shaking them well in a bowl of cold water.

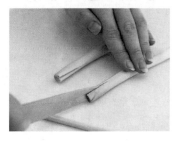

5 If leeks appear dirty only at the top end and you want to cook the leek whole, cut a short slit in the leek. Then either wash the leeks under the cold tap or soak them in a bowl of cold, well-salted water for 30 minutes to draw out the dirt. Soaking also leaches out vitamins, so this should be a last resort.

Preparing in advance
It is unwise to prepare any of the onion family too far in advance. Raw alliums can develop "off-flavours" as a result of the sulphur compounds that are released when their cell walls are broken. Though safe to eat, they can taint delicate dishes of eggs, cream and butter. If you want to prepare alliums ahead of time, fry them briefly in a little fat from the recipe (or blanch them in boiling water for a few minutes).

SLICING AND CHOPPING ONIONS, SHALLOTS AND LEEKS

1 The easiest way to slice an onion is to cut it in half with a sharp knife, from neck to root.

2 Place the halves, cut sides down, on the chopping board.

3 Hold down one half firmly, but tuck your fingertips in, away from the blade of the knife, then, using the knuckles to guide the knife blade, cut down to make slices. Repeat with the other half.

Cutting crescent-shaped slices

Crescent-shaped slices of onion are good in salads and stir-fries. Thicker wedges are excellent for roasting.

1 Leave the root end of the onion intact and cut the bulb in half vertically, from neck to root.

2 Lay the onion, cut side down, on a board and, using a sharp knife, cut thin slices following the curve of the onion.

3 Leave these thin slices attached at the base for frying or separate them into layers for salad garnishes.

Cutting onion rings

1 Choose evenly shaped round onions. Look at the neck of the bulb and check that there is only one shoot, or neck – this means that there is more chance of getting perfectly round onion rings.

2 Cut a thin slice from one side so that it will not slip on the chopping board.

3 Cut down to form thin or thick slices. Push out to separate into rings.

Chopping onions

1 Slice the onion in half from top to bottom and lay it cut side down.

2 Slice across the onion, leaving a small section uncut at the root end.

3 Slice down through the onion at right angles to these cuts from neck to root. Leave the root end uncut to prevent the onion falling apart.

4 Finally, slice across the onion at right angles to the second set of cuts and the onion will fall into dice on the chopping board as you cut.

Slicing leeks

1 Cut across the width of the leek in the thickness you require.

COOK'S TIP
The green part of the leek often takes a little longer to cook than the tender white part, so put it into the pan a few minutes earlier.

2 When stir-frying, cut across the leek obliquely in a series of diagonal cuts. This exposes a larger surface area of the central portion of the leek to the heat, ensuring that it cooks quickly.

Chopping leeks

1 Using a sharp knife, carefully cut the leek in half vertically, from top to root. Lay the leek, cut side down, on the chopping board.

2 Make a series of cuts along the length of the leek from bottom to top, leaving the root end intact to prevent the leek falling apart.

3 Cut across the leek and it will fall into dice on the chopping board.

PREPARING SPRING ONIONS AND BUNCHING ONIONS

Spring onions and bunching onions are easily prepared. Cut off only tough or damaged green leaves. Peel the thin, outer layer from the onion and trim the root end. Wash thoroughly in a bowl of cold water or under a cold tap. For stir-frying, simply slice at an oblique angle, holding the knife blade at about 40 degrees to the length of the onion.

Spring onion brushes

These are traditionally served with Peking duck. The fringed end of the onion may be used to dip into the hoisin or plum sauce for brushing it on to the pancakes.

1 Cut the spring onion into 6–7.5cm/ 2½–3in lengths.

2 Make a series of lengthways cuts at one end of the spring onion, using a sharp knife or kitchen scissors to produce a tassel effect. Leave at least half the onion uncut to form a handle.

3 Place the spring onions in a bowl of iced water and chill in the fridge for 30–45 minutes to allow them to curl.

Making spring onion curls

1 Cut the spring onion into 6–7.5cm/ 2½–3in lengths.

2 Cut each piece in half lengthways, then cut these pieces lengthways into long, thin shreds.

3 Place in a bowl of iced water and chill in the fridge for 30 minutes to allow the shreds to curl.

Making spring onion tassels

1 Make a series of short, lengthways cuts at each end of the onions using a sharp knife or kitchen scissors to produce a tassel effect. Make sure you leave at least 2.5cm/1in of onion uncut at the centre.

2 Chill the spring onions in iced water for 30–45 minutes until the ends curl.

CUTTING CHIVES

1 Hold a bunch of chives in your hand, snip the bunch level at one end with kitchen scissors, then snip off the amount you require.

2 Cut straight across to form little rings, or obliquely to form slanting chives.

PREPARING GARLIC

The taste of garlic differs depending on how it is prepared. This is because varying amounts of the natural sulphur compounds, which are contained in garlic, are released depending on how you cut it. The finer you chop or crush garlic, the stronger the flavour will be.

Peeling garlic

The easiest way to peel garlic is to place it on a chopping board and use the blade of a wide-bladed knife flat to crush the clove.

1 Lay the blade of a knife flat on the clove and press down firmly on the blade with your fist or the heel of your hand, breaking the skin of the garlic.

2 The skin will then peel off easily. This also bruises the garlic, which allows the flavour to come out.

COOK'S TIP

To remove the smell of garlic from your hands, sprinkle them with salt, then rinse in cold water before washing them with hot water and soap. Alternatively, rub them all over with the cut side of a lemon before washing in hot water.

Blanching garlic

If peeling a lot of garlic, you can blanch the cloves to make them easier to peel.

1 Cut off the top and bottom of each garlic clove and place in a bowl of boiling water for 2–3 minutes. Drain, then slip the cloves out of their skins.

Chopping garlic

1 When chopping or crushing garlic, first remove any green shoot at the centre of the cloves. The shoot is most apparent in late winter/spring and can taste bitter. Cut out the shoot with the tip of a knife or pinch it out.

2 For a mild flavour, cut garlic into thin slices, across the clove, or chop roughly.

3 For a stronger flavour, finely chop the garlic by first cutting the clove in half from top to bottom, then cutting along and then across the clove.

Crushing garlic

To attain a much stronger flavour, crush the garlic rather than chopping it.

1 Crush the garlic in a mortar with a pestle or, alternatively, crush it on a chopping board with the flat blade of a knife to make a paste. Adding a few flakes of sea salt to the garlic will make crushing much easier.

2 Easier still, press the peeled clove through a specially designed garlic press or crusher.

GARLIC GADGETS

The only tools you really need to prepare garlic are a good, small, sharp knife, a chopping board and, of course, your hands. However, there are plenty of pieces of equipment on the market that are designed to help with the preparation of garlic. Most of this equipment has just one aim in mind – to minimize handling the garlic and therefore preventing the hands from smelling of it.

Garlic peeler

Garlic peelers are made of a simple rubber tube with a textured inside surface. The garlic clove is placed inside the tube, which is then pressed down on and rolled back and forth on the work surface to loosen the skin for easier peeling.

Garlic press (pump action)

A pump action garlic press is the most familiar type of garlic crusher. Some presses have a very useful reverse action that helps to extract the garlic that can become trapped in the holes. Garlic presses can also be used for preparing onion and ginger juice.

Garlic press (screw action)

A different type of press to the pump action but the result is basically the same. As you screw down the handle, the garlic is pressed out of the head. It is easy to use, but not so easy to clean.

Mortar and pestle

These are very useful pieces of general kitchen equipment and are excellent for crushing large quantities of garlic or making garlicky pastes, such as aioli.

Below: A mortar and pestle are the traditional devices for crushing garlic.

Garlic crush

A garlic crush is similar to a pestle but has a larger domed base. It is most effective when used with a bowl-shaped board. It produces a similar result to garlic crushed with the flat blade of a large knife.

Garlic slicer

A garlic slicer acts like a miniature mandolin. The garlic clove is placed in the holder, then slid back and forth over the sharp blade. This gadget is particularly useful if you are slicing large quantities of garlic or ginger.

COOKING ONIONS AND OTHER ALLIUMS

There are many ways of cooking onions, all of which will produce very different results both in the flavour of the onion and in the dish in which it is used.

FRYING ONIONS

Onions can be fried in a number of different ways and each gives its own unique result. Onions that are quickly fried until they are brown will retain all the pungency of the raw onion and may taste quite bitter if allowed to get too brown. Quick-fried onions are generally used in dishes where they will receive further cooking, such as stews and casseroles – dishes that also benefit from the dark colour the browned onions impart to the sauce.

Slow-fried onions, cooked over a low heat in a covered saucepan and not allowed to brown at all, will develop a wonderful, mellow, sweet taste that can add a great depth of flavour to the finished dish. This process is called sweating, and is an essential first step in preparing many soups and sauces. It works well with leeks, too.

Caramelizing onions is a combination of these two methods. First the onions are cooked slowly until soft but not browned, then the heat is turned up and the onions are cooked uncovered until they brown. In some recipes, a little sugar is added to speed up the caramelizing process. When the onions are cooked slowly to a mahogany brown, they are used as the base of many rich, brown soups and many classic sauces. They are also good to eat just as they are as an accompaniment to meat, poultry or cheese.

Different kinds of onion, or onions at different stages of growth, react in different ways to these basic cooking techniques. Green, unripened onions will not fry to a dry crispness. Red onions tend to be "wetter" than yellow Spanish onions and so they tend not to brown and caramelize so easily. Shallots, on the other hand, are quite dry-fleshed and will soon dry out and turn bitter and hard if they are fried and browned too quickly. To keep onions soft and prevent them browning when frying, add a pinch of salt to draw out their moisture.

Quick frying

1 Heat whatever fat the recipe calls for in a large, heavy-based frying pan over a medium heat until hot. Add the thinly sliced or chopped onions and cook for about 5 minutes, stirring frequently to prevent them sticking to the pan, until the onions begin to turn brown at the edges. Do not allow to burn as this will spoil the flavour.

Slow frying

1 Cook the onions over a very low heat for 10–15 minutes until they collapse and turn a deep golden yellow colour. Stir the onions occasionally while they cook to prevent them from sticking to the pan and browning as this will spoil their mellow flavour.

Sweating

This cooking process can be used for onions or leeks and is often the first step in soup making, as it concentrates and mellows the flavour, producing a rounder taste. Sweating or slow-frying requires a very low heat that cooks, but does not brown the onions or leeks as this destroys the mellow, sweet flavour.

1 Cook the onions as for shallow frying, but cover the saucepan with a lid to produce a much softer, sweeter result.

2 Some cooks like to press a piece of greaseproof or non-stick baking paper on top of the onions before covering them with the lid. This sweats the onions even more intensely.

Remedies for onion odours
• Try rubbing the soles of your feet with pure peppermint oil. Within 30 minutes the smell on your breath should be of mint.
• Chewing fresh parsley is the best-known antidote to onions and garlic on the breath. The chlorophyll in the parsley neutralizes the sulphur

chemicals released by the alliums, which cause odours.
• Cover over the onion smells by chewing cardamom or fennel seeds – these seeds are traditionally offered after Indian meals as breath fresheners and an aid to digestion.
• Drink a herbal infusion of mint, fennel and/or sage.

Thai crisp-fried shallots

These are excellent for garnishing salads, rice and soups.

1 Peel the shallots and slice to a medium thickness.

2 Cook the shallots gently in oil for about 8 minutes until they soften.

3 Raise the heat and fry the shallots briskly until they brown and crisp. Remove with a slotted spoon and drain well on kitchen paper.

COOK'S TIP
Dried shallot or onion slices can be fried from dry to form a crisp-fried garnish. Take care not to burn them.

CARAMELIZING

To caramelize onions or shallots, they need to be cooked slowly until their natural sugars turn an appetizing brown colour. Caramelized onions or shallots add a depth of flavour to soups, sauces and stews. They are also good served with liver, steak or sausages.

The speed with which onions will caramelize depends on the heat of the pan. Onions or shallots caramelized over a very low heat for 45 minutes will slowly turn a deep mahogany brown. The cooking time will depend on the onions' sugar content. Caramelized onions are used most famously in *soupe à l'oignon*. For a quicker result, raise the heat and add just a little sugar to aid caramelization, but stir frequently to prevent the onions sticking to the pan.

Caramelizing onions in a saucepan

1 Cook onions slowly, covered, in butter or oil until they soften and turn golden.

2 Continue cooking, uncovered, until they begin to brown at the edges, stirring them frequently.

3 Add 2.5–5ml/½–1 tsp sugar to help the onions to caramelize more quickly.

Caramelizing onions in the oven

This technique can be quite useful if you are busy, because the onions do not need to be stirred quite so often as onions caramelized in a saucepan.

1 Place thickly sliced onions in a roasting tin or on a baking tray, season with salt and pepper to taste, add herbs, such as thyme or rosemary, and sprinkle with a little olive oil.

2 Cover the onions with foil and cook at 190°C/375°F/Gas 5 for 30 minutes.

3 Uncover the tin, stir in 5ml/1 tsp sugar and sprinkle a little wine or balsamic vinegar over the onions.

4 Return the baking sheet to the oven, uncovered this time, and cook for another 25–35 minutes, stirring once or twice, by which time the onions should be very soft and browned.

COOK'S TIP
A thick layer of onions will caramelize better than a thin layer, which will brown too quickly. Keep an eye on them in the oven. If they brown too quickly, lower the heat and be sure to stir once or twice.

Caramelizing shallots or baby onions

Shallots and baby onions are usually caramelized whole, but they can also be cooked in thick slices.

1 Brown the shallots or baby onions lightly on all sides in a little butter or oil. Raise the heat slightly, sprinkle in a little sugar, then let the shallots cook until the sugar begins to caramelize.

2 Add seasoning, herbs, if using, and a fairly shallow layer of a liquid to suit the recipe, such as wine, stock or vinegar. Cook gently, covered, until the shallots or onions are tender but still whole.

3 Then cook, uncovered, at a higher heat until all the liquid has evaporated.

FRYING GARLIC

Because of garlic's relatively low moisture content, it fries and browns more quickly than onions. It will burn easily and develops a bitter, acrid taste. Therefore, when a recipe calls for onions and garlic to be fried together, add the garlic to the pan when the onions are almost cooked.

In Chinese and Asian cooking, garlic is often fried in oil at the beginning of cooking. Sometimes it is removed and discarded afterwards because only the flavoured oil is wanted in the dish; at other times, the garlic is an integral part of the dish. Again, care needs to be taken that the garlic cooks to an even, light brown, when it has a delicious toasty flavour.

Frying garlic slices

1 Heat a wok or deep frying pan until hot, add some cooking oil and allow it to become hot.

2 Add finely sliced garlic to the wok or pan and immediately stir it through the oil. It will begin to colour at once.

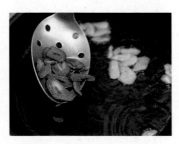

3 Remove the garlic with a slotted spoon as soon as it is a light brown.

Frying whole garlic cloves

Fried cloves of garlic make a delicious addition to green salads, especially those with goat's cheese.

1 Choose large, plump garlic cloves and peel them. Bring a large saucepan of water to the boil and throw in the garlic, cook for 3–4 minutes, then drain.

2 Repeat the blanching process, then drain and dry thoroughly.

3 Heat a shallow layer of oil in a wok or frying pan, then fry the garlic gently until it turns an even, medium brown.

4 Remove with a slotted spoon and drain well on kitchen paper.

GRILLING

Cooking onions, leeks and spring onions in this way gives a delicious result. They are perfect for serving as a vegetable accompaniment. Grilling – either under a grill, over hot coals or using a griddle pan – gives onions, leeks and spring onions a sweet, mellow flavour.

Grilling onions

Onions, particularly mild, sweet onions such as Spanish onions, grill very successfully and are especially good when cooked over hot coals.

1 Peel the onions and slice them horizontally into thick slices, discarding the thin slices from the top and bottom of the onion. Carefully spear the slices on an oiled metal skewer, passing the skewer through the slice so that all the layers are kept flat.

2 Brush the skewered onion slices with oil, season, then grill for 5–6 minutes on each side or until the onions are soft and slightly charred.

3 Alternatively, place the onion slices in a grill cage, brush with oil and season, then grill each side for 5–6 minutes.

Grilling spring onions

Spring onions are delicious grilled and are very good as an accompaniment to grilled fish, poultry and meat dishes or served with cheese. They are very popular in Mexico and Cataluña where they are known as *calçots* and eaten with a spicy chilli sauce.

1 Choose big, fat spring onions with large bulbs for grilling.

2 Trim off any damaged leaves and the outer skin; trim off the root, too, but leave the end intact.

3 Brush with a little oil and grill, either over charcoal on a barbecue or on a cast-iron, ridged grill pan, for about 2 minutes each side, or until softened and browned but not too charred. In Cataluña the outer skin is often peeled off before eating.

COOK'S TIP
Whole grilled cipolla onions make unusual and delicious canapés. After cooking, marinate the grilled cipolla onions in French dressing and serve on rounds of toasted bread or simply with thick slices of fresh crusty bread.

Grilling leeks

Baby leeks, when very small, may be grilled in a similar way to spring onions. However, leeks are usually blanched for a few minutes in boiling water before grilling, since they have tougher skins than spring onions.

1 Bring a large pan of lightly salted water to the boil and throw in the trimmed leeks. Cook baby leeks for 2–3 minutes and cook larger leeks for 4–5 minutes, then drain.

2 Cool a little, then gently squeeze the excess water out of the leeks. Leave baby leeks whole. Cut large leeks in half lengthways or into short logs. Dry on a clean dish towel or kitchen paper.

3 Brush the leeks with oil, season with salt and pepper to taste, then grill baby leeks as for spring onions, allowing 3–4 minutes each side. Grill large leeks for about 4–5 minutes each side.

COOK'S TIP
Grilled leeks may be served hot, warm or cold. They are particularly delicious with a simple dressing of oil, tarragon vinegar and a little mustard.

ROASTING ONIONS

Onions are delicious roasted. They can be roasted in their skins, which will produce a soft, juicy, sweet centre, or they can be peeled, which produces a more caramelized taste and a much crisper texture.

Roasting onions in their skins

1 Remove any damaged skin and cut off excess root, leaving the base intact.

2 Brush with oil if you like, then roast at 190°C/375°F/Gas 5 until they feel soft when gently squeezed (1–1½ hours).

3 To serve, cut a cross in the top and add butter or cheese. A flavoured butter with herbs or chilli is especially good.

Roasting peeled onions

1 Small, peeled onions may be roasted whole. Larger onions may be cut into wedges (leaving them attached at the root base, so they don't fall apart on cooking) or, alternatively, they can be cut into halves or quarters.

2 Alternatively, make 2–3 cross-cuts from the top down to 1cm/½in from the root base. As they roast, the layers of the onion will open out.

3 Whole onions will roast more quickly if first blanched in boiling water for 3–4 minutes. Toss in oil, season, and cook, uncovered at 190–200°C/375–400°F/Gas 5–6. Whole onions take about 40 minutes; wedges about 30 minutes.

STUFFING ONIONS

Onions make natural containers for stuffings, and these may be prepared in two ways.

Preparing raw onion cups for stuffing

1 Choose round, even-shaped onions, not flat or pointed onions. Large Spanish onions are best.

2 Peel, and cut a thin slice off each end so that the cups will stay upright.

3 Using a sharp knife, cut the onion in half horizontally.

4 Using a sharp, pointed knife, cut round the second or third layer of onion, counting in from the outer layer.

5 Gradually loosen the centre of the onion from the outer layers, leaving a cup of 2–3 layers.

6 If any of the cups has a hole in the base, cover it with a small piece of the removed onion. Fill with stuffing and cook according to the recipe.

To prepare whole onions for stuffing

Whole onions need to be blanched first so that they will cook evenly. The flesh can then be scooped out and mixed with the stuffing. Allow one large onion per person.

1 Choose round, even-shaped onions, peel, but leave the top and especially the root base intact.

2 Cover in boiling lightly salted water and cook for 15 minutes, then drain thoroughly and set aside until cool enough to handle.

3 Cut off and remove a cap from the top of the onion.

4 Using a small, sharp knife and a pointed or serrated teaspoon, remove the centre of the onion to leave a shell 2–3 layers thick.

Making stuffing

The most popular stuffings for onions are either meat, or breadcrumbs with herbs, spices and cheese. The stuffing usually incorporates the chopped onion that has been removed.

Raw onion cups are best suited to meaty fillings as they need cooking for 1–1½ hours at 180–190°C/350–375°F/ Gas 4–5. They cook best if sat on a bed of sauce or a mixture of olive oil and lemon juice, so that the onions may be basted while they cook. This helps to stop them drying out and keeps them moist. Blanched, partially cooked whole onions should be brushed with a little oil or melted butter and baked for 45–60 minutes.

Watering eyes

Peeling and chopping onions makes you cry because these actions release the volatile chemicals that give onions their strength and bite. They travel to the eyes and nasal cavities through the water vapour in juicy onions. The stronger and juicier the onion, the more it will make you cry. Shallots and garlic, though often containing more of the offending allicins, contain less water, so produce less vapour and hence fewer tears. Leeks are very mild and hardly ever cause tears during preparation.

Most cures for onion tears have to be taken with a pinch of salt, but here are a few that people claim help.
• Chilling an onion in the fridge for several hours (or the freezer for a few minutes) is said to "lock-in" the water vapour and prevent it from reaching your eyes.
• Peeling onions under water will prevent the water vapour reaching your nose and eyes, but no one's suggesting you try chopping onions underwater!
• The chemicals mostly reach your tear ducts through your nose, so try breathing through your mouth rather than your nose.
• If you are preparing a lot of small onions, try peeling them by the blanching method – this reduces the chemical spray that's released when onions are peeled.
• When preparing onions, try leaving the base (root) end intact, or cut it last of all. This basal portion of the onion contains the highest concentration of tear-causing allicins.
• An old wives' tale suggests that if you bite on a crust of bread while preparing onions, then you won't cry. Maybe the crust forms a barrier to prevent the onion's water vapour from reaching your nose and eyes.

PICKLING AND PRESERVING

Once, pickling was an important way of storing vegetables through the lean winter months but nowadays onions are pickled because people like the taste. Although onions, shallots and garlic keep well in their natural state, pickling has always been a popular way of keeping them because their naturally strong flavour survives the pickling process so well and stands up to the strong tastes of vinegar and spices.

Pickling onions

Choose small, firm even-shaped onions for pickling and peel them by the blanching method. Onions to be pickled are usually salted to remove water and to ensure they keep well.

For crisp pickled onions, cover with cold vinegar. For a softer pickle, the onions may be cooked in the hot vinegar for up to 10 minutes.

1 The onions can be layered with sea salt in a non-reactive (i.e. non-metallic) bowl.

2 Alternatively, put the onions in a bowl and cover with a strong brine solution. Set aside to soak.

3 Weight the onions to ensure that they are covered by the brine.

4 After 1–2 days in the brine (this depends on the size of the onions), the onions should be rinsed and patted dry, then packed into clean, sterilized jars.

5 Pour spiced vinegar over the onions.

6 Extra spices can be added to the jar if liked, then tightly seal the jars for storage.

COOK'S TIP

Spices, which can be added for extra flavouring, may include mustard seeds, peppercorns, coriander seeds, allspice, chillies and cloves.

Simple spiced vinegar

Heat together 1.2 litres/2 pints/5 cups vinegar (light or dark malt has the best keeping qualities) with 2 pieces of dried ginger root, 2 blades of mace, 2–3 dried red chillies and 15ml/1 tbsp each mustard seeds, coriander seeds and black peppercorns. Add a few bay leaves, a piece of cinnamon stick or 2 or 3 star anise to taste. The longer you heat the flavourings with the vinegar, the stronger the taste will become. For a sweeter vinegar, dissolve 45ml/3 tbsp of muscovado sugar in the vinegar.

To sterilize jars

Wash, rinse and dry thoroughly. Heat the oven to 180°C/350°F/Gas 4. Making sure you remove any rubber seals first, place the jars on a tray, then heat the jars for about 20 minutes. Cool a little before handling them – the jars will be very hot.

Jars can also be sterilized by putting them in a pan of boiling water for 10 minutes. Stand them on a trivet so that they are not directly over the heat.

OTHER WAYS OF PRESERVING ALLIUMS

Drying onions

In the past, drying was a popular way of preserving onions, but it is less so now, since onions are available fresh all year round. However, dried onions can make a useful store-cupboard ingredient for emergencies. To use dried onions, add them directly to stews or casseroles, or reconstitute them in a little warm water for about 10–15 minutes first. Dried shallots may be fried in a little oil over a medium heat to produce excellent crisp-fried shallots, which are useful as a garnish for many Thai and South-east Asian dishes.

1 Peel and thinly slice the onions, then lay them on racks.

2 Leave them in a very low oven (110°C/225°F/Gas ¼) until very dry. This will take anything up to 12 hours. Turn the slices once as they dry.

3 Store the onions in a cloth or paper bag in a dry place or in a jar with a cloth or paper lid to absorb any residual moisture. Shallots may be dried in the same way.

Making roasted garlic purée

This makes a very useful flavouring to have in the fridge. It will store for several weeks as long as you keep the purée covered with at least 1cm/½in of oil. Top up the oil when you remove some purée. As a rough guide, 1 head of garlic should yield about 15–30ml/1–2 tbsp of purée.

The purée is useful in many dishes. To make a simple sauce for pasta, stir 2–3 tbsp of the purée into 150ml/¼ pint/⅔ cup of heated, bubbling double cream, season with salt and pepper to taste and add a little lemon juice and some chopped thyme or basil. This is good with many vegetarian dishes too. The purée is also good in soufflés, omelettes and tarts, or simply spread on good bread and eaten with some grilled or baked goat's cheese.

Roasted garlic purée

The following quantities make approximately 120ml/4fl oz/ ½ cup purée.

5 large heads garlic
2–3 sprigs thyme or rosemary
   or both
extra virgin olive oil
salt and ground black pepper

COOK'S TIP

When puréeing this amount of garlic, it is easier to purée the garlic, skins and all, in a food mill or mouli legumes. The mill will force through the soft garlic, leaving all the papery skins and debris behind.

Using a dehydrator

If you are planning on drying a lot of onions, it may be worthwhile for you to invest in a domestic dehydrator. They are easy to use and will enable you to dry large quantities of onions quickly and efficiently. They are also useful for drying other vegetables and fruit, as well as being handy for quick-drying fresh herbs. Follow the manufacturer's instructions for timing.

1 Cut a thin slice off the top of each head of garlic.

2 Wrap the garlic heads in foil with the herbs and drizzle over 45ml/3 tbsp oil. Bake at 190°C/ 375°F/Gas 5 for 50–60 minutes, or until the garlic is soft, then cool.

3 Squeeze the garlic out of its skin into a bowl, then mash, beat in the oil and season.

4 Spoon into a sterilized jar. Pour over oil to cover by about 1cm/½in. Cover and store in the fridge for up to 3 weeks.

Freezing

It is not recommended to freeze raw alliums, since they can develop "off flavours" because of the sulphur compounds that are released when they are cut. Sauces that contain raw garlic or onion should also be frozen with caution. With pesto, for instance, prepare and freeze the basil, pine nut and oil paste and only add the garlic and grated cheeses on thawing.

THE RECIPES

With few exceptions, the onion has become an essential part of the cooking of every culture across the globe. However, onions and their relations are often taken for granted and tend to be used simply as the basis for whatever savoury dish we are cooking. The wonderful selection of recipes that follow redress the balance in the alliums' favour, and celebrate the onion family not just as kitchen staples, but as star attractions in their own right — from soups and starters to meat, poultry and fish dishes to breads and pickles.

Is there anything more restorative than a steaming bowl of onion soup? Whatever the varying fortunes in alliums' popularity, onions in soups have always been favourites. They are an essential flavouring in good stock, and star in soups as diverse as thick French Onion Soup and velvety, chilled Vichyssoise. Garlic soups cure many ills; thick soupy stews of leeks ward off winter chills; buttery, saffron-scented onion soup is simply delicious to eat.

Soups without onions would be hard to imagine.

Soups

SHERRIED ONION <u>AND</u> ALMOND SOUP
<u>WITH</u> SAFFRON

*THE SPANISH COMBINATION OF ONIONS, SHERRY AND SAFFRON GIVES THIS PALE YELLOW SOUP A
BEGUILING FLAVOUR THAT IS PERFECT AS THE OPENING COURSE OF A SPECIAL MEAL.*

2 Add the saffron strands and cook, uncovered, for 3–4 minutes, then add the ground almonds and cook, stirring constantly, for another 2–3 minutes. Pour in the stock and sherry and stir in 5ml/1 tsp salt. Season with plenty of black pepper. Bring to the boil, then lower the heat and simmer gently for about 10 minutes.

<u>SERVES FOUR</u>

INGREDIENTS
  40g/1½oz/3 tbsp butter
  2 large yellow onions, thinly sliced
  1 small garlic clove, finely chopped
  good pinch of saffron strands (about 12 strands)
  50g/2oz blanched almonds, toasted and finely ground
  750ml/1¼ pints/3 cups good chicken or vegetable stock
  45ml/3 tbsp dry sherry
  salt and ground black pepper
  30ml/2 tbsp flaked or slivered almonds, toasted, and chopped fresh parsley to garnish

1 Melt the butter in a heavy-based saucepan over a low heat. Add the onions and garlic, stirring to coat them thoroughly in the butter, then cover the pan and cook very gently, stirring frequently, for 15–20 minutes, until the onions are soft and golden yellow.

VARIATION
This soup is also delicious served chilled. Use olive oil rather than butter and add a little more chicken or vegetable stock to make a slightly thinner soup, then leave to cool and chill for at least 4 hours. Just before serving, taste for seasoning. Float 1–2 ice cubes in each bowl.

3 Process the soup in a blender or food processor until smooth, then return it to the rinsed pan. Reheat slowly, without allowing the soup to boil, stirring occasionally. Taste for seasoning, adding more salt and pepper if required.

4 Ladle the soup into heated bowls, garnish with the toasted flaked or slivered almonds and a little parsley and serve immediately.

SIMPLE CREAM OF ONION SOUP

THIS WONDERFULLY SOOTHING SOUP HAS A DEEP, BUTTERY FLAVOUR THAT IS COMPLEMENTED BY CRISP CROÛTONS OR SNIPPED CHIVES, SPRINKLED OVER JUST BEFORE SERVING.

SERVES FOUR

INGREDIENTS

115g/4oz/½ cup unsalted butter
1kg/2¼lb yellow onions, sliced
1 fresh bay leaf
105ml/7 tbsp dry white vermouth
1 litre/1¾ pints/4 cups good chicken
   or vegetable stock
150ml/¼ pint/⅔ cup double cream
a little lemon juice (optional)
salt and ground black pepper
croûtons or snipped fresh chives,
   to garnish

COOK'S TIP
Adding the second batch of onions gives texture and a lovely buttery flavour to this soup. Make sure the onions do not brown.

1 Melt 75g/3oz/6 tbsp of the butter in a large heavy-based saucepan. Set about 200g/7oz of the onions aside and add the rest to the pan with the bay leaf. Stir to coat in the butter, then cover and cook very gently for about 30 minutes. The onions should be very soft and tender, but not browned.

2 Add the vermouth, increase the heat and boil rapidly until the liquid has evaporated. Add the stock, 5ml/1 tsp salt and pepper to taste. Bring to the boil, lower the heat and simmer for 5 minutes, then remove from the heat.

3 Leave the soup to cool, then discard the bay leaf and process it in a blender or food processor. Return the soup to the rinsed pan.

4 Meanwhile, melt the remaining butter in another pan and cook the remaining onions slowly, covered, until soft but not browned. Uncover and continue to cook gently until golden yellow.

5 Add the cream to the soup and reheat it gently until hot, but do not allow it to boil. Taste and adjust the seasoning, adding a little lemon juice if liked. Add the buttery onions and stir for 1–2 minutes, then ladle the soup into bowls. Sprinkle with croûtons or snipped chives and serve.

French Onion Soup
with Gruyère Croûtes

This is perhaps the most famous of all onion soups. Traditionally, it was served as a sustaining early morning meal to the porters and workers of Les Halles market in Paris.

SERVES SIX

INGREDIENTS
    50g/2oz/¼ cup butter
    15ml/1 tbsp olive or groundnut oil
    2kg/4½lb yellow onions, peeled
        and sliced
    5ml/1 tsp chopped fresh thyme
    5ml/1 tsp caster sugar
    15ml/1 tbsp sherry vinegar
    1.5 litres/2½ pints/6¼ cups good
        beef, chicken or duck stock
    25ml/1½ tbsp plain flour
    150ml/¼ pint/⅔ cup dry white wine
    45ml/3 tbsp brandy
    salt and ground black pepper
For the croûtes
    6–12 thick slices day-old French
        stick or baguette, about 2.5cm/
        1in thick
    1 garlic clove, halved
    15ml/1 tbsp French mustard
    115g/4oz/1 cup coarsely grated
        Gruyère cheese

1 Melt the butter with the oil in a large saucepan. Add the onions and stir to coat them in the fat. Cook over a medium heat for 5–8 minutes, stirring once or twice, until the onions begin to soften. Stir in the thyme.

2 Reduce the heat to very low, cover the pan and cook the onions for 20–30 minutes, stirring frequently, until they are very soft and golden yellow.

3 Uncover the pan and increase the heat slightly. Stir in the sugar and cook for 5–10 minutes, until the onions start to brown. Add the sherry vinegar and increase the heat again, then continue cooking, stirring frequently, until the onions turn a deep, golden brown – this could take up to 20 minutes.

COOK'S TIP
The long slow cooking of the onions is the key to success with this soup. If the onions brown too quickly the soup will be bitter.

4 Meanwhile, bring the stock to the boil in another saucepan. Stir the flour into the onions and cook for about 2 minutes, then gradually pour in the hot stock. Add the wine and brandy and season the soup to taste with salt and pepper. Simmer for 10–15 minutes.

5 For the croûtes, preheat the oven to 150°C/300°F/Gas 2. Place the slices of bread on a greased baking tray and bake for 15–20 minutes, until dry and lightly browned. Rub the bread with the cut surface of the garlic and spread with the mustard, then sprinkle the grated Gruyère cheese over the slices.

6 Preheat the grill on the hottest setting. Ladle the soup into a large flameproof pan or six flameproof bowls. Float the croûtes on the soup, then grill until the cheese melts, bubbles and browns. Serve immediately.

CHILLED GARLIC AND ALMOND SOUP WITH GRAPES

THIS CREAMY CHILLED SUMMER SOUP IS BASED ON AN ANCIENT MOORISH RECIPE FROM ANDALUCIA IN SOUTHERN SPAIN. ALMONDS AND PINE NUTS ARE TYPICAL INGREDIENTS OF THIS REGION.

SERVES SIX

INGREDIENTS
   75g/3oz/¾ cup blanched almonds
   50g/2oz/½ cup pine nuts
   6 large garlic cloves, peeled
   200g/7oz good-quality day-old bread,
      crusts removed
   900ml–1 litre/1½–1¾ pints/3¾–4 cups
      still mineral water, chilled
   120ml/4fl oz/½ cup extra virgin olive
      oil, plus extra to serve
   15ml/1 tbsp sherry vinegar
   30–45ml/2–3 tbsp dry sherry
   250g/9oz grapes, peeled, halved
      and seeded
   salt and ground white pepper
   ice cubes and snipped fresh chives,
      to garnish

1 Roast the almonds and pine nuts together in a dry saucepan over a moderate heat until they are very lightly browned. Cool, then grind to a powder.

2 Blanch the garlic in boiling water for 3 minutes. Drain and rinse.

3 Soak the bread in 300ml/½ pint/1¼ cups of the water for 10 minutes, then squeeze dry. Process the garlic, bread, nuts and 5ml/1 tsp salt in a food processor or blender until they form a paste.

4 Gradually blend in the olive oil and sherry vinegar, followed by sufficient water to make a smooth soup with a creamy consistency.

5 Stir in 30ml/2 tbsp of the sherry. Adjust the seasoning and add more dry sherry to taste. Chill for at least 3 hours, then adjust the seasoning again and stir in a little more chilled water if the soup has thickened. Reserve a few of the grapes for the garnish and stir the remainder into the soup.

6 Ladle the soup into bowls (glass bowls look particularly good) and garnish with ice cubes, the reserved grapes and snipped fresh chives. Serve with additional extra virgin olive oil to drizzle over the soup to taste just before it is eaten.

COOK'S TIPS
• Toasting the nuts slightly accentuates their flavour, but you can omit this step if you prefer a paler soup.
• Blanching the garlic softens its flavour.

VICHYSSOISE

THIS CLASSIC, CHILLED SUMMER SOUP WAS FIRST CREATED IN THE 1920S BY LOUIS DIAT, CHEF AT THE NEW YORK RITZ-CARLTON. HE NAMED IT AFTER VICHY NEAR HIS HOME IN FRANCE. IT IS BASED ON A SIMPLE LEEK AND POTATO SOUP, MADE LUXURIOUSLY VELVETY BY ADDING DOUBLE CREAM.

SERVES FOUR TO SIX

INGREDIENTS
50g/2oz/¼ cup unsalted butter
450g/1lb leeks, white parts only,
   thinly sliced
3 large shallots, sliced
250g/9oz floury potatoes (such as
   King Edward or Maris Piper), peeled
   and cut into chunks
1 litre/1¾ pints/4 cups light chicken
   stock or water
300ml/½ pint/1¼ cups
   double cream
iced water (optional)
a little lemon juice (optional)
salt and ground black pepper
snipped fresh chives,
   to garnish

1 Melt the butter in a heavy-based saucepan and cook the leeks and shallots gently, covered, for 15–20 minutes, until soft but not browned.

2 Add the potatoes and cook, uncovered, for a few minutes.

3 Stir in the stock or water, 5ml/1 tsp salt and pepper to taste. Bring to the boil, then reduce the heat and partly cover the pan. Simmer for 15 minutes, or until the potatoes are soft.

4 Cool, then process the soup until smooth in a blender or food processor. Sieve the soup into a bowl and stir in the cream. Taste and adjust the seasoning and add a little iced water if the consistency of the soup seems too thick.

5 Chill the soup for at least 4 hours or until very cold. Taste the chilled soup for seasoning and add a squeeze of lemon juice, if required. Pour the soup into bowls and sprinkle with snipped chives. Serve immediately.

VARIATIONS
• **Potage Bonne Femme** For this hot leek and potato soup, use 1 chopped onion instead of the shallots and 450g/1lb potatoes. Halve the quantity of double cream and reheat it in the puréed soup, adding a little milk if the consistency of the soup seems very thick. Deep-fried shredded leek may be used to garnish the soup instead of snipped fresh chives.
• **Chilled Leek and Sorrel or Watercress Soup** Add about 50g/2oz/1 cup shredded sorrel to the soup at the end of cooking. Finish and chill as in the main recipe, then serve the soup garnished with a little pile of finely shredded sorrel. The same quantity of watercress can be used in the same way.

CHICKEN AND LEEK SOUP WITH PRUNES AND BARLEY

THIS RECIPE IS BASED ON THE TRADITIONAL SCOTTISH SOUP, COCK-A-LEEKIE. THE UNUSUAL COMBINATION OF LEEKS AND PRUNES IS SURPRISINGLY DELICIOUS.

SERVES SIX

INGREDIENTS
1 chicken, weighing about 2kg/4¼lb
900g/2lb leeks
1 fresh bay leaf
a few each fresh parsley stalks and
   thyme sprigs
1 large carrot, thickly sliced
2.4 litres/4 pints/10 cups chicken or
   beef stock
115g/4oz/generous ½ cup
   pearl barley
400g/14oz ready-to-eat prunes
salt and ground black pepper
chopped fresh parsley, to garnish

1 Cut the breasts off the chicken and set aside. Place the remaining chicken carcass in a large saucepan. Cut half the leeks into 5cm/2in lengths and add them to the pan. Tie the bay leaf, parsley and thyme into a bouquet garni and add to the pan with the carrot and the stock. Bring to the boil, then reduce the heat and cover. Simmer gently for 1 hour. Skim off any scum when the water first boils and occasionally during simmering.

2 Add the chicken breasts and cook for another 30 minutes, until they are just cooked. Leave until cool enough to handle, then strain the stock. Reserve the chicken breasts and meat from the chicken carcass. Discard all the skin, bones, cooked vegetables and herbs. Skim as much fat as you can from the stock, then return it to the pan.

3 Meanwhile, rinse the pearl barley thoroughly in a sieve under cold running water, then cook it in a large saucepan of boiling water for about 10 minutes. Drain, rinse well again and drain thoroughly.

4 Add the pearl barley to the stock. Bring to the boil over a medium heat, then lower the heat and cook very gently for 15–20 minutes, until the barley is just cooked and tender. Season the soup with 5ml/1 tsp salt and black pepper.

5 Add the prunes. Slice the remaining leeks and add them to the pan. Bring to the boil, then simmer for 10 minutes or until the leeks are just cooked.

6 Slice the chicken breasts and add them to the soup with the remaining chicken meat, sliced or cut into neat pieces. Reheat if necessary, then ladle the soup into deep plates and sprinkle with chopped parsley.

MEDITERRANEAN LEEK AND FISH SOUP WITH TOMATOES

THIS CHUNKY SOUP, WHICH IS ALMOST A STEW, MAKES A ROBUST AND WONDERFULLY AROMATIC MEAL IN A BOWL. SERVE IT WITH CRISP-BAKED CROÛTES SPREAD WITH A SPICY GARLIC MAYONNAISE.

SERVES FOUR

INGREDIENTS
30ml/2 tbsp olive oil
2 large thick leeks, white and green
  parts separated, both thinly sliced
5ml/1 tsp crushed coriander seeds
good pinch of dried red chilli flakes
300g/11oz small salad potatoes,
  thickly sliced
200g/7oz can Italian peeled
  chopped plum tomatoes
600ml/1 pint/2½ cups fish stock
150ml/¼ pint/⅔ cup fruity white wine
1 fresh bay leaf
1 star anise
strip of pared orange rind
good pinch of saffron strands
450g/1lb white fish fillets, such as
  monkfish, sea bass, cod or haddock
450g/1lb small squid, cleaned
250g/9oz uncooked peeled prawns
30–45ml/2–3 tbsp chopped parsley
salt and ground black pepper
To serve
1 short French loaf, sliced and toasted
spicy garlic mayonnaise

1 Gently heat the oil in a pan, then add the green part of the leeks, the coriander and the chilli, and cook for 5 minutes.

2 Add the potatoes and tomatoes and pour in the stock and wine. Add the bay leaf, star anise, orange rind and saffron.

3 Bring to the boil, reduce the heat and part-cover the pan. Simmer for 20 minutes or until the potatoes are tender. Taste and adjust the seasoning.

4 Cut the fish into chunks. Cut the squid sacs into rectangles and score a criss-cross pattern into them without cutting right through.

5 Add the fish to the stew and cook gently for 4 minutes. Add the prawns and cook for 1 minute. Add the squid and the shredded white part of the leek and cook, stirring occasionally, for 2 minutes.

6 Stir in the chopped parsley and serve with toasted French bread and spicy garlic mayonnaise.

CHICKEN, LEEK AND CELERY SOUP

THIS MAKES A SUBSTANTIAL MAIN COURSE SOUP WITH FRESH CRUSTY BREAD. YOU WILL NEED NOTHING MORE THAN A SALAD AND CHEESE, OR JUST FRESH FRUIT TO FOLLOW.

SERVES FOUR TO SIX

INGREDIENTS
1.4kg/3lb free-range chicken
1 small head of celery, trimmed
1 onion, coarsely chopped
1 fresh bay leaf
a few fresh parsley stalks
a few fresh tarragon sprigs
2.4 litres/4 pints/10 cups cold water
3 large leeks
65g/2½oz/5 tbsp butter
2 potatoes, cut into chunks
150ml/¼ pint/⅔ cup dry white wine
30–45ml/2–3 tbsp single
  cream (optional)
salt and ground black pepper
90g/3½oz pancetta, grilled until
  crisp, to garnish

1 Cut the breasts off the chicken and set aside. Chop the rest of the chicken carcass into 8–10 pieces and place in a large saucepan.

2 Chop 4–5 of the outer sticks of the celery and add them to the pan with the onion. Tie the bay leaf, parsley and tarragon together and add to the pan. Pour in the cold water to cover the ingredients and bring to the boil. Reduce the heat and cover the pan, then simmer for 1½ hours.

3 Remove the chicken and cut off and reserve the meat. Strain the stock, then return it to the pan and boil rapidly until it has reduced to about 1.5 litres/ 2½ pints/6¼ cups.

4 Meanwhile, set about 150g/5oz of the leeks aside. Slice the remaining leeks and the remaining celery, reserving any celery leaves. Chop the celery leaves and set aside to garnish the soup.

5 Melt half the butter in a large, heavy-based saucepan. Add the sliced leeks and celery, cover and cook over a low heat for about 10 minutes, or until softened but not browned. Add the potatoes, wine and 1.2 litres/2 pints/ 5 cups of the stock.

6 Season well with salt and pepper, bring to the boil and reduce the heat. Part-cover the pan and simmer the soup for 15–20 minutes, or until the potatoes are cooked.

7 Meanwhile, skin the reserved chicken breasts and cut the flesh into small pieces. Melt the remaining butter in a frying pan, add the chicken and fry for 5–7 minutes, until cooked.

8 Thickly slice the remaining leeks, add to the pan and cook, stirring occasionally, for a further 3–4 minutes, until just cooked.

9 Process the soup with the cooked chicken from the stock in a blender or food processor. Taste and adjust the seasoning, and add more stock if the soup is very thick.

10 Stir in the cream, if using, and the chicken and leek mixture. Reheat the soup gently. Serve in warmed bowls. Crumble the pancetta over the soup and sprinkle with the chopped celery leaves.

GARLIC AND CORIANDER SOUP

THIS RECIPE IS BASED ON THE WONDERFUL BREAD SOUPS OR AÇORDAS OF PORTUGAL. BEING A SIMPLE SOUP IT SHOULD BE MADE WITH THE BEST INGREDIENTS — PLUMP GARLIC, FRESH CORIANDER, HIGH-QUALITY CRUSTY COUNTRY BREAD AND EXTRA VIRGIN OLIVE OIL.

SERVES SIX

INGREDIENTS
  25g/1oz fresh coriander, leaves and
    stalks chopped separately
  1.5 litres/2½ pints/6¼ cups vegetable
    or chicken stock, or water
  5–6 plump garlic cloves, peeled
  6 eggs
  275g/10oz day-old bread, most of
    the crust removed and torn into
    bite-size pieces
  salt and ground black pepper
  90ml/6 tbsp extra virgin olive oil,
    plus extra to serve

1 Place the coriander stalks in a saucepan. Add the stock or water and bring to the boil. Lower the heat and simmer for 10 minutes, then process in a blender or food processor and sieve back into the pan.

2 Crush the garlic with 5ml/1 tsp salt, then stir in 120ml/4fl oz/½ cup hot soup. Return the mixture to the pan.

3 Meanwhile, poach the eggs in a frying pan of simmering water for about 3–4 minutes, until just set. Use a draining spoon to remove them from the pan and transfer to a warmed plate. Trim off any untidy bits of white.

4 Bring the soup back to the boil and add seasoning. Stir in the chopped coriander leaves and remove from the heat.

5 Place the bread in six soup plates or bowls and drizzle the oil over it. Ladle in the soup and stir. Add a poached egg to each bowl and serve immediately, offering olive oil at the table so that it can be drizzled over the soup to taste.

ROASTED GARLIC AND BUTTERNUT SQUASH SOUP WITH TOMATO SALSA

THIS IS A WONDERFUL, RICHLY FLAVOURED DISH. A SPOONFUL OF THE HOT AND SPICY TOMATO SALSA GIVES BITE TO THE SWEET-TASTING SQUASH AND GARLIC SOUP.

SERVES FOUR TO FIVE

INGREDIENTS
  2 garlic bulbs, outer papery
    skin removed
  75ml/5 tbsp olive oil
  a few fresh thyme sprigs
  1 large butternut squash, halved
    and seeded
  2 onions, chopped
  5ml/1 tsp ground coriander
  1.2 litres/2 pints/5 cups vegetable or
    chicken stock
  30–45ml/2–3 tbsp chopped fresh
    oregano or marjoram
  salt and ground black pepper
For the salsa
  4 large ripe tomatoes, halved
    and seeded
  1 red pepper, halved and seeded
  1 large fresh red chilli, halved
    and seeded
  30–45ml/2–3 tbsp extra virgin
    olive oil
  15ml/1 tbsp balsamic vinegar
  pinch of caster sugar (optional)

1 Preheat the oven to 220°C/425°F/
Gas 7. Place the garlic bulbs on a piece
of foil and pour over half the olive oil.
Add the thyme sprigs, then fold the foil
around the garlic bulbs to enclose them
completely. Place the foil parcel on a
baking sheet with the butternut squash
and brush the squash with 15ml/1 tbsp
of the remaining olive oil. Add the
tomatoes, red pepper and fresh chilli
for the salsa.

2 Roast the vegetables for 25 minutes,
then remove the tomatoes, pepper and
chilli. Reduce the temperature to
190°C/375°F/Gas 5 and cook the
squash and garlic for 20–25 minutes
more, or until the squash is tender.

3 Heat the remaining oil in a large,
heavy-based saucepan and cook the
onions and ground coriander gently for
about 10 minutes, or until softened.

4 Skin the pepper and chilli and
process in a food processor or blender
with the tomatoes and 30ml/2 tbsp olive
oil. Stir in the vinegar and seasoning to
taste, adding a pinch of caster sugar, if
necessary. Add the remaining oil if you
think the salsa needs it.

5 Squeeze the roasted garlic out of its
papery skin into the onions and scoop
the squash out of its skin, adding it
to the pan. Add the stock, 5ml/1 tsp
salt and plenty of black pepper. Bring
to the boil and simmer for 10 minutes.

6 Stir in half the oregano or marjoram
and cool the soup slightly, then process
it in a blender or food processor.
Alternatively, press the soup through a
fine sieve.

7 Reheat the soup without allowing it
to boil, then taste for seasoning before
ladling it into warmed bowls. Top each
with a spoonful of salsa and sprinkle
over the remaining chopped oregano
or marjoram. Serve immediately.

MISO BROTH WITH SPRING ONIONS AND TOFU

THE JAPANESE EAT MISO BROTH, A SIMPLE BUT HIGHLY NUTRITIOUS SOUP, ALMOST EVERY DAY — IT IS STANDARD BREAKFAST FARE AND IT IS EATEN WITH RICE OR NOODLES LATER IN THE DAY.

SERVES FOUR

INGREDIENTS

1 bunch of spring onions or
    5 baby leeks
15g/½ oz fresh coriander
3 thin slices fresh root ginger
2 star anise
1 small dried red chilli
1.2 litres/2 pints/5 cups dashi stock
    or vegetable stock
225g/8oz pak choi or other Asian
    greens, thickly sliced
200g/7oz firm tofu, cut into
    2.5cm/1in cubes
60ml/4 tbsp red miso
30–45ml/2–3 tbsp Japanese soy
    sauce (shoyu)
1 fresh red chilli, seeded and
    shredded (optional)

1 Cut the coarse green tops off the spring onions or baby leeks and slice the rest of the spring onions or leeks finely on the diagonal. Place the coarse green tops in a large saucepan with the coriander stalks, fresh root ginger, star anise, dried chilli and dashi or vegetable stock.

2 Heat the mixture gently until boiling, then lower the heat and simmer for 10 minutes. Strain, return to the pan and reheat until simmering. Add the green portion of the sliced spring onions or leeks to the soup with the pak choi or greens and tofu. Cook for 2 minutes.

3 Mix 45ml/3 tbsp of the miso with a little of the hot soup in a bowl, then stir it into the soup. Taste the soup and add more miso with soy sauce to taste.

4 Coarsely chop the coriander leaves and stir most of them into the soup with the white part of the spring onions or leeks. Cook for 1 minute, then ladle the soup into warmed serving bowls. Sprinkle with the remaining coriander and the fresh red chilli, if using, and serve at once.

COOK'S TIP
Dashi powder is available in most Asian and Chinese stores. Alternatively, make your own by gently simmering 10–15cm/ 4–6in kombu seaweed in 1.2 litres/ 2 pints/5 cups water for 10 minutes. Do not boil the stock vigorously as this makes the dashi bitter. Remove the kombu, then add 15g/½oz dried bonito flakes and bring to the boil. Strain immediately through a fine sieve.

COCONUT AND SEAFOOD SOUP
WITH GARLIC CHIVES

THE LONG LIST OF INGREDIENTS IN THIS THAI-INSPIRED RECIPE COULD MISLEAD YOU INTO THINKING THAT THIS SOUP IS COMPLICATED. IN FACT, IT IS VERY EASY TO PUT TOGETHER.

SERVES FOUR

INGREDIENTS
600ml/1 pint/2½ cups
  fish stock
5 thin slices fresh galangal or
  fresh root ginger
2 lemon grass stalks, chopped
3 kaffir lime leaves, shredded
25g/1oz garlic chives (1 bunch)
15g/½oz fresh coriander
15ml/1 tbsp vegetable oil
4 shallots, chopped
400ml/14fl oz can coconut milk
30–45ml/2–3 tbsp Thai fish sauce
  (*nam pla*)
45–60ml/3–4 tbsp Thai green
  curry paste
450g/1lb uncooked large prawns,
  peeled and deveined
450g/1lb prepared squid
a little lime juice (optional)
salt and ground black pepper
60ml/4 tbsp crisp fried shallot
  slices, to serve

1 Pour the fish stock into a saucepan and add the slices of galangal or ginger, lemon grass and half the shredded kaffir lime leaves.

2 Reserve a few garlic chives for the garnish, then snip the remainder. Add half the snipped garlic chives to the pan with the coriander stalks. Bring to the boil, reduce the heat and cover the pan, then simmer gently for 20 minutes. Strain the stock.

3 Rinse the pan. Add the oil and shallots. Cook over a medium heat for 5–10 minutes, until the shallots are just beginning to brown.

4 Stir in the strained stock, coconut milk, the remaining kaffir lime leaves and 30ml/2 tbsp of the fish sauce. Heat gently until simmering and cook over a low heat for 5–10 minutes.

VARIATIONS
• Instead of squid, you could add 400g/14oz firm white fish, such as monkfish, cut into small pieces.
• You could also replace the squid with mussels. Steam 675g/1½lb closed live mussels in a tightly covered pan for 3–4 minutes, or until the shells have opened. Discard any that remain shut, then remove the mussels from their shells.

5 Stir in the curry paste and prawns, then cook for 3 minutes. Add the squid and cook for a further 2 minutes. Add the lime juice, if using, and season, adding more fish sauce to taste.

6 Stir in the remaining chives and the coriander. Serve in bowls sprinkled with fried shallots and whole garlic chives.

As we gather around the table, keen to share food with family and friends, the intensely savoury smell and flavour of onions make them a good choice to start the meal. Throughout history, onions have been praised for their ability to stimulate the appetite and help us enjoy our food. In this section you'll find a large variety of onion dishes suitable for starting different types of meal and some that are substantial enough to form a light meal on their own with salad and good bread.

Starters and
Light Meals

SPICED ONION KOFTAS

THESE DELICIOUS INDIAN ONION FRITTERS ARE MADE WITH CHICK-PEA FLOUR, OTHERWISE KNOWN AS GRAM FLOUR OR BESAN. SERVE WITH CHUTNEY OR YOGURT DIP.

SERVES FOUR TO FIVE

INGREDIENTS
  675g/1½lb onions, halved and
    thinly sliced
  5ml/1 tsp salt
  5ml/1 tsp ground coriander
  5ml/1 tsp ground cumin
  2.5ml/½ tsp ground turmeric
  1–2 green chillies, seeded and
    finely chopped
  45ml/3 tbsp chopped
    fresh coriander
  90g/3½oz/¾ cup chick-pea flour
  2.5ml/½ tsp baking powder
  vegetable oil, for deep-frying
To serve
  lemon wedges (optional)
  fresh coriander sprigs
  yogurt and herb dip or yogurt and
    cucumber dip

1 Place the onions in a colander, add the salt and toss. Place on a plate and leave to stand for 45 minutes, tossing once or twice. Rinse the onions, then squeeze out any excess moisture.

2 Place the onions in a bowl. Add the ground coriander, cumin, turmeric, chillies and fresh coriander. Mix well.

COOK'S TIPS
• To make a yogurt and herb dip, stir 30ml/2 tbsp each of chopped fresh coriander and mint into about 250ml/ 8fl oz/1 cup set yogurt. Season with salt, ground toasted cumin seeds and a pinch of muscovado sugar.
• For a cucumber dip, stir half a diced cucumber and 1 seeded and chopped fresh green chilli into 250ml/8fl oz/1 cup set yogurt. Season with salt and cumin.

3 Add the chick-pea flour and baking powder, then use your hand to mix all the ingredients thoroughly.

4 Shape the mixture by hand into 12–15 koftas about the size of golf balls.

5 Heat the oil for deep-frying to 180–190°C/350–375°F or until a cube of day-old bread browns in about 30–45 seconds. Fry the koftas, 4–5 at a time, until deep golden brown all over. Drain each batch on kitchen paper and keep warm until all the koftas are cooked. Serve with lemon wedges, coriander sprigs and a yogurt dip.

LITTLE ONIONS COOKED WITH WINE, CORIANDER AND OLIVE OIL

IF YOU CAN FIND THE SMALL, FLAT ITALIAN CIPOLLA OR BORETTANE ONIONS, THEY ARE EXCELLENT IN THIS RECIPE — OTHERWISE USE PICKLING ONIONS, SMALL RED ONIONS OR SHALLOTS.

3 Add the currants, reduce the heat and cook gently for 15–20 minutes, or until the onions are tender but not falling apart. Use a draining spoon to transfer the onions to a serving dish.

4 Boil the liquid over a high heat until it reduces considerably. Taste and adjust the seasoning, if necessary, then pour the reduced liquid over the onions. Scatter the oregano over the onions, set aside to cool and then chill them.

5 Just before serving, stir in the grated lemon rind, chopped parsley and toasted pine nuts

SERVES SIX

INGREDIENTS
105ml/7 tbsp olive oil
675g/1½lb small onions, peeled
150ml/¼ pint/⅔ cup dry white wine
2 bay leaves
2 garlic cloves, bruised
1–2 small dried red chillies
15ml/1 tbsp coriander seeds,
   toasted and lightly crushed
2.5ml/½ tsp sugar
a few fresh thyme sprigs
30ml/2 tbsp currants
10ml/2 tsp chopped fresh oregano
5ml/1 tsp grated lemon rind
15ml/1 tbsp chopped fresh flat
   leaf parsley
30–45ml/2–3 tbsp pine nuts, toasted
salt and ground black pepper

1 Place 30ml/2 tbsp olive oil in a wide saucepan. Add the onions and cook gently over a medium heat for about 5 minutes, or until they begin to colour. Remove from the pan and set aside.

2 Add the remaining oil, the wine, bay leaves, garlic, chillies, coriander, sugar and thyme to the pan. Bring to the boil and cook briskly for 5 minutes. Return the onions to the pan.

COOK'S TIP
Serve this dish as one of several small dishes – an antipasto – perhaps with mustard mayonnaise-dressed celeriac salad and some thinly sliced prosciutto or other air-dried ham.

Roast Garlic with Goat's Cheese, Walnut and Herb Pâté

The combination of sweet, mellow roasted garlic and goat's cheese is a classic one. This is particularly good made with the new season's walnuts, sometimes known as "wet" walnuts, which are available in the early autumn.

SERVES FOUR

INGREDIENTS
    4 large garlic bulbs
    4 fresh rosemary sprigs
    8 fresh thyme sprigs
    60ml/4 tbsp olive oil
    sea salt and ground black pepper
For the pâté
    200g/7oz soft goat's cheese
    5ml/1 tsp finely chopped fresh thyme
    15ml/1 tbsp chopped fresh parsley
    50g/2oz shelled walnuts, chopped
    15ml/1 tbsp walnut oil (optional)
    fresh thyme, to garnish
To serve
    4–8 slices sourdough bread
    shelled walnuts

1 Preheat the oven to 180°C/350°F/ Gas 4. Strip the papery skin from the garlic bulbs. Place them in an ovenproof dish large enough to hold them snugly. Tuck in the rosemary and thyme, drizzle the oil over and season to taste.

2 Cover the garlic closely with foil and bake for 50–60 minutes, basting once. Leave to cool.

3 Preheat the grill. To make the pâté, cream the cheese with the thyme, parsley and chopped walnuts. Beat in 15ml/1 tbsp of the cooking oil from the garlic and season to taste, then transfer the pâté to a serving bowl.

4 Brush the sourdough bread with the remaining cooking oil from the garlic, then grill until toasted.

5 Drizzle the walnut oil, if using, over the goat's cheese pâté and grind some black pepper over it. Place a bulb of garlic on each plate and serve with the pâté and some toasted bread. Garnish with a little fresh thyme and serve a few freshly shelled walnuts and a little sea salt with each portion.

POTATO AND CHIVE PANCAKES WITH PICKLED HERRING AND ONION RINGS

THESE PANCAKES ARE FULL OF DELICIOUS SCANDINAVIAN FLAVOURS. SERVE THEM AS A FIRST COURSE OR AS A LIGHT MAIN COURSE WITH SALAD. SMALL PANCAKES MAKE EXCELLENT CANAPÉS TO SERVE WITH ICE-COLD SHOTS OF VODKA OR OTHER PRE-DINNER DRINKS.

SERVES SIX

INGREDIENTS
275g/10oz peeled potatoes
2 eggs, beaten
150ml/¼ pint/⅔ cup milk
40g/1½oz plain flour
30ml/2 tbsp snipped fresh chives
vegetable oil or butter, for greasing
salt and ground black pepper
For the topping
2 small red or yellow onions, thinly
   sliced into rings
60ml/4 tbsp soured cream or
   crème fraîche
5ml/1 tsp wholegrain mustard
15ml/1 tbsp chopped fresh dill
6 pickled herring fillets
To garnish
fresh dill sprigs
fresh chives or chive flowers

1 Cut the potatoes into chunks and cook them in boiling salted water for about 15 minutes, or until tender, then drain and mash or sieve to form a smooth purée.

2 Meanwhile prepare the topping. Place the onions in a bowl and cover with boiling water. Set aside for 2–3 minutes, then drain thoroughly and dry on kitchen paper.

3 Mix the onions with the soured cream or crème fraîche, mustard and chopped dill. Season to taste.

4 Using a sharp knife, cut the pickled herring fillets into 12–18 pieces. Set them aside.

5 Put the potato purée in a bowl and beat in the eggs, milk and flour with a wooden spoon to make a batter. Season to taste with salt and pepper and whisk in the snipped chives.

6 Heat a non-stick frying pan over a medium heat and grease it with a little oil or butter. Spoon about 30ml/2 tbsp of batter into the pan to make a pancake, measuring about 7.5cm/3in across. Cook for 3–4 minutes, until the underside is set and golden brown. Turn the pancake over and cook the other side for 3–4 minutes, until golden brown. Transfer to a plate and keep warm while you make the remaining pancakes in batches of 3–4. The mixture will make 12 pancakes.

7 Place two pancakes on each of six warmed plates and distribute the pickled herring fillets and onions equally among them. Garnish with dill sprigs, fresh chives and/or chive flowers. Season with black pepper and serve immediately.

Deep-fried Spring Onions ᴵᴺ Beer Batter ᵂᴵᵀᴴ Romesco Sauce

THIS PIQUANT, BUT NOT HOT, SAUCE FROM TARRAGONA IN SPAIN ADMIRABLY CUTS THE RICHNESS OF DEEP-FRIED FOOD, AND IT IS EXCELLENT WITH DEEP-FRIED SPRING ONIONS IN THEIR CRISP BATTER.

SERVES SIX

INGREDIENTS
　3 bunches plump spring onions,
　　18–24 in all
　sea salt and ground black pepper
　lemon wedges, to serve
For the batter
　225g/8oz/2 cups self-raising flour
　150ml/¼ pint/⅔ cup lager
　175–200ml/6–7fl oz/¾–scant 1 cup
　　ice-cold water
　groundnut oil, for deep-frying
　1 large egg white
　2.5ml/½ tsp cream of tartar
For the sauce
　2–3 large mild dried red chillies,
　　such as Spanish *ñoras* or Mexican
　　anchos or *guajillos*
　1 large red pepper, halved and seeded
　2 large tomatoes, halved and seeded
　4–6 large garlic cloves, unpeeled
　75–90ml/5–6 tbsp olive oil
　25g/1oz/¼ cup hazelnuts, blanched
　4 slices French bread, each about
　　2cm/¾in thick
　15ml/1 tbsp sherry vinegar
　squeeze of lemon juice (optional)
　chopped fresh parsley, to garnish

1 First prepare the sauce. Soak the dried chillies in hot water for about 30 minutes. Preheat the oven to 220°C/425°F/Gas 7.

2 Place the pepper halves, tomatoes and garlic on a baking sheet and drizzle with 15ml/1 tbsp olive oil.

3 Roast, uncovered, for about 30–40 minutes, until the pepper is blistered and blackened and the garlic is soft. Cool slightly, then peel the pepper, tomatoes and garlic.

4 Heat the remaining oil in a small frying pan and fry the hazelnuts until lightly browned, then transfer them to a plate. Fry the bread in the same oil until light brown on both sides, then transfer to the plate with the nuts and leave to cool. Reserve the oil from cooking.

5 Drain the chillies, discard as many of their seeds as you can, then place them in a food processor. Add the pepper, tomatoes, garlic, hazelnuts and bread with the reserved oil. Add the vinegar and process to a paste. Check the seasoning and thin the sauce with a little more oil or lemon juice, if necessary. Set aside.

6 Trim roots from the spring onions. Trim the leaves to leave the onions about 15–18cm/6–7in long.

7 To make the batter, sift the flour into a bowl and add a good pinch each of salt and black pepper. Make a well in the centre, then gradually whisk in the lager, followed by the water. The batter should be the consistency of thick cream, so adjust the volume of water to produce this consistency.

8 Heat the oil for deep-frying to 180°C/350°F or until a cube of day-old bread browns in 30–45 seconds. Whisk the egg white with the cream of tartar until stiff, then fold it into the batter.

9 Dip the spring onions individually in the batter, drain off the excess and fry them in batches for 4–5 minutes. Drain thoroughly on kitchen paper and sprinkle with a little sea salt. Keep each batch warm until the next is cooked. Garnish with a little chopped parsley and serve hot with the sauce and lemon wedges.

STILTON-STUFFED MUSHROOMS BAKED IN GARLIC BREADCRUMBS

SERVE THESE SUCCULENT STUFFED MUSHROOMS WITH CHUNKS OF WARM, CRUSTY BREAD OR FRESH ROLLS TO SOAK UP ALL THEIR DELICIOUS GARLIC-FLAVOURED JUICES.

SERVES FOUR

INGREDIENTS

450g/1lb chestnut mushrooms
3 garlic cloves, finely chopped
90g/3½oz/7 tbsp butter, melted
juice of ½ lemon
115g/4oz Stilton cheese, crumbled
50g/2oz/½ cup walnuts, chopped
90g/3½oz/1½ cups fresh
  white breadcrumbs
25g/1oz Parmesan cheese, grated
30ml/2 tbsp chopped fresh parsley
salt and ground black pepper

COOK'S TIP

A simple sauce of fromage frais or thick Greek yogurt with some chopped fresh herbs and a little Dijon mustard stirred through goes well with these Stilton-stuffed mushrooms.

1 Preheat the oven to 200°C/400°F/ Gas 6. Place the mushrooms in an ovenproof dish and scatter half the garlic over them. Drizzle with 60ml/ 4 tbsp of the butter and the lemon juice. Season with salt and pepper and bake for 15–20 minutes. Leave to cool.

2 Cream the crumbled Stilton with the chopped walnuts and mix in 30ml/ 2 tbsp of the breadcrumbs.

3 Divide the Stilton mixture among the mushrooms.

4 Preheat the grill. Mix the remaining garlic, breadcrumbs and melted butter together. Stir in the Parmesan and parsley and season with pepper. Cover the mushrooms with the breadcrumb mixture and grill for about 5 minutes, or until crisp and browned. Serve at once.

Spring Onion and Ricotta Fritters with Avocado Salsa

THE FRESH-FLAVOURED SALSA SPIKED WITH A LITTLE RED ONION AND CHILLI IS EXCELLENT WITH THESE MELT-IN-THE-MOUTH HERBY SPRING ONION FRITTERS.

SERVES FOUR TO SIX

INGREDIENTS

250g/9oz/generous 1 cup
  ricotta cheese
1 large egg, beaten
90ml/6 tbsp self-raising flour
90ml/6 tbsp milk
1 bunch spring onions, finely sliced
30ml/2 tbsp chopped fresh coriander
sunflower oil, for shallow frying
salt and ground black pepper
200ml/7fl oz/scant 1 cup crème
  fraîche, to serve
For the salsa
2 ripe, but not soft, avocados
1 small red onion, diced
grated rind and juice of 1 lime
½–1 fresh green or red chilli, seeded
  and finely chopped
225g/8oz tomatoes, peeled, seeded
  and diced
30–45ml/2–3 tbsp chopped mixed
  fresh mint and coriander
pinch of caster sugar
5–10ml/1–2 tsp Thai fish sauce
  (*nam pla*)
To garnish
fresh coriander sprigs
lime wedges

2 Beat the ricotta until smooth, then beat in the egg and flour, followed by the milk to make a smooth, thick batter. Beat in the spring onions and coriander. Season well with pepper and a little salt.

3 Heat a little oil in a non-stick frying pan over a medium heat. Add spoonfuls of the mixture to make fritters about 7.5cm/3in across and fry for about 4–5 minutes each side, until set and browned. The mixture makes 12 fritters.

4 Taste the salsa and adjust the seasoning, adding more lime juice and/or sugar to taste. Serve the fritters immediately, with the salsa and a dollop of crème fraîche. Garnish with coriander sprigs and lime wedges.

VARIATION
The fritters are also good served with thinly sliced smoked salmon.

1 Make the salsa first. Peel, stone and dice the avocados. Place in a bowl with the red onion, lime rind and juice. Add chilli to taste, the tomatoes, mint and coriander. Season with salt, pepper, sugar and Thai fish sauce. Mix well and set aside for 30 minutes.

MUSSELS IN GARLIC BUTTER

GARLIC AND HERB BUTTER IS A CLASSIC TREATMENT FOR SNAILS IN BURGUNDY, BUT BECAME VERY POPULAR IN THE 1960s WITH MUSSELS, AND MAKES A DELICIOUS FIRST COURSE.

SERVES FOUR

INGREDIENTS

2kg/4½lb mussels, scrubbed
2 large shallots, finely chopped
200ml/7fl oz/scant 1 cup dry
  white wine
115g/4oz/½ cup unsalted
  butter, softened
2–3 garlic cloves, finely chopped
grated rind of 1 lemon
60ml/4 tbsp finely chopped mixed
  herbs, such as parsley, chervil,
  tarragon and chives
115g/4oz/1 cup fresh
  white breadcrumbs
salt and ground black pepper
lemon wedges, to serve

1 Check that all the mussels are closed after cleaning and discard any that remain open when sharply tapped.

2 Place the shallots and wine in a large saucepan and bring to the boil. Throw in the mussels and cover tightly. Cook over a high heat for 4–5 minutes, shaking the pan vigorously 2–3 times.

3 The mussels should be cooked and gaping open. Discard any that do not open after 5 minutes' cooking. Drain, reserving the cooking liquid.

4 Discard the top (empty) half of each shell. Place the mussels in a large roasting tin or heatproof dish.

5 Pour the cooking liquid into a clean saucepan and boil it vigorously until reduced to about 45ml/3 tbsp. Remove from the heat and leave to cool.

6 Cream the butter with the shallots from the reduced liquid, the garlic, lemon rind and herbs. Season well and chill until firm.

7 Distribute the flavoured butter among the mussels. Sprinkle with the cooking liquid, then scatter the breadcrumbs over the top.

8 Preheat the grill and position the shelf about 10cm/4in below the heat. Grill the mussels until the butter is bubbling and the breadcrumbs are golden and crisp. Serve immediately, with wedges of lemon.

TAPENADE WITH QUAIL'S EGGS AND CRUDITÉS

TAPENADE MAKES A SOCIABLE START TO A MEAL. SERVE WITH HARD-BOILED QUAIL'S EGGS AND VEGETABLE CRUDITÉS AND LET EVERYONE HELP THEMSELVES.

SERVES SIX

INGREDIENTS
 225g/8oz/2 cups stoned black olives
 2 large garlic cloves, peeled
 15ml/1 tbsp salted capers, rinsed
 6 canned or bottled anchovy
   fillets, drained
 50g/2oz good-quality canned tuna
 5–10ml/1–2 tsp cognac (optional)
 5ml/1 tsp chopped fresh thyme
 30ml/2 tbsp chopped fresh parsley
 30–60ml/2–4 tbsp extra virgin
   olive oil
 a dash of lemon juice
 30ml/2 tbsp crème fraîche or
   fromage frais (optional)
 12–18 quail's eggs
 ground black pepper
For the crudités
 bunch of spring onions, halved
   if large
 bunch of radishes, trimmed
 bunch of baby fennel, trimmed and
   halved if large, or 1 large fennel
   bulb, cut into thin wedges
To serve
 French bread
 unsalted butter
 sea salt

1 Process the olives, garlic, capers, anchovies and tuna in a food processor or blender. Blend in the cognac, if using, the thyme, parsley and enough olive oil to make a paste. Season to taste with pepper and a dash of lemon juice. Stir in the crème fraîche or fromage frais, if using, and transfer to a serving bowl.

2 Place the quail's eggs in a saucepan, cover with cold water and bring to the boil. Cook for only 2 minutes, then immediately drain and plunge the eggs into iced water to stop them from cooking further and to make them easier to shell.

3 When the eggs are cold, carefully part-shell them.

4 Arrange the tapenade with the eggs and crudités and serve, offering French bread, unsalted butter and sea salt to accompany them.

COOK'S TIPS
• Crème fraîche or fromage frais softens the flavour of the olives for a milder tapenade.
• In Provence, where tapenade comes from, it is traditional to serve it with crudités of celery, fennel and tomato.
• Tapenade is also delicious spread on thin slices of toasted French bread and served as an appetizer with pre-dinner drinks. It may be garnished with chopped hard-boiled egg.

RED ONION AND MUSHROOM TARTLETS WITH GOAT'S CHEESE

CRISP AND SAVOURY, THESE ATTRACTIVE LITTLE TARTS ARE DELICIOUS SERVED WITH A FEW MIXED SALAD LEAVES DRIZZLED WITH A GARLIC-INFUSED FRENCH DRESSING.

SERVES SIX

INGREDIENTS
60ml/4 tbsp olive oil
25g/1oz/2 tbsp butter
4 red onions, thinly sliced
5ml/1 tsp brown sugar
15ml/1 tbsp balsamic vinegar
15ml/1 tbsp soy sauce
200g/7oz button mushrooms,
  thinly sliced
1 garlic clove, finely chopped
2.5ml/½ tsp chopped fresh tarragon
30ml/2 tbsp chopped fresh parsley
250g/9oz goat's cheese
  log (*chèvre*)
salt and ground black pepper
mixed salad leaves,
  to serve
For the pastry
200g/7oz/1¾ cups plain flour
pinch of cayenne pepper
90g/3½oz/7 tbsp butter
40g/1½oz/½ cup freshly grated
  Parmesan cheese
45–60ml/3–4 tbsp iced water

1 First make the pastry. Sift the flour and cayenne into a bowl, add the butter, then rub in with the fingertips until the mixture looks like breadcrumbs.

2 Stir in the grated Parmesan, then bind the pastry with the iced water, adding just enough to give a firm dough. Press the pastry together into a ball, then wrap it in clear film and chill for at least 45 minutes.

3 Heat 15ml/1 tbsp of the oil and half the butter in a heavy frying pan, then add the onions, cover and cook gently for 15 minutes, stirring occasionally.

4 Uncover the pan, increase the heat slightly and sprinkle in the brown sugar. Cook, stirring frequently, until the onions begin to caramelize and brown. Add the vinegar and soy sauce and cook briskly until the liquid evaporates. Season to taste then set aside.

5 Heat another 30ml/2 tbsp of the oil and the remaining butter in a saucepan, then add the mushrooms and garlic and cook fairly briskly for 5–6 minutes, until the mushrooms are browned and cooked.

6 Set a few mushrooms and onion rings aside then stir the rest of the mushrooms into the onions with the tarragon and parsley. Adjust the seasoning to taste. Preheat the oven to 190°C/375°F/Gas 5.

7 Roll out the pastry and use to line 6 × 10cm/4in tartlet tins, preferably loose-based and metal. Prick the pastry bases with a fork and line the sides with strips of foil. Bake for 10 minutes, remove the foil and bake for another 5–7 minutes, or until the pastry is lightly browned and cooked. Remove from the oven and increase the temperature to 200°C/400°F/Gas 6.

8 Remove the pastry shells from the tins and arrange them on a baking sheet. Distribute the onion mixture equally among the pastry shells. Cut the goat's cheese into 6 equal slices and place 1 slice on each tartlet. Add a few reserved mushrooms and onion slices to each tartlet, drizzle with the remaining oil and season with pepper.

9 Return the tartlets to the oven and bake for 5–8 minutes, or until the goat's cheese is just beginning to turn brown. Serve with mixed salad leaves.

CHICKEN LIVER PÂTÉ WITH GARLIC

THIS SMOOTH, GARLICKY PÂTÉ IS WICKEDLY INDULGENT BUT ABSOLUTELY DELICIOUS. IT IS IDEAL AS A FIRST COURSE, WITH TOAST AND SOME SMALL PICKLED GHERKINS (CORNICHONS). IT IS ALSO GOOD WITH CONFIT OF SLOW-COOKED ONIONS.

SERVES SIX TO EIGHT

INGREDIENTS

225g/8oz/1 cup unsalted butter
400g/14oz chicken livers, chopped
45–60ml/3–4 tbsp Madeira
3 large shallots, chopped
2 large garlic cloves, finely chopped
5ml/1 tsp finely chopped fresh thyme
pinch of ground allspice
30ml/2 tbsp double cream (optional)
salt and ground black pepper
small fresh bay leaves or fresh thyme
   sprigs, to garnish

VARIATIONS
• Cognac, Armagnac or port can be used instead of the Madeira.
• Use duck livers instead of chicken and add 2.5ml/½ tsp grated orange rind.

1 Melt 75g/3oz/6 tbsp butter in a small saucepan over a low heat, then allow it to bubble gently until it is clear. Pour off the clarified butter into a bowl.

2 Melt 40g/1½oz/3 tbsp butter in a frying pan and fry the chicken livers for 4–5 minutes, until browned.

3 Add the Madeira and set it alight, then scrape the contents of the pan into a food processor or blender.

4 Melt 25g/1oz/2 tbsp butter in the pan over a low heat and cook the shallots for 5 minutes, until soft. Add the garlic, thyme and allspice and cook for another 2–3 minutes. Add this mixture to the livers with the remaining butter and cream, if using, then process until smooth.

5 Add about 7.5ml/1½ tsp each of salt and pepper and more Madeira to taste. Scrape the pâté into a serving dish and place a few bay leaves or thyme sprigs on top. Melt the clarified butter, if necessary, then pour it over the pâté. Cool and chill for 4 hours or overnight.

COOK'S TIP
The flavour of the pâté deepens and matures on chilling, so it is best if you make it a day before it is required.

BAGNA CAUDA

THIS HOT GARLIC DIP FROM PIEDMONT IN NORTHERN ITALY IS OUTRAGEOUSLY RICH AS IT CONTAINS OLIVE OIL, BUTTER AND CREAM. LITERALLY TRANSLATED, THE NAME MEANS "A HOT BATH" AND IN PIEDMONT IT IS TRADITIONALLY EATEN TO CELEBRATE THE END OF THE GRAPE HARVEST.

2 Place the olive oil in a small saucepan over a very low heat, then add the fresh rosemary and sliced or chopped garlic. Keep the heat low for about 5 minutes so that the flavour of the garlic permeates the oil, but do not allow the garlic to brown.

3 Add the anchovies, remove the rosemary and cook for 3–5 minutes, mashing the anchovies into the oil with a wooden spoon. Keep the heat low to ensure the garlic does not brown.

SERVES FOUR

INGREDIENTS
150ml/¼ pint/⅔ cup extra virgin olive oil
5cm/2in sprig fresh rosemary
6 garlic cloves, thinly sliced or finely chopped
50g/2oz can anchovy fillets, drained and chopped
90g/3½oz/7 tbsp unsalted butter
75ml/5 tbsp double cream (optional)
ground black pepper
To serve
a selection of vegetables, such as new potatoes, baby artichokes, cardoons, cauliflower florets, fennel, celery, baby carrots
crusty bread
large cooked prawns

1 Prepare the serving ingredients you have chosen for dipping according to type. Cook them if necessary – new potatoes and baby artichokes, for example – and cut the bread and large vegetables into small portions.

VARIATIONS
• In Piedmont they sometimes add a little very finely shaved white truffle. Add this at the very end to appreciate the wonderful aroma of the truffle.
• The rosemary is not traditional but the slight bitterness it imparts cuts the rich sauce. Omit it if you prefer.
• Omit the cream for a stronger-tasting, less rich dip, and use a light olive oil from Provence or Liguria instead.

4 When the anchovies have broken down completely, add the butter and cream and whisk gently until the butter has melted. Season to taste with a little pepper

5 Pour the mixture into a fondue pan or small earthenware container and stand this over a spirit stove or nightlight to keep the bagna cauda warm. Surround with the bread, vegetables and prawns for dipping and serve immediately.

Leek, Saffron and Mussel Tarts

Serve these vividly coloured little tarts as a first course, with a few salad leaves, such as watercress, rocket and frisée. Alternatively, cook the filling in one 23cm/9in tart shell and serve it as a main course with salad and fresh bread.

2 Soak the saffron in the hot water for 10 minutes. Fry the leeks in the oil in a large saucepan over a medium heat for 6–8 minutes, until softened and beginning to brown. Add the pepper strips and cook for another 2 minutes.

3 Bring 2.5cm/1in depth of water to a rolling boil in a large saucepan and add 10ml/2 tsp salt. Discard any open mussels that do not shut when tapped sharply, then throw the rest into the pan. Cover and cook over a high heat, shaking the pan occasionally, for 3–4 minutes or until the mussels open. Discard any mussels that do not open. Shell the mussels.

SERVES SIX

INGREDIENTS
    350g/12oz shortcrust pastry, thawed
      if frozen
    large pinch of saffron strands (about
      15 strands)
    15ml/1 tbsp hot water
    2 large leeks, sliced
    30ml/2 tbsp olive oil
    2 large yellow peppers, halved,
      seeded, grilled and peeled, then
      cut into strips
    900g/2lb mussels, scrubbed and
      beards removed
    2 large eggs
    300ml/½ pint/1¼ cups single cream
    30ml/2 tbsp finely chopped
      fresh parsley
    salt and ground black pepper
    salad leaves, to serve

1 Preheat the oven to 190°C/375°F/ Gas 5. Roll out the pastry and use to line 6 × 10cm/4in tartlet tins, 2.5cm/1in deep. Prick the bases and line the sides with strips of foil. Bake for 10 minutes. Remove the foil and bake for another 5–8 minutes, until lightly coloured. Remove from the oven. Reduce the temperature to 180°C/350°F/Gas 4.

4 Beat the eggs, cream and saffron liquid together. Season well with salt and pepper and whisk in the parsley.

5 Arrange the leeks, peppers and mussels in the pastry cases, add the egg mixture and bake for 20–25 minutes, until risen and just firm. Serve at once with salad leaves.

BAKED EGGS EN COCOTTE
WITH WILD MUSHROOMS AND CHIVES

THESE SIMPLE, BUT UTTERLY DELICIOUS, BAKED EGGS MAKE A SPLENDID START TO A LIGHT MEAL OR AN EXCELLENT DISH FOR BRUNCH. SERVE WITH HOT, BUTTERED WHOLEMEAL TOAST.

SERVES FOUR TO SIX

INGREDIENTS
65g/2½oz/5 tbsp butter
2 shallots, finely chopped
1 small garlic clove, finely chopped
250g/9oz mixed mushrooms,
  finely chopped
15ml/1 tbsp lemon juice
5ml/1 tsp chopped fresh tarragon
30ml/2 tbsp crème fraîche
30ml/2 tbsp snipped fresh chives
4–6 eggs
salt and ground black pepper
whole chives, to garnish
buttered wholemeal toast, to serve

COOK'S TIP
The eggs may also be cooked by standing the dishes in a covered frying pan containing 2.5cm/1in boiling water. Cook over a medium heat for 8–10 minutes.

1 Melt 50g/2oz/4 tbsp of the butter in a saucepan over a medium-low heat and cook the shallots and garlic gently, stirring occasionally, for 5 minutes, until softened but not browned.

2 Increase the heat and add the mushrooms, then cook briskly, stirring frequently, until the mushrooms lose their moisture and begin to brown.

3 Stir in the lemon juice and tarragon and continue to cook over a medium heat, stirring occasionally, until the mushrooms absorb the liquid. Stir in half the crème fraîche and half the snipped chives and season to taste.

4 Preheat the oven to 190°C/375°F/ Gas 5. Distribute the mushroom mixture equally among 4–6 large ramekins or small ovenproof dishes of about 150–175ml/5–6fl oz/⅔–¾ cup capacity. Sprinkle the remaining snipped chives over the mushrooms.

5 Break an egg into each dish, add a dab of crème fraîche and season to taste with black pepper. Dot with the remaining butter and bake in the centre of the oven for 10–15 minutes, or until the whites of the eggs are set and the yolks cooked to your liking.

6 Serve immediately, garnished with fresh chives and accompanied by lots of hot, buttered wholemeal toast.

LEEK TERRINE <u>WITH</u> RED PEPPERS

THIS PRESSED LEEK TERRINE LOOKS VERY PRETTY WHEN SLICED AND SERVED ON INDIVIDUAL PLATES WITH THE DRESSING DRIZZLED OVER AND AROUND THE SLICES.

SERVES SIX TO EIGHT

INGREDIENTS
- 1.8kg/4lb slender leeks
- 4 large red peppers, halved and seeded
- 15ml/1 tbsp extra virgin olive oil
- 10ml/2 tsp balsamic vinegar
- 5ml/1 tsp ground roasted cumin seeds
- salt and ground black pepper

For the dressing
- 120ml/4fl oz/½ cup extra virgin olive oil
- 1 garlic clove, bruised and peeled
- 5ml/1 tsp Dijon mustard
- 5ml/1 tsp soy sauce
- 15ml/1 tbsp balsamic vinegar
- pinch of caster sugar
- 2.5–5ml/½–1 tsp ground roasted cumin seeds
- 15–30ml/1–2 tbsp chopped mixed fresh basil and flat leaf parsley

COOK'S TIP
It is easier to slice the terrine if you leave the clear film on and use a very sharp knife or an electric carving knife. Use a fish slice to transfer the slices to the plates, then remove the clear film.

1 Line a 23cm/9in-long terrine or loaf tin with clear film, leaving the ends overhanging the tin. Cut the leeks to the same length as the tin.

2 Cook the leeks in boiling salted water for 5–7 minutes, until just tender. Drain thoroughly and allow to cool, then squeeze out as much water as possible from the leeks and leave them to drain on a clean dish towel.

3 Grill the red peppers, skin side uppermost, until the skin blisters and blackens. Place in a bowl, cover and leave for 10 minutes. Peel the peppers and cut the flesh into long strips, then place them in a bowl and add the oil, balsamic vinegar and ground roasted cumin. Season to taste with salt and pepper and toss well.

4 Layer the leeks and strips of red pepper in the lined tin, alternating the layers so that the white of the leeks in one row is covered by the green of the next row. Season the leeks with a little more salt and pepper.

5 Cover with the overhanging clear film. Top with a plate and weigh it down with heavy food cans or scale weights. Chill for several hours or overnight.

6 To make the dressing, place the oil, garlic, mustard, soy sauce and vinegar in a jug and mix thoroughly. Season and add the caster sugar. Add ground cumin to taste and leave to stand for several hours. Discard the garlic and add the fresh herbs to the dressing.

7 Unmould the terrine and cut it into thick slices. Put 1–2 slices on each plate, drizzle with dressing and serve.

GRILLED LEEK AND COURGETTE SALAD WITH FETA AND MINT

SERVED ON CRISP, SWEET LETTUCE, THIS MAKES A DELICIOUS SUMMERY STARTER. TRY TO OBTAIN GENUINE EWE'S MILK FETA FOR THE BEST FLAVOUR AND TEXTURE.

SERVES SIX

INGREDIENTS
12 slender, baby leeks
6 small courgettes
90ml/6 tbsp extra virgin olive oil
finely shredded rind and juice
 of ½ lemon
1–2 garlic cloves, finely chopped
½ fresh red chilli, seeded and diced
pinch of caster sugar (optional)
50g/2oz/½ cup black olives, stoned
 and roughly chopped
30ml/2 tbsp chopped fresh mint
150g/5oz feta cheese, sliced
 or crumbled
salt and ground black pepper
fresh mint leaves, to garnish
crisp lettuce leaves, to serve

1 Bring a large saucepan of salted water to the boil. Add the leeks and cook for 2–3 minutes. Drain, refresh under cold water, then squeeze out excess water and leave to drain.

2 Cut the courgettes in half lengthways. Place in a colander, adding 5ml/1 tsp salt to the layers, and leave to drain for 45 minutes. Rinse and dry thoroughly on kitchen paper.

3 Heat the grill. Toss the leeks and courgettes in 30ml/2 tbsp of the oil. Grill the leeks for 2–3 minutes each side and the courgettes for about 5 minutes on each side. Cut the leeks into serving pieces and place them in a shallow dish with the courgettes.

4 Place the remaining oil in a small bowl and whisk in the lemon rind, 15ml/1 tbsp of the lemon juice, the garlic, chilli and a pinch of sugar, if using. Season to taste with salt and pepper. Add more lemon juice to taste.

5 Pour the dressing over the leeks and courgettes. Stir in the olives and mint, then set aside to marinate for a few hours, turning the vegetables in the dressing once or twice. If the salad has been marinated in the fridge, remove it 30 minutes before serving and bring back to room temperature.

6 Add the feta cheese just before serving. Serve with crisp lettuce leaves or spoon the salad on to the leaves arranged on individual serving plates and garnish with fresh mint leaves.

BRAISED BABY LEEKS IN RED WINE WITH AROMATICS

CORIANDER SEEDS AND OREGANO LEND A GREEK FLAVOUR TO THIS DISH OF BRAISED LEEKS. SERVE IT AS PART OF A MIXED HORS D'OEUVRE OR AS A PARTNER FOR BAKED WHITE FISH.

SERVES SIX

INGREDIENTS
12 baby leeks or 6 thick leeks
15ml/1 tbsp coriander seeds,
   lightly crushed
5cm/2in piece cinnamon stick
120ml/4fl oz/½ cup olive oil
3 fresh bay leaves
2 strips pared orange rind
5–6 fresh or dried oregano sprigs
5ml/1 tsp caster sugar
150ml/¼ pint/⅔ cup fruity red wine
10ml/2 tsp balsamic or sherry vinegar
30ml/2 tbsp coarsely chopped fresh
   oregano or marjoram
salt and ground black pepper

1 Leave baby leeks whole, but cut thick ones into 5–7.5cm/2–3in lengths.

2 Place the coriander seeds and cinnamon in a pan wide enough to take all the leeks in a single layer. Cook over a medium heat for 2–3 minutes, until the spices are fragrant, then stir in the oil, bay leaves, orange rind, oregano, sugar, wine and vinegar. Bring to the boil and simmer for 5 minutes.

3 Add the leeks. Bring back to the boil, reduce the heat and cover the pan. Cook gently for 5 minutes. Uncover and simmer gently for another 5–8 minutes, until the leeks are just tender when tested with the tip of a sharp knife.

4 Use a draining spoon to transfer the leeks to a serving dish. Boil the juices rapidly until reduced to about 75–90ml/ 5–6 tbsp. Add salt and pepper to taste and pour the liquid over the leeks. Leave to cool.

5 The leeks can be left to stand for several hours. If you chill them, bring them back to room temperature again before serving. Scatter chopped oregano or marjoram over the leeks just before serving them.

GRILLED SPRING ONIONS <u>AND</u> ASPARAGUS <u>WITH</u> PARMA HAM

THIS IS A GOOD CHOICE OF FIRST COURSE AT THE BEGINNING OF SUMMER, WHEN BOTH SPRING ONIONS AND ASPARAGUS ARE AT THEIR BEST. THE SLIGHT SMOKINESS OF THE GRILLED VEGETABLES GOES VERY WELL WITH THE SWEETNESS OF THE AIR-DRIED HAM.

SERVES FOUR TO SIX

INGREDIENTS
  2 bunches plump spring onions
    (about 24)
  500g/1¼lb asparagus
  45–60ml/3–4 tbsp olive oil
  20ml/4 tsp balsamic vinegar
  8–12 slices Parma or San
    Daniele ham
  50g/2oz Pecorino cheese
  sea salt and ground black pepper
  extra virgin olive oil, to serve

COOK'S TIP
The spring onions can be cooked on a cast-iron ridged grill pan. If more convenient, the asparagus can be roasted at 200°C/400°F/Gas 6 for 15 minutes.

1 Trim the root, outer papery skin and the top off the spring onions.

2 Cut off and discard the woody ends of the asparagus and use a vegetable peeler to peel the bottom 7.5cm/3in of the spears.

3 Heat the grill. Toss the spring onions and asparagus in 30ml/2 tbsp of the oil. Place on 2 baking sheets and season.

4 Grill the asparagus for 5 minutes on each side, until just tender when tested with the tip of a sharp knife. Protect the tips with foil if they seem to char too much. Grill the spring onions for about 3–4 minutes on each side, until tinged with brown. Brush both vegetables with more oil when you turn them.

5 Distribute the vegetables among 4–6 plates. Season with pepper and drizzle over the vinegar. Lay 2–3 slices of ham on each plate and shave the Pecorino over the top. Serve more extra virgin olive oil for drizzling at the table.

FLASH-FRIED SQUID WITH PAPRIKA AND GARLIC

THESE QUICK-FRIED SQUID ARE GOOD SERVED WITH A DRY SHERRY OR MANZANILLA AS AN APPETIZER OR AS PART OF MIXED TAPAS. ALTERNATIVELY, SERVE THEM ON A BED OF SALAD LEAVES AND OFFER WARM BREAD AS AN ACCOMPANIMENT FOR A MORE SUBSTANTIAL FIRST COURSE.

SERVES SIX TO EIGHT AS AN APPETIZER,
FOUR AS A FIRST COURSE

INGREDIENTS

500g/1¼lb very small squid, cleaned
90ml/6 tbsp olive oil, plus extra
1 red chilli, seeded and
 finely chopped
10ml/2 tsp Spanish mild smoked
 paprika (*pimentón*)
30ml/2 tbsp plain flour
2 garlic cloves, finely chopped
15ml/1 tbsp sherry vinegar
5ml/1 tsp grated lemon rind
30–45ml/2–3 tbsp finely chopped
 fresh parsley
salt and ground black pepper

1 Choose small squid that are no longer than 10cm/4in. Cut the body sacs into rings and cut the tentacles into bite-size pieces.

2 Place the squid in a bowl and add 30ml/2 tbsp of the oil, half the chilli and the paprika. Season with a little salt and some pepper, cover and marinate for 2–4 hours in the fridge.

COOK'S TIPS
• Make sure the wok or pan is very hot as the squid should cook for only 1–2 minutes: any longer and it will begin to toughen.
• Smoked paprika, known as *pimentón* in Spain, has a wonderful smoky flavour. If you cannot find it, use mild paprika.

3 Toss the squid in the flour and divide it into 2 batches. Heat the remaining oil in a preheated wok or deep frying pan over a high heat until very hot. Add the first batch of squid and stir-fry for 1–2 minutes, or until the squid becomes opaque and the tentacles have curled.

4 Sprinkle in half the garlic. Stir, then turn out on to a plate. Repeat with the second batch, adding more oil if needed.

5 Sprinkle over the sherry vinegar, lemon rind, remaining chilli and parsley. Season and serve hot or cool.

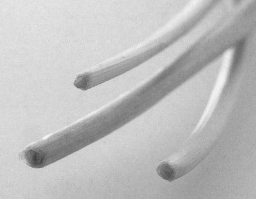

A little onion will often take a salad into new realms. But raw onion needs some discretion: use red onions or spring onions for their mild, sweet flavour. Onions also make some of the most delicious cooked salads. Try lightly blanched leeks or grilled onions, mixed with herby, mustardy dressings. Cheese, from mild mozzarella to salty feta, makes a great addition. And don't restrict chives to pretty garnishes - they pack a surprising punch of flavour in dressings for salads with potatoes, beetroot or egg.

Salads

GRILLED ONION AND AUBERGINE SALAD WITH GARLIC AND TAHINI DRESSING

THIS IS A DELICIOUSLY SMOKY SALAD THAT BALANCES SWEET AND SHARP FLAVOURS. IT MAKES A GOOD FILLING FOR PITTA BREAD, WITH SOME CRISP LETTUCE AND SWEET, RIPE TOMATOES.

SERVES SIX

INGREDIENTS
- 3 aubergines, cut into 1cm/½in thick slices
- 675g/1½lb round, not flat, onions, thickly sliced
- 75–90ml/5–6 tbsp olive oil
- 5ml/1 tsp powdered sumac (optional)
- 45ml/3 tbsp roughly chopped flat leaf parsley
- 45ml/3 tbsp pine nuts, toasted
- salt and ground black pepper
For the dressing
- 2 garlic cloves, crushed
- 150ml/¼ pint/⅔ cup light tahini
- juice of 1–2 lemons
- 45–60ml/3–4 tbsp water

1 Place the aubergines on a rack or in a colander and sprinkle generously with salt. Leave for 45–60 minutes, then rinse thoroughly under cold running water and pat dry with kitchen paper.

2 Thread the onions on to skewers or place them in an oiled wire grill cage.

COOK'S TIPS
• Sumac is a Mediterranean spice with a sharp, lemony taste. Buy it ready ground at Middle Eastern stores, good wholefood shops or delicatessens.
• Tahini is a thick, smooth, oily paste made from sesame seeds. It is also available from Middle Eastern stores, wholefood shops and delicatessens and from some supermarkets.

3 Brush the aubergines and onions with about 45ml/3 tbsp of the oil and grill for 6–8 minutes on each side. Brush with more oil, if necessary, when you turn the vegetables. The vegetables should be browned and soft when cooked. The onions may need a little longer than the aubergines.

4 Arrange the vegetables on a serving dish and sprinkle with the sumac, if using, and season with salt and pepper to taste. Sprinkle with the remaining oil if they seem dry.

5 For the dressing, crush the garlic in a mortar with a pinch of salt and gradually work in the tahini. Gradually work in the juice of 1 lemon, followed by the water. Taste and add more lemon juice if you think the dressing needs it. Thin with more water, if necessary, so that the dressing is fairly runny.

6 Drizzle the dressing over the salad and leave for 30–60 minutes, then sprinkle with the chopped parsley and pine nuts. Serve immediately at room temperature, not chilled.

BEETROOT AND RED ONION SALAD

THIS SALAD LOOKS ESPECIALLY ATTRACTIVE WHEN MADE WITH A MIXTURE OF RED AND YELLOW BEETROOT. TRY IT WITH ROAST BEEF OR COOKED HAM AS IT TASTES EXCELLENT WITH THESE RICH MEATS.

SERVES SIX

INGREDIENTS

500g/1¼lb small beetroot
75ml/5 tbsp water
60ml/4 tbsp olive oil
90g/3½oz/scant 1 cup walnut or pecan halves
5ml/1 tsp caster sugar, plus a little extra for the dressing
30ml/2 tbsp walnut oil
15ml/1 tbsp sherry vinegar or balsamic vinegar
5ml/1 tsp soy sauce
5ml/1 tsp grated orange rind
2.5ml/½ tsp ground roasted coriander seeds
5–10ml/1–2 tsp orange juice
1 red onion, halved and very thinly sliced
15–30ml/1–2 tbsp chopped fresh fennel
75g/3oz watercress or mizuna leaves
handful of baby red chard or beetroot leaves (optional)
salt and ground black pepper

3 Meanwhile, heat 15ml/1 tbsp of the olive oil in a small frying pan and cook the walnuts or pecans until they begin to brown. Add the sugar and cook, stirring, until the nuts begin to caramelize. Season with 2.5ml/½ tsp salt and lots of pepper, then turn the nuts out on to a plate and leave to cool.

4 In a jug or bowl, whisk together the remaining olive oil, the walnut oil, sherry or balsamic vinegar, soy sauce, orange rind and ground roasted coriander to make the dressing. Season with salt and pepper to taste and add a pinch of caster sugar. Whisk in orange juice to taste.

5 Separate the red onion slices into half-rings and add them to the strips of beetroot. Add the dressing and toss thoroughly to mix.

6 When ready to serve, toss the salad with the fennel, watercress or mizuna and red chard or beetroot leaves, if using. Transfer to individual bowls or plates and sprinkle with the caramelized nuts. Serve immediately.

1 Preheat the oven to 180°C/350°F/ Gas 4. Place the beetroot in an ovenproof dish just large enough to hold them in a single layer and add the water. Cover tightly and cook in the oven for about 1–1½ hours, or until they are just tender.

2 Cool, then peel the beetroot, then slice them or cut them into strips and toss with 15ml/1 tbsp of the olive oil. Transfer to a bowl and set aside.

MOROCCAN ORANGE, ONION AND OLIVE SALAD

THIS IS A REFRESHING SALAD TO FOLLOW A RICH MAIN DISH, SUCH AS A MOROCCAN TAGINE OF LAMB, OR TO LIGHTEN ANY SPICY MEAL. IT IS ALSO DELICIOUS WITH COLD ROAST DUCK.

SERVES SIX

INGREDIENTS
 5 large oranges
 90g/3½oz/scant 1 cup black olives
 1 red onion, thinly sliced
 1 large fennel bulb, thinly sliced,
  feathery tops reserved
 15ml/1 tbsp chopped fresh mint,
  plus a few extra sprigs
 15ml/1 tbsp chopped fresh coriander,
  plus a few extra sprigs
 2.5ml/½ tsp orange flower water
For the dressing
 60ml/4 tbsp olive oil
 10ml/2 tsp lemon juice
 2.5ml/½ tsp ground toasted
  coriander seeds
 salt and ground black pepper

1 Peel the oranges with a sharp knife, making sure you remove all the white pith, and cut them into 5mm/¼in slices. Remove any pips and work over a bowl to catch all the orange juice. Set the juice aside.

2 Stone the olives, if wished. In a bowl, toss the orange slices, onion and fennel together with the olives, chopped mint and fresh coriander.

3 Make the dressing. In a bowl or jug, whisk together the olive oil, 15ml/1 tbsp of the reserved fresh orange juice and the lemon juice. Add the ground toasted coriander seeds and season to taste with a little salt and pepper. Whisk thoroughly to mix.

4 Toss the dressing into the salad and leave to stand for 30–60 minutes.

5 Drain off any excess dressing and place the salad on a serving dish. Scatter with the herbs and fennel tops, and sprinkle with the orange flower water.

TOMATO, MOZZARELLA AND RED ONION SALAD WITH BASIL AND CAPER DRESSING

SWEET TOMATOES AND THE HEADY SCENT OF BASIL CAPTURE THE ESSENCE OF SUMMER IN THIS SIMPLE SALAD. VINE-RIPENED TOMATOES USUALLY HAVE THE BEST FLAVOUR.

SERVES FOUR

INGREDIENTS
 5 large ripe tomatoes, peeled if liked
 2 buffalo mozzarella cheeses,
  drained and sliced
 1 small red onion, chopped
For the dressing
 ½ small garlic clove, peeled
 15g/½oz fresh basil
 30ml/2 tbsp chopped fresh flat
  leaf parsley
 25ml/5 tsp small salted
  capers, rinsed
 2.5ml/½ tsp mustard
 75–90ml/5–6 tbsp extra virgin
  olive oil
 5–10ml/1–2 tsp balsamic vinegar
 salt and ground black pepper
For the garnish
 fresh basil leaves
 fresh parsley sprigs

1 First make the dressing. Put the garlic, basil, parsley, half the capers and the mustard in a food processor or blender and process briefly to chop. Then, with the motor running, gradually pour in the olive oil through the feeder tube to make a smooth purée with a dressing consistency. Add the balsamic vinegar to taste and season with ground black pepper.

2 Slice the tomatoes. Arrange the tomato and mozzarella slices on a plate. Scatter the onion over and season with a little pepper.

3 Drizzle the dressing over the salad, then scatter a few basil leaves, parsley sprigs and the remaining capers on top as a garnish. Leave for 10–15 minutes before serving.

SALAD ᴼꟳ ROASTED SHALLOTS ᴬᴺᴰ BUTTERNUT SQUASH ᵂᴵᵀᴴ FETA CHEESE

THIS IS ESPECIALLY GOOD SERVED WITH A GRAIN OR STARCHY SALAD, BASED ON RICE OR COUSCOUS, FOR EXAMPLE. SERVE PLENTY OF GOOD BREAD TO MOP UP THE JUICES.

SERVES FOUR TO SIX

INGREDIENTS
    75ml/5 tbsp olive oil
    15ml/1 tbsp balsamic vinegar, plus a
      little extra if liked
    15ml/1 tbsp sweet soy sauce
    350g/12oz shallots, peeled but
      left whole
    3 fresh red chillies
    1 butternut squash, peeled, seeded
      and cut into chunks
    5ml/1 tsp finely chopped fresh thyme
    15g/½oz flat leaf parsley
    1 small garlic clove, finely chopped
    75g/3oz walnuts, chopped
    150g/5oz feta cheese
    salt and ground black pepper

1 Preheat the oven to 200°C/400°F/ Gas 6. Beat the oil, vinegar and soy sauce together in a large bowl, then season with salt and pepper.

2 Toss the shallots and 2 of the chillies in the oil mixture and turn into a large roasting tin or ovenproof dish. Roast for 15 minutes, stirring once or twice.

3 Add the butternut squash and roast for a further 30–35 minutes, stirring once, until the squash is tender and browned. Remove from the oven, stir in the chopped thyme and set the vegetables aside to cool.

4 Chop the parsley and garlic together and mix with the walnuts. Seed and finely chop the remaining chilli.

5 Stir the parsley, garlic and walnut mixture into the vegetables. Add chopped chilli to taste and adjust the seasoning, adding a little extra balsamic vinegar if liked. Crumble the feta and add to the salad. Transfer to a serving dish and serve immediately.

POTATO AND MUSSEL SALAD WITH SHALLOT AND CHIVE DRESSING

SHALLOT AND CHIVES IN A CREAMY DRESSING ADD BITE TO THIS SALAD OF POTATO AND SWEET MUSSELS. SERVE WITH A BOWL OF FULL-FLAVOURED WATERCRESS AND PLENTY OF WHOLEMEAL BREAD.

SERVES FOUR

INGREDIENTS

675g/1½lb salad potatoes
1kg/2¼lb mussels, scrubbed and
  beards removed
200ml/7fl oz/ scant 1 cup dry
  white wine
15g/½oz flat leaf parsley, chopped
salt and ground black pepper
snipped fresh chives, to garnish
watercress sprigs, to serve
For the dressing
105ml/7 tbsp mild olive oil
15–30ml/1–2 tbsp white wine vinegar
5ml/1 tsp Dijon mustard
1 large shallot, very finely chopped
15ml/1 tbsp snipped fresh chives
45ml/3 tbsp double cream
pinch of caster sugar (optional)

1 Cook the potatoes in boiling, salted water for 15–20 minutes, or until tender. Drain, cool, then peel. Slice the potatoes into a bowl and toss with 30ml/2 tbsp of the oil for the dressing.

2 Discard any open mussels that do not close when sharply tapped. Bring the white wine to the boil in a large, heavy-based saucepan. Add the mussels, cover and boil vigorously, shaking the pan occasionally, for 3–4 minutes, until the mussels have opened. Discard any mussels that have not opened after 5 minutes' cooking. Drain and shell the mussels, reserving the cooking liquid.

3 Boil the reserved cooking liquid until reduced to about 45ml/3 tbsp. Strain this through a fine sieve over the potatoes and toss to mix.

4 For the dressing, whisk together the remaining oil, 15ml/1 tbsp vinegar, the mustard, shallot and chives.

5 Add the cream and whisk again to form a thick dressing. Adjust the seasoning, adding more vinegar and/or a pinch of sugar to taste.

6 Toss the mussels with the potatoes, then mix in the dressing and chopped parsley. Sprinkle with extra snipped chives and serve with watercress sprigs.

COOK'S TIP
Potato salads, such as this one, should not be chilled if at all possible as the cold alters the texture of the potatoes and of the creamy dressing. For the best flavour and texture, serve this salad just cool or at room temperature.

GRILLED LEEK <u>AND</u> FENNEL SALAD
<u>WITH</u> SPICY TOMATO DRESSING

THIS IS AN EXCELLENT SALAD TO MAKE IN THE EARLY AUTUMN WHEN YOUNG LEEKS ARE AT THEIR BEST AND RIPE TOMATOES ARE FULL OF FLAVOUR. SERVE WITH GOOD BREAD AS A STARTER OR SERVE TO ACCOMPANY SIMPLY GRILLED WHITE FISH FOR A MAIN COURSE.

SERVES SIX AS A STARTER

INGREDIENTS
  675g/1½lb leeks
  2 large fennel bulbs
  120ml/4fl oz/½ cup extra virgin
    olive oil
  2 shallots, chopped
  150ml/¼ pint/⅔ cup dry white wine or
    white vermouth
  5ml/1 tsp fennel seeds, crushed
  6 fresh thyme sprigs
  2–3 bay leaves
  good pinch of dried red chilli flakes
  350g/12oz tomatoes, peeled, seeded
    and diced
  5ml/1 tsp sun-dried tomato
    paste (optional)
  good pinch of caster sugar (optional)
  75g/3oz/¾ cup small black olives
  salt and ground black pepper

2 Trim the fennel bulbs, reserving any feathery tops for the garnish and cut the bulbs either into thin slices or into thicker wedges, according to taste.

3 Cook the fennel in the reserved cooking water for about 5 minutes, then drain thoroughly and toss with 30ml/ 2 tbsp of the olive oil. Season to taste with black pepper.

6 Add the diced tomatoes and cook briskly for 5–8 minutes, or until reduced and thickened.

7 Add the tomato paste, if using, and adjust the seasoning, adding a good pinch of caster sugar if you think the dressing needs it.

1 Cook the leeks in boiling salted water for 4–5 minutes. Use a draining spoon to remove the leeks and place them in a colander to drain thoroughly and cool. Reserve the cooking water in the pan. Squeeze out excess water and cut the leeks into 7.5cm/3in lengths.

COOK'S TIP
When buying fennel, look for rounded bulbs; they have a better shape for this dish. The flesh should be crisp and white, with no signs of bruising. Avoid specimens with broken leaves or with brown or dried out patches.

4 Heat a ridged cast-iron griddle. Arrange the leeks and fennel on the griddle and cook until tinged deep brown, turning once. Remove the vegetables from the griddle, place in a large shallow dish and set aside.

5 Place the remaining olive oil, the shallots, white wine or vermouth, crushed fennel seeds, thyme, bay leaves and chilli flakes in a large saucepan and bring to the boil over a medium heat. Lower the heat and simmer for 10 minutes.

8 Pour the dressing over the leeks and fennel, toss to mix and leave to cool. The salad may be made several hours in advance and kept in the fridge, but bring it back to room temperature before serving.

9 When ready to serve, stir the salad then scatter the chopped fennel tops and black olives over the top.

LEEK SALAD WITH ANCHOVIES, EGGS AND PARSLEY

CHOPPED HARD-BOILED EGGS AND COOKED LEEKS ARE A CLASSIC COMBINATION IN FRENCH-STYLE SALADS. THIS ONE MAKES A GOOD FIRST COURSE, WITH SOME CRUSTY BREAD, OR A LIGHT MAIN DISH THAT CAN BE FINISHED WITH A TOMATO SALAD AND/OR A POTATO SALAD.

3 To make the dressing, whisk the mustard with the vinegar. Gradually whisk in the oil, followed by the cream. Stir in the shallot, then season to taste with salt, pepper and a pinch of caster sugar, if liked.

4 Leave the leeks whole or thickly slice them, then place in a serving dish. Pour most of the dressing over them and stir to mix. Leave for at least 1 hour, or until ready to serve, bringing them back to room temperature first, if necessary.

SERVES FOUR

INGREDIENTS
675g/1½lb thin or baby
  leeks, trimmed
2 large or 3 medium eggs
50g/2oz good-quality anchovy
  fillets in olive oil, drained
15g/½oz flat leaf parsley, chopped
a few black olives, stoned
  (optional)
salt and ground black pepper
For the dressing
  5ml/1 tsp Dijon mustard
  15ml/1 tbsp tarragon vinegar
  75ml/5 tbsp olive oil
  30ml/2 tbsp double cream
  1 small shallot, very finely
    chopped
  pinch of caster sugar (optional)

1 Cook the leeks in boiling salted water for 3–4 minutes. Drain, plunge into cold water, then drain again. Squeeze out excess water, then pat dry.

2 Place the eggs in a saucepan of cold water, bring to the boil and cook for 6–7 minutes. Drain, plunge into cold water, then shell and chop the eggs.

5 Arrange the anchovies on the leeks, then scatter the eggs and parsley over the top. Drizzle with the remaining dressing, season with black pepper and dot with a few olives, if using. Serve immediately.

COOK'S TIP
Make sure the leeks are well drained and squeezed of excess water or they will dilute the dressing and spoil the flavour.

PARSLEY AND ROCKET SALAD WITH BLACK OLIVE AND GARLIC DRESSING

BEING LIGHT BUT FULL OF FLAVOUR, THIS MAKES A WELL-ROUNDED FIRST COURSE; IT IS ALSO GOOD SERVED ALONGSIDE RARE ROAST BEEF. USE THE BEST PARMESAN CHEESE — PARMIGIANO REGGIANO — TO ENSURE THAT THIS SALAD IS SPECIAL.

SERVES SIX

INGREDIENTS
1 garlic clove, halved
115g/4oz good white bread, cut into 1cm/½in thick slices
45ml/3 tbsp olive oil, plus extra for shallow frying
75g/3oz rocket leaves
75g/3oz baby spinach
25g/1oz flat leaf parsley, leaves only
45ml/3 tbsp salted capers, rinsed and dried
40g/1½oz Parmesan cheese, pared into shavings
For the dressing
25ml/5 tsp black olive paste
1 garlic clove, finely chopped
5ml/1 tsp Dijon mustard
75ml/5 tbsp olive oil
10ml/2 tsp balsamic vinegar
ground black pepper

1 First make the dressing. Whisk the black olive paste, garlic and mustard together in a bowl. Gradually whisk in the olive oil, then the vinegar. Adjust the seasoning with black pepper – the dressing should be sufficiently salty.

2 Heat the oven to 190°C/375°F/Gas 5. Rub the halved garlic clove over the bread and cut or tear the slices into bite-size croûtons. Toss them in the oil and place on a small baking tray. Bake for 10–15 minutes, stirring once, until golden brown. Cool on kitchen paper.

3 Mix the rocket, spinach and parsley in a large salad bowl.

4 Heat a shallow layer of olive oil in a frying pan. Add the capers and fry briefly until crisp. Scoop out straight away and drain on kitchen paper.

5 Toss the dressing and croûtons into the salad and divide it among 6 bowls or plates. Scatter the Parmesan shavings and the fried capers over the top and serve immediately.

COOK'S TIP
Use a swivel-action or fixed-blade potato peeler to cut thin shavings from a block of Parmigiano Reggiano – some supermarkets sell tubs of ready-shaved cheese. It is easier to make shavings if you choose a relatively young cheese rather than an older, drier and much harder Parmesan.

LENTIL AND SPINACH SALAD WITH ONION, CUMIN AND GARLIC

THIS WONDERFUL, EARTHY SALAD IS GREAT FOR A PICNIC OR WITH BARBECUED FOOD. IT IMPROVES WITH STANDING AND IS AT ITS BEST SERVED AT ROOM TEMPERATURE RATHER THAN CHILLED.

SERVES SIX

INGREDIENTS
  225g/8oz/1 cup Puy lentils
  1 fresh bay leaf
  1 celery stick
  fresh thyme sprig
  30ml/2 tbsp olive oil
  1 onion or 3–4 shallots,
    finely chopped
  10ml/2 tsp crushed toasted
    cumin seeds
  400g/14oz young spinach
  salt and ground black pepper
  30–45ml/2–3 tbsp chopped fresh
    parsley, plus a few extra sprigs
For the dressing
  75ml/5 tbsp extra virgin olive oil
  5ml/1 tsp Dijon mustard
  15–25ml/3–5 tsp red wine vinegar
  1 small garlic clove, finely chopped
  2.5ml/½ tsp finely grated lemon rind

4 Heat the oil in a deep frying pan and cook the onion or shallots over a low heat for about 4–5 minutes, until they are beginning to soften. Add the cumin and cook for 1 minute.

5 Add the spinach and season to taste, cover and cook for 2 minutes. Stir, then cook again briefly until wilted.

6 Stir the spinach into the lentils and leave the salad to cool. Bring back to room temperature if necessary. Stir in the remaining dressing and chopped parsley. Adjust the seasoning, adding extra red wine vinegar if necessary.

7 Turn the salad on to a serving platter and scatter over some parsley sprigs.

1 Rinse the lentils and place them in a large saucepan. Add plenty of water to cover. Tie the bay leaf, celery and thyme into a bundle and add to the pan, then bring to the boil. Reduce the heat so that the water boils steadily. Cook the lentils for 30–45 minutes, until just tender. Do not add salt at this stage, as it toughens the lentils.

2 Meanwhile, to make the dressing, mix the oil, mustard, 15ml/3 tsp vinegar, the garlic and lemon rind, and season well with salt and pepper.

3 Thoroughly drain the lentils and turn them into a bowl. Add most of the dressing and toss well, then set the lentils aside, stirring occasionally.

COOK'S TIP
Originally grown around the town of Puy in south-west France, these grey-green lentils have an excellent, earthy flavour and keep their shape on cooking. Do not add salt when cooking as it toughens the outer skin. Season when cooked.

BEAN SALAD WITH TUNA AND RED ONION

THIS MAKES A GREAT FIRST COURSE OR EVEN A LIGHT MAIN MEAL IF SERVED WITH A GREEN SALAD,
SOME GARLIC MAYONNAISE AND PLENTY OF WARM, CRUSTY BREAD.

SERVES FOUR

INGREDIENTS
  250g/9oz/1⅓ cups dried haricot
    or cannellini beans, soaked
    overnight in cold water
  1 bay leaf
  200–250g/7–9oz fine French
    beans, trimmed
  1 large red onion, very thinly sliced
  45ml/3 tbsp chopped fresh flat
    leaf parsley
  200–250g/7–9oz good-quality canned
    tuna in olive oil, drained
  200g/7oz cherry tomatoes, halved
  salt and ground black pepper
  a few onion rings, to garnish
For the dressing
  90ml/6 tbsp extra virgin olive oil
  15ml/1 tbsp tarragon vinegar
  5ml/1 tsp tarragon mustard
  1 garlic clove, finely chopped
  5ml/1 tsp grated lemon rind
  a little lemon juice
  pinch of caster sugar (optional)

1 Drain the beans and bring them to the boil in fresh water with the bay leaf added. Boil rapidly for 10 minutes, then reduce the heat and boil steadily for 1–1½ hours, until tender. The cooking time depends on the age of the beans. Drain well. Discard the bay leaf.

3 Blanch the French beans in plenty of boiling water for 3–4 minutes. Drain, refresh under cold water and drain thoroughly again.

2 Meanwhile, place all the dressing ingredients apart from the lemon juice and sugar in a jug or bowl and whisk until mixed. Season to taste with salt, pepper, lemon juice and a pinch of caster sugar, if liked. Leave to stand.

4 Place both types of beans in a bowl. Add half the dressing and toss to mix. Stir in the onion and half the chopped parsley, then season to taste with salt and pepper.

5 Flake the tuna into large chunks with a knife and toss it into the beans with the tomato halves.

6 Arrange the salad on four individual plates. Drizzle the remaining dressing over the salad and scatter the remaining chopped parsley on top. Garnish with a few onion rings and serve immediately, at room temperature.

THAI PRAWN SALAD <u>WITH</u> GARLIC DRESSING <u>AND</u> FRIZZLED SHALLOTS

IN THIS INTENSELY FLAVOURED SALAD, SWEET PRAWNS AND MANGO ARE PARTNERED WITH A SWEET-SOUR GARLIC DRESSING HEIGHTENED WITH THE HOT TASTE OF CHILLI. THE CRISP FRIZZLED SHALLOTS ARE A TRADITIONAL ADDITION TO THAI SALADS.

SERVES FOUR TO SIX

INGREDIENTS
  675g/1½lb medium-size raw prawns,
    shelled and deveined with tails on
  finely shredded rind of 1 lime
  ½ fresh red chilli, seeded and
    finely chopped
  30ml/2 tbsp olive oil, plus extra
    for brushing
  1 ripe but firm mango
  2 carrots, cut into long thin shreds
  10cm/4in piece cucumber, sliced
  1 small red onion, halved and
    thinly sliced
  a few sprigs of fresh coriander
  a few sprigs of fresh mint
  45ml/3 tbsp roasted peanuts,
    roughly chopped
  4 large shallots, thinly sliced and
    fried until crisp in 30ml/2 tbsp
    peanut oil
  salt and ground black pepper
For the dressing
  1 large garlic clove, chopped
  10–15ml/2–3 tsp caster sugar
  juice of 2 limes
  15–30ml/1–2 tbsp Thai fish sauce
    (*nam pla*)
  1 red chilli, seeded
  5–10ml/1–2 tsp light rice vinegar

1 Place the prawns in a glass or china dish and add the lime rind and chilli. Season with salt and pepper and spoon the oil over them. Toss to mix and leave to marinate for 30–40 minutes.

2 For the dressing, place the garlic in a mortar with 10ml/2 tsp caster sugar and pound until smooth, then work in the juice of 1½ limes and 15ml/1 tbsp of the Thai fish sauce.

3 Transfer the dressing to a jug. Finely chop half the chilli. and add it to the dressing. Taste the dressing and add more sugar, lime juice, fish sauce and the rice vinegar to taste.

COOK'S TIP
To devein prawns, make a shallow cut down the back of the prawn using a small, sharp knife. Using the tip of the knife, lift out the thin, black vein, then rinse the prawn thoroughly under cold, running water.

4 Peel and stone the mango, then cut it into very fine strips.

5 Toss together the mango, carrots, cucumber and onion, and half the dressing. Arrange the salad on individual plates or in bowls.

6 Heat a ridged, cast-iron grill pan or heavy-based frying pan until very hot. Brush with a little oil, then sear the prawns for 2–3 minutes on each side, until they turn pink and are patched with brown on the outside. Arrange the prawns on the salads.

7 Sprinkle the remaining dressing over the salads and scatter the sprigs of coriander and mint over. Finely shred the remaining chilli and sprinkle it over the salads with the peanuts and crisp-fried shallots. Serve immediately.

BEEF AND GRILLED SWEET POTATO SALAD WITH SHALLOT AND HERB DRESSING

THIS SALAD MAKES A GOOD MAIN DISH FOR A SUMMER BUFFET, ESPECIALLY IF THE BEEF HAS BEEN CUT INTO FORK-SIZE STRIPS. IT IS ABSOLUTELY DELICIOUS WITH A SIMPLE POTATO SALAD AND SOME PEPPERY LEAVES, SUCH AS WATERCRESS, MIZUNA OR ROCKET.

SERVES SIX TO EIGHT

INGREDIENTS
 800g/1¾lb fillet of beef
 5ml/1 tsp black peppercorns, crushed
 10ml/2 tsp chopped fresh thyme
 60ml/4 tbsp olive oil
 450g/1lb orange-fleshed sweet
  potato, peeled
 salt and ground black pepper
For the dressing
 1 garlic clove, chopped
 15g/½oz flat leaf parsley
 30ml/2 tbsp chopped fresh coriander
 15ml/1 tbsp small salted
  capers, rinsed
 ½–1 fresh green chilli, seeded
  and chopped
 10ml/2 tsp Dijon mustard
 10–15ml/2–3 tsp white wine vinegar
 75ml/5 tbsp extra virgin olive oil
 2 shallots, finely chopped

1 Roll the beef fillet in the crushed peppercorns and thyme, then set aside to marinate for a few hours. Preheat the oven to 200°C/400°F/Gas 6.

2 Heat half the olive oil in a heavy-based frying pan. Add the beef and brown it all over, turning frequently, to seal it. Place on a baking tray and cook in the oven for 10–15 minutes.

3 Remove the beef from the oven, and cover with foil, then leave to rest for 10–15 minutes.

4 Meanwhile, preheat the grill. Cut the sweet potatoes into 1cm/½in slices. Brush with the remaining olive oil, season to taste with salt and pepper, and grill for about 5–6 minutes on each side, until tender and browned. Cut the sweet potato slices into strips and place them in a bowl.

5 Cut the beef into slices or strips and toss with the sweet potato, then set the bowl aside.

6 For the dressing, process the garlic, parsley, coriander, capers, chilli, mustard and 10ml/2 tsp of the vinegar in a food processor or blender until chopped. With the motor still running, gradually pour in the oil to make a smooth dressing. Season the dressing with salt and pepper and add more vinegar, to taste. Stir in the shallots.

7 Toss the dressing into the sweet potatoes and beef and leave to stand for up to 2 hours before serving.

EGG AND BACON CAESAR SALAD

CAESAR CARDINI INVENTED THE CLASSIC CAESAR SALAD IN 1924 AT HIS RESTAURANT IN TIJUANA, JUST SOUTH OF THE US BORDER. THE ESSENTIALS ARE GOOD, SWEET LITTLE GEM, COS OR ROMAINE LETTUCE, CRISP GARLIC CROÛTONS AND A CREAMY MAYONNAISE-LIKE DRESSING.

SERVES SIX AS A STARTER OR
FOUR AS A LIGHT MAIN COURSE

INGREDIENTS
   3 × 1cm/½in thick slices white bread
   45ml/3 tbsp olive oil
   1 large garlic clove, finely chopped
   3–4 Little Gem lettuces or 2 larger
     cos or romaine lettuces
   12–18 quail's eggs
   115g/4oz thinly sliced Parma, San
     Daniele or Serrano ham
   40–50g/1½–2oz Parmesan
     cheese, grated
   salt and ground black pepper
For the dressing
   1 large egg
   1–2 garlic cloves, chopped
   4 anchovy fillets in oil, drained
   120ml/4fl oz/½ cup olive oil
   lemon juice or white wine vinegar

1 Preheat the oven to 190°C/375°F/ Gas 5. Cut the bread into bite-size squares or chunks and toss them with the oil and garlic. Season to taste with salt and pepper.

2 Turn out on to a baking tray. Bake for 10–14 minutes, stirring once or twice, until golden brown all over.

3 Meanwhile, for the dressing, bring a saucepan of water to the boil and add the egg, then boil it for 90 seconds. Plunge the egg into cold water and shell it into a food processor or blender.

4 Add the garlic and anchovy fillets and process to mix. With the motor still running, gradually add the olive oil in a thin stream. When all the oil is incorporated and the dressing is creamy, add 10–15ml/2–3 tsp lemon juice or wine vinegar and season to taste with salt and pepper.

5 Trim the lettuces, cutting the Little Gem lettuces into quarters or separating the larger lettuces into leaves. Place in a large salad bowl.

6 Place the quail's eggs in a saucepan, cover with cold water, then bring to the boil and boil for 2 minutes. Plunge the eggs into cold water, then part-shell them. Grill the ham for 2–3 minutes on each side, or until crisp.

7 Toss the dressing into the lettuce with 25g/1oz of the Parmesan. Add the croûtons. Cut the quail's eggs in half and add them to the salad. Crumble the ham into large pieces and scatter it over the salad with the remaining cheese. Serve immediately.

Flavour-packed onions make superb partners for the delicate flavours of seafood. They are essential in pickled fish dishes, as an aromatic bed for baked fish or in stuffings for mackerel, snapper or trout. Garlic complements seafood - think of mussels in garlic breadcrumbs. Aioli, the rich garlic mayonnaise from Provence, is wonderful with salt cod and Mediterranean fish stews. On the milder side, leeks and chives are perfect with fine-flavoured seafood such as sole and scallops.

Fish and
Seafood

CEVICHE ^{WITH} RED ONION, AVOCADO AND SWEET POTATO

CEVICHE IS A SOUTH AMERICAN DISH OF FISH MARINATED IN CITRUS JUICE AND ONION, WHICH HAS A SIMILAR EFFECT TO COOKING, MAKING THE FISH OPAQUE AND FIRM IN TEXTURE.

SERVES SIX AS A STARTER

INGREDIENTS

500–675g/1¼–1½lb white fish
  fillets, skinned
1 red onion, thinly sliced
pinch of dried red chilli flakes
grated rind of 1 small lime and
  juice of 5 limes
450–500g/1–1¼lb sweet potatoes
75ml/5 tbsp mild olive oil
15–25ml/3–5 tsp rice vinegar
2.5–5ml/½–1 tsp caster sugar
2.5 ml/½ tsp ground toasted
  cumin seeds
½–1 fresh red or green chilli, seeded
  and finely chopped
1 large or 2 small avocados, peeled,
  stoned and sliced
225g/8oz peeled cooked prawns
45ml/3 tbsp chopped
  fresh coriander
30ml/2 tbsp roasted
  peanuts, chopped
salt and ground black pepper

1 Cut the fish into strips or chunks. Scatter half the onion over the base of a glass dish and lay the fish on top. Sprinkle on the dried red chilli flakes and pour in the lime juice. Cover and chill for 2–3 hours, spooning the lime juice over the fish once or twice. Drain, and discard the onion.

2 Steam or boil the sweet potatoes for 20–25 minutes, or until just tender. Peel and slice, or cut into wedges.

3 Place the oil in a bowl and whisk in the rice vinegar and sugar to taste, then add the cumin, season, and whisk in the fresh chilli and grated lime rind.

4 In a glass bowl, toss together the fish, sweet potatoes, avocado slices, prawns and most of the coriander, and the dressing.

5 Toss in the remaining half of the sliced red onion. Sprinkle with the remaining coriander and the peanuts and serve at once.

COOK'S TIP
Choose orange-fleshed sweet potatoes if you can for this dish.

MOUCLADE

THIS IS A TRADITIONAL DISH OF MUSSELS COOKED WITH SHALLOTS, GARLIC AND SAFFRON FROM THE WEST ATLANTIC COAST OF FRANCE. IT TASTES AS SUPERB AS IT LOOKS.

SERVES SIX

INGREDIENTS

2kg/4½lb fresh mussels, scrubbed
  and beards removed
250g/9oz shallots, finely chopped
300ml/½ pint/1¼ cups medium white
  wine, such as Vouvray
generous pinch of saffron strands
  (about 12 strands)
75g/3oz/6 tbsp butter
2 celery sticks, finely chopped
5ml/1 tsp fennel seeds,
  lightly crushed
2 large garlic cloves, finely chopped
250ml/8fl oz/1 cup fish or
  vegetable stock
1 bay leaf
pinch of cayenne pepper
2 large egg yolks
150ml/¼ pint/⅔ cup double cream
juice of ½–1 lemon
30–45ml/2–3 tbsp chopped
  fresh parsley
salt and ground black pepper

1 Discard any mussels that do not shut when tapped sharply.

2 Place 30ml/2 tbsp of the shallots with the wine in a wide saucepan and bring to the boil. Add half the mussels and cover, then boil rapidly for 1 minute, shaking the pan once. Remove all the mussels, discarding any that remain closed. Repeat with the remaining mussels. Remove the top half-shell from each mussel. Strain the cooking liquid through a fine sieve into a bowl and stir in the saffron, then set aside.

3 Melt 50g/2oz/4 tbsp of the butter in a heavy-based saucepan. Add the remaining shallots and celery and cook over a low heat, stirring occasionally, for 5–6 minutes, until softened but not browned. Add the fennel seeds and half of the garlic, then cook for another 2–3 minutes.

4 Pour in the reserved mussel liquid, bring to the boil and then simmer for 5 minutes before adding the stock, bay leaf and cayenne. Season with salt and pepper to taste, then simmer, uncovered, for 5–10 minutes.

5 Beat the egg yolks with the cream, then whisk in a ladleful of the hot liquid followed by the juice of ½ lemon. Whisk this mixture back into the sauce. Cook over a very low heat, without allowing it to boil, for 5–10 minutes until slightly thickened. Taste for seasoning and add more lemon juice if necessary.

6 Stir the remaining garlic, butter and most of the parsley into the sauce with the mussels and reheat for 30–60 seconds. Distribute the mussels among 6 soup plates and ladle the sauce over. Sprinkle with the remaining parsley and serve.

Salt Cod Fritters with Aioli

Aioli is a fiercely garlicky, olive oil mayonnaise from Provence in the south of France and is a traditional accompaniment to salt cod.

<u>SERVES SIX</u>

INGREDIENTS
    450g/1lb salt cod
    500g/1¼lb floury potatoes
    300ml/½ pint/1¼ cups milk
    6 spring onions, finely chopped
    30ml/2 tbsp extra virgin olive oil
    30ml/2 tbsp chopped fresh parsley
    juice of ½ lemon, to taste
    2 eggs, beaten
    60ml/4 tbsp plain flour
    90g/3½oz/1⅓ cups dry
        white breadcrumbs
    vegetable oil, for shallow frying
    salt and ground black pepper
    lemon wedges and salad, to serve
For the aioli
    2 large garlic cloves
    2 egg yolks
    300ml/½ pint/1¼ cups olive oil
    lemon juice, to taste

1 Soak the salt cod in cold water for 24–36 hours, changing the water 5–6 times. The cod should swell as it rehydrates and a tiny piece should not taste unpleasantly salty when tried. Drain well.

2 Cook the potatoes, unpeeled, in a saucepan of boiling salted water for about 20 minutes, until tender. Drain, then peel and mash the potatoes.

3 Poach the cod very gently in the milk with half the spring onions for 10–15 minutes, or until it flakes easily. Remove the cod and flake it with a fork into a bowl, discarding bones and skin.

4 Add 60ml/4 tbsp mashed potato to the flaked cod and beat with a wooden spoon. Work in the olive oil, then gradually add the remaining potato. Beat in the remaining spring onions and the parsley. Season with lemon juice and pepper to taste – the mixture may need a little salt. Beat in 1 egg, then chill the mixture until firm.

5 Shape the mixture into 12–18 small round cakes. Coat them in flour, then dip them in the remaining egg and coat with the breadcrumbs. Chill until ready to fry.

COOK'S TIPS
• Try to find a thick, creamy white piece of salt cod, preferably cut from the middle of the fish rather than the tail and fin ends. Avoid thin, yellowish salt cod, as it will be too dry and salty.
• Mash potatoes by hand, never in a food processor, as it makes them gluey.
• Aioli traditionally has a sharp bite from the raw garlic. However, if you prefer a milder flavour, blanch the garlic once or twice in boiling water for about 3 minutes each time before using it.

6 Meanwhile, make the aioli. Place the garlic and a good pinch of salt in a mortar and pound to a paste with a pestle. Using a small whisk or a wooden spoon, gradually work in the egg yolks.

7 Add the olive oil, a drop at a time, until about half is incorporated. When the sauce is as thick as soft butter, beat in 5–10ml/1–2 tsp lemon juice, then continue adding oil until the aioli is very thick. Adjust the seasoning, adding lemon juice to taste.

8 Heat about 2cm/¾in depth of oil in a large, heavy-based frying pan. Add the fritters and cook over a medium-high heat for about 4 minutes. Turn them over and cook for a further 4 minutes on the other side, until crisp and golden. Drain on crumpled kitchen paper, then serve with the aioli, lemon wedges and salad leaves.

SEAFOOD AND SPRING ONION SKEWERS WITH TARTARE SAUCE

IF YOU MAKE THESE SKEWERS QUITE SMALL, THEY ARE GOOD AS A CANAPÉ TO SERVE AT A DRINKS PARTY OR BEFORE DINNER, WITH THE TARTARE SAUCE OFFERED AS A DIP.

MAKES NINE

INGREDIENTS
675g/1½lb monkfish tail, filleted,
  skinned and membrane removed
1 bunch thick spring onions
75ml/5 tbsp olive oil
1 garlic clove, finely chopped
15ml/1 tbsp lemon juice
5ml/1 tsp dried oregano
30ml/2 tbsp chopped fresh flat
  leaf parsley
12–18 small scallops or large
  raw prawns
75g/3oz/1½ cups fine fresh
  breadcrumbs
salt and ground black pepper
For the tartare sauce
2 egg yolks
300ml/½ pint/1¼ cups olive oil, or
  vegetable oil and olive oil mixed
15–30ml/1–2 tbsp lemon juice
5ml/1 tsp French mustard, preferably
  tarragon mustard
15ml/1 tbsp chopped gherkin or
  pickled cucumber
15ml/1 tbsp chopped capers
30ml/2 tbsp chopped fresh flat
  leaf parsley
30ml/2 tbsp snipped fresh chives
5ml/1 tsp chopped fresh tarragon

2 Whisk in 15ml/1 tbsp lemon juice, then a little more oil. Stir in all the mustard, gherkin or cucumber, capers, parsley, chives and tarragon. Add more lemon juice and seasoning to taste.

4 Mix the breadcrumbs and remaining parsley together. Toss the seafood and spring onions in the mixture to coat. Soak 9 bamboo skewers in cold water.

1 First make the tartare sauce. Whisk the egg yolks and a pinch of salt. Whisk in the oil, a drop at a time at first. When about half the oil is incorporated, add it in a thin stream, whisking all the time. Stop when the mayonnaise is very thick.

3 Cut the monkfish into 18 pieces and cut the spring onions into 18 pieces about 5–6cm/2–2½in long. Mix the oil, garlic, lemon juice, oregano and half the parsley with seasoning. Add the monkfish, scallops or prawns and spring onions, then marinate for 15 minutes.

5 Preheat the grill. Drain the skewers and thread the monkfish, scallops or prawns and spring onions on to them. Drizzle with a little marinade then grill for 5–6 minutes in total, turning once and drizzling with the marinade, until the fish is just cooked. Serve immediately with the tartare sauce.

MARINATED RED MULLET <u>WITH</u> ONION, PEPPER <u>AND</u> AUBERGINE

SNAPPER, SEA BREAM OR TILAPIA ARE ALL GOOD ALTERNATIVES TO MULLET IN THIS RECIPE, BASED ON A SPANISH WAY OF COOKING FISH EN ESCABECHE BY FIRST FRYING IT, THEN MARINATING IT.

SERVES SIX

INGREDIENTS
7.5ml/1½ tsp mild Spanish
   paprika, preferably Spanish
   smoked *pimentón*
45ml/3 tbsp plain flour
120ml/4fl oz/½ cup olive oil
6 red mullet, each weighing about
   300g/11oz, filleted
2 aubergines, sliced or cut into
   long wedges
2 red or yellow peppers, seeded and
   thickly sliced
1 large red onion, thinly sliced
2 garlic cloves, sliced
15ml/1 tbsp sherry vinegar
juice of 1 lemon
brown sugar, to taste
15ml/1 tbsp chopped fresh oregano
18–24 black olives
45ml/3 tbsp chopped fresh flat
   leaf parsley
salt and ground black pepper

3 Add another 30ml/2 tbsp oil to the pan and cook the peppers and onion gently for 6–8 minutes, until softened but not browned. Add the garlic and remaining paprika, then cook for a further 2 minutes. Stir in the sherry vinegar and lemon juice with 30ml/2 tbsp water and heat until simmering. Season to taste with a pinch of sugar.

4 Stir in the oregano and olives, then spoon over the fish. Set aside to cool, then cover and marinate in the fridge for several hours or overnight.

5 About 30 minutes before serving, bring the fish and vegetables back to room temperature. Stir in the parsley just before serving.

1 Mix 5ml/1 tsp of the paprika with the flour and season well with salt and pepper. Heat half the oil in a large frying pan. Dip the fish into the flour, turning to coat both sides, and fry for 4–5 minutes, until browned on each side. Place the fish in a glass or china dish suitable for marinating it.

2 Add 30ml/2 tbsp of the remaining oil to the pan and fry the aubergines until softened and browned. Drain on kitchen paper and add to the fish.

GRILLED SOLE WITH CHIVE AND LEMON GRASS BUTTER

CHIVES ARE AT THEIR BEST WHEN BARELY COOKED, AND THEY MAKE A DELICIOUS BUTTER TO SERVE WITH SIMPLE GRILLED FISH. SOLE IS THE IDEAL CHOICE, BUT HALIBUT, TURBOT AND SWORDFISH ARE ALSO GOOD. SERVE WITH STEAMED NEW POTATOES AND A SIMPLE VEGETABLE ACCOMPANIMENT.

SERVES FOUR

INGREDIENTS
115g/4oz/½ cup unsalted butter,
  softened, plus extra melted butter
5ml/1 tsp minced lemon grass
pinch of finely grated lime rind
1 kaffir lime leaf, very finely
  shredded (optional)
45ml/3 tbsp snipped chives or
  chopped chive flowers, plus extra
  chives or chive flowers to garnish
2.5–5ml/½–1 tsp Thai fish sauce
4 sole, skinned
salt and ground black pepper
lemon or lime wedges, to serve

COOK'S TIP
Finer white fish fillets, such as plaice,
can be cooked in this way, but reduce
the cooking time slightly.

1 Cream the butter with the lemon grass, lime rind, lime leaf, if using, and chives or chive flowers. Season to taste with Thai fish sauce, salt and pepper.

2 Chill the butter mixture to firm it for a short while, then form it into a roll and wrap in foil, clear film or greaseproof paper. Chill until firm. Preheat the grill.

3 Brush the fish with a little melted butter. Place it on the grill rack and season. Grill for about 5 minutes on each side, until firm and just cooked. Meanwhile, cut the chilled butter into thin slices. Serve the fish topped with slices of the butter. Serve immediately, garnished with chives. Offer lemon or lime wedges with the fish.

SEARED TUNA STEAKS
WITH RED ONION SALSA

RED ONIONS ARE IDEAL FOR THIS SALSA, NOT ONLY FOR THEIR MILD AND SWEET FLAVOUR, BUT ALSO BECAUSE THEY LOOK SO APPETIZING. SALAD, RICE OR BREAD AND A BOWL OF THICK YOGURT FLAVOURED WITH CHOPPED FRESH HERBS ARE GOOD ACCOMPANIMENTS.

SERVES FOUR

INGREDIENTS

4 tuna loin steaks, each weighing
  about 175–200g/6–7oz
5ml/1 tsp cumin seeds, toasted
  and crushed
pinch of dried red chilli flakes
grated rind and juice of 1 lime
30–60ml/2–4 tbsp extra virgin
  olive oil
salt and ground black pepper
lime wedges and fresh coriander
  sprigs, to garnish
For the salsa
1 small red onion,
  finely chopped
200g/7oz red or yellow cherry
  tomatoes, roughly chopped
1 avocado, peeled, stoned
  and chopped
2 kiwi fruit, peeled and chopped
1 fresh red chilli, seeded and
  finely chopped
15g/½oz fresh coriander, chopped
6 fresh mint sprigs, leaves
  only, chopped
5–10ml/1–2 tsp Thai fish sauce
  (*nam pla*)
about 5ml/1 tsp muscovado sugar

1 Wash the tuna steaks and pat dry. Sprinkle with half the cumin, the dried chilli, salt, pepper and half the lime rind. Rub in 30ml/2 tbsp of the oil and set aside in a glass or china dish for about 30 minutes.

2 Meanwhile, make the salsa. Mix the onion, tomatoes, avocado, kiwi fruit, fresh chilli, chopped coriander and mint. Add the remaining cumin, the rest of the lime rind and half the lime juice. Add Thai fish sauce and sugar to taste. Set aside for 15–20 minutes, then add more Thai fish sauce, lime juice and olive oil if required.

3 Heat a ridged, cast iron grill pan. Cook the tuna, allowing about 2 minutes on each side for rare tuna or a little longer for a medium result.

4 Serve the tuna steaks garnished with lime wedges and coriander sprigs. Serve the salsa separately or spoon on to the plates with the tuna.

PISSALADIÈRE

THIS FAMOUS .ONION AND ANCHOVY DISH IS A TRADITIONAL MARKET FOOD OF NICE IN SOUTHERN FRANCE. IT CAN BE MADE USING EITHER SHORTCRUST PASTRY OR, AS HERE, YEASTED DOUGH, SIMILAR TO A PIZZA BASE. EITHER WAY, IT IS MOST DELICIOUS EATEN LUKEWARM RATHER THAN PIPING HOT.

SERVES SIX

INGREDIENTS
  250g/9oz/2¼ cups strong plain white
    flour, plus extra for dusting
  50g/2oz/⅓ cup fine polenta
    or semolina
  5ml/1 tsp salt
  175ml/6fl oz/¾ cup lukewarm water
  5ml/1 tsp dried yeast
  5ml/1 tsp caster sugar
  30ml/2 tbsp extra virgin olive oil
For the topping
  60–75ml/4–5 tbsp extra virgin
    olive oil
  6 large sweet Spanish onions,
    thinly sliced
  2 large garlic cloves, thinly sliced
  5ml/1 tsp chopped fresh thyme, plus
    several sprigs
  1 fresh rosemary sprig
  1–2 × 50g/2oz cans anchovies in
    olive oil
  50–75g/2–3oz small black olives,
    preferably small Niçoise olives
  salt and ground black pepper

1 Mix the flour, polenta or semolina and salt in a large mixing bowl. Pour half the water into a bowl. Add the yeast and sugar, then leave in a warm place for 10 minutes, until frothy. Pour the yeast mixture into the flour mixture with the remaining water and the olive oil.

2 Using your hands, mix all the ingredients together to form a dough, then turn out and knead for 5 minutes, until smooth, springy and elastic.

3 Return the dough to the clean, floured bowl and place it in a plastic bag or cover with oiled clear film, then set the dough aside at room temperature for 30–60 minutes to rise and double in bulk.

4 Meanwhile, start to prepare the topping. Heat 45ml/3 tbsp of the olive oil in a large, heavy-based saucepan and add the sliced onions. Stir well to coat the onions in the oil, then cover the pan and cook over a very low heat, stirring occasionally, for 20-30 minutes. (Use a heat-diffuser mat to keep the heat low, if possible.)

5 Add a little salt to taste and the garlic, chopped thyme and rosemary sprig. Stir well and continue cooking for another 15–25 minutes, or until the onions are soft and deep golden yellow but not browned at all. Uncover the pan for the last 5–10 minutes' cooking if the onions seem very wet. Remove and discard the rosemary. Set the onions aside to cool.

6 Preheat the oven to 220°C/425°F/ Gas 7. Roll out the dough thinly and use to line a large baking sheet, about 30 × 23–25cm/12 × 9–10in. Taste the onions for seasoning before spreading them over the dough.

7 Drain the anchovies, cut them in half lengthways and arrange them in a lattice pattern over the onions. Scatter the olives and thyme sprigs over the top of the pissaladière and drizzle with the remaining olive oil. Bake for about 20–25 minutes, or until the dough is browned and cooked. Season with pepper and serve warm, cut into slices.

VARIATIONS
• Shortcrust pastry can be used instead of yeast dough as a base: bake it blind for 10–15 minutes before adding the filling.
• If you enjoy anchovies, try spreading about 60ml/4 tbsp anchovy purée (*anchoïade*) over the base before adding the onions. Alternatively, spread black olive paste over the base.

JANSSON'S TEMPTATION

A TRADITIONAL SWEDISH FAVOURITE, THIS RICH GRATIN IS UTTERLY MORE-ISH. AS FOOD WRITER JANE GRIGSON POINTED OUT, THE NAME PROBABLY DOES NOT REFER TO A SPECIFIC JANSSON BUT MEANS "EVERYONE'S TEMPTATION", AS JANSSON IS A COMMON SWEDISH SURNAME.

SERVES FOUR TO SIX

INGREDIENTS

50g/2oz/¼ cup butter
900g/2lb potatoes (preferably Estima
or Desirée)
2 large sweet Spanish onions, sliced
2 × 50g/2oz cans anchovies in olive
oil, drained
450ml/¾ pint/scant 2 cups whipping
cream or half and half double and
single cream
a little milk (optional)
salt and ground black pepper

1 Preheat the oven to 200°C/400°F/
Gas 6. Use 15g/½oz/1 tbsp of the butter
to grease a 1.5 litre/2½ pint/6¼ cup
ovenproof dish.

2 Using a sharp knife, carefully cut the
potatoes into fine matchstick strips.

3 Toss the potato strips with salt and
freshly ground black pepper and scatter
half of them in the base of the prepared
ovenproof dish.

4 Lay half of the onions on top of the
potatoes, season with black pepper and
dot with butter. Lay the anchovies on
top of the onions, then add the rest of
the sliced onions and top with the
remaining potatoes.

5 Mix the cream with 30ml/2 tbsp cold
water and pour this over the potatoes.
Add a little milk, if necessary, to bring
the liquid to just below the top of the
final layer of potatoes.

6 Dot the potatoes with the remaining
butter then cover with foil and bake for
1 hour.

7 Reduce the heat to 180°C/350°F/
Gas 4 and uncover the dish. Bake for
a further 40–50 minutes or until the
potatoes are tender and brown.

COOK'S TIPS
• Cover the gratin with foil for the first
half of cooking so that the potatoes don't
brown or dry out too much. If using
whole, salted anchovies or Swedish
salted sprats they will need to be boned.
If they are very salty, soak in a little milk
for 30 minutes before using.
• Serve with small glasses of chilled
schnapps and cold beer for an authentic
Swedish flavour.

BAKED MONKFISH <u>WITH</u> POTATOES <u>AND</u> GARLIC

THIS SIMPLE SUPPER DISH CAN BE MADE WITH OTHER FISH. SAUCE TARTARE OR A THICK VINAIGRETTE FLAVOURED WITH CHOPPED GHERKINS AND HARD-BOILED EGG ARE DELICIOUS ACCOMPANIMENTS.

<u>SERVES FOUR</u>

INGREDIENTS
    1kg/2¼lb waxy potatoes, cut
      into chunks
    50g/2oz/¼ cup butter
    2 onions, thickly sliced
    4 garlic cloves
    few fresh thyme sprigs
    2–3 fresh bay leaves
    450ml/¾ pint/scant 2 cups
      vegetable or fish stock,
      plus 45ml/3 tbsp
    900g/2lb monkfish tail in one piece,
      skin and membrane removed
    30–45ml/2–3 tbsp white wine
    50g/2oz/1 cup fresh
      white breadcrumbs
    15g/½oz fresh parsley, chopped
    15ml/1 tbsp olive oil
    salt and ground black pepper

1 Preheat the oven to 190°C/375°F/Gas 5. Put the chunks of potato in an ovenproof dish. Melt half the butter in a large frying pan and cook the onions gently for 5–6 minutes. Add the onions to the potatoes and mix.

2 Slice 2–3 of the garlic cloves and add to the potatoes with the thyme and bay leaves, and season with salt and freshly ground black pepper.

3 Pour in the main batch of stock over the potatoes and bake, stirring once or twice, for 50–60 minutes, until the potatoes are just tender.

4 Nestle the monkfish into the potatoes and season with salt and pepper. Bake for 10–15 minutes. Mix the 45ml/3 tbsp stock with the wine and use to baste the monkfish 2–3 times during cooking.

5 Finely chop the remaining garlic. Melt the remaining butter and toss it with the breadcrumbs, chopped garlic, most of the chopped parsley and seasoning. Spoon over the monkfish, pressing it down gently with the back of a spoon.

6 Drizzle the olive oil over the crumb-covered fish, return the dish to the oven and bake for a final 10–15 minutes, until the breadcrumbs are crisp and golden and all the liquid has been absorbed. Sprinkle the remaining parsley on to the potatoes and serve immediately.

SALMON EN PAPILLOTE WITH LEEKS AND YELLOW PEPPERS

COOKING FISH "EN PAPILLOTE" MAKES A LOT OF SENSE, ENSURING THAT THE FISH RETAINS ITS FLAVOUR WHILE IT COOKS IN ITS STEAMY PARCEL WITH AROMATIC INGREDIENTS SUCH AS LEEKS AND HERBS. IT IS ALSO EXCELLENT WHEN ENTERTAINING, AS THE PARCELS MAY BE PREPARED AHEAD OF COOKING.

SERVES SIX

INGREDIENTS

25ml/1½ tbsp groundnut oil
2 yellow peppers, seeded and
   thinly sliced
4cm/1½in fresh root ginger, peeled
   and finely shredded
1 large fennel bulb, finely sliced,
   feathery tops chopped and reserved
1 green chilli, seeded and
   finely shredded
2 large leeks, cut into 10cm/4in
   lengths and shredded lengthways
30ml/2 tbsp snipped chives
10ml/2 tsp light soy sauce
6 portions salmon fillet, each
   weighing 150–175g/5–6oz, skinned
10ml/2 tsp toasted sesame oil
salt and ground black pepper

1 Heat the oil in a large non-stick frying pan and cook the peppers, ginger and fennel for 5–6 minutes, until they are softened but not browned. Add the chilli and leeks and cook for a further 2–3 minutes. Stir in half the chives and the soy sauce with seasoning to taste. Set aside to cool.

2 Preheat the oven to 190°C/375°F/ Gas 5. Cut 6 × 35cm/14in circles of baking parchment or foil. Divide the vegetable mixture between the 6 circles and place a portion of salmon on each pile of vegetables. Drizzle with sesame oil and sprinkle with the remaining chives and the chopped fennel tops. Season with salt and pepper.

3 Fold the paper or foil over to enclose the fish, rolling and twisting the edges together to seal the parcels. Place the parcels on a baking sheet and bake for 15–20 minutes, until the parcels are puffed up and, if made with paper, lightly browned. Transfer the parcels to warmed individual plates and serve immediately.

BACON-WRAPPED TROUT WITH OATMEAL AND ONION STUFFING

THIS STUFFING IS BASED ON A SCOTTISH SPECIALITY, A MIXTURE OF OATMEAL AND ONION CALLED SKIRLIE. HERRING CAN BE COOKED IN THE SAME WAY. THIS IS VERY GOOD WITH SLICES OF COOKED POTATOES, BRUSHED WITH OLIVE OIL AND GRILLED UNTIL GOLDEN ON EACH SIDE.

SERVES FOUR

INGREDIENTS

10 dry-cured streaky bacon rashers
40g/1½oz/3 tbsp butter or
  bacon fat
1 onion, finely chopped
115g/4oz/1 cup oatmeal
30ml/2 tbsp chopped fresh parsley
30ml/2 tbsp snipped fresh chives
4 trout, about 350g/12oz each,
  gutted and boned
juice of ½ lemon
salt and ground black pepper
watercress, cherry tomatoes and
  lemon wedges, to serve
For the herb mayonnaise
6 watercress sprigs
15ml/1 tbsp snipped fresh chives
30ml/2 tbsp roughly chopped parsley
90ml/6 tbsp lemon mayonnaise
30ml/2 tbsp fromage frais or
  crème fraîche
2.5–5ml/½–1 tsp tarragon mustard

1 Preheat oven to 190°C/375°F/Gas 5. Chop 2 of the bacon rashers. Melt 25g/1oz/2 tbsp of the butter or bacon fat in a large frying pan and cook the bacon briefly. Add the finely chopped onion and fry gently for 5–8 minutes, until softened.

2 Add the oatmeal and cook until the oatmeal darkens and absorbs the fat, but do not allow it to overbrown. Stir in the parsley, chives and seasoning. Cool.

3 Wash and dry the trout, then stuff with the oatmeal mixture. Wrap each fish in 2 bacon rashers and place in an ovenproof dish. Dot with the remaining butter and sprinkle with the lemon juice. Bake for 20–25 minutes, until the bacon browns and crisps a little.

4 Meanwhile, make the mayonnaise. Place the watercress, chives and parsley in a sieve and pour boiling water over them. Drain, rinse under cold water, and drain well on kitchen paper.

5 Purée the herbs in a mortar with a pestle. (This is easier than using a food processor for this small quantity.) Stir the puréed herbs into the lemon mayonnaise together with the fromage frais or crème fraîche. Add tarragon mustard to taste and stir to combine.

6 When cooked, transfer the trout to warmed serving plates and serve immediately with watercress, tomatoes and lemon wedges, accompanied by the herb mayonnaise.

SEARED SCALLOPS WITH CHIVE SAUCE ON LEEK AND CARROT RICE

SCALLOPS ARE ONE OF THE MOST DELICIOUS SHELLFISH. HERE THEY ARE PARTNERED WITH A DELICATE CHIVE SAUCE AND A PILAFF OF WILD AND WHITE RICE WITH SWEET LEEKS AND CARROTS.

SERVES FOUR

INGREDIENTS
 12–16 shelled scallops
 45ml/3 tbsp olive oil
 50g/2oz/⅓ cup wild rice
 65g/2½ oz/5 tbsp butter
 4 carrots, cut into long thin strips
 2 leeks, cut into thick,
  diagonal slices
 1 small onion, finely chopped
 115g/4oz/⅔ cup long grain rice
 1 fresh bay leaf
 200ml/7fl oz/scant 1 cup white wine
 450ml/¾ pint/scant 2 cups fish stock
 60ml/4 tbsp double cream
 a little lemon juice
 25ml/5 tsp snipped fresh chives
 30ml/2 tbsp chervil sprigs
 salt and ground black pepper

1 Lightly season the scallops, brush with 15ml/1 tbsp of the olive oil and set aside.

2 Cook the wild rice in plenty of boiling water for about 30 minutes, until tender, then drain.

3 Melt half the butter in a small frying pan and cook the carrots fairly gently for 4–5 minutes. Add the leeks and fry for another 2 minutes. Season with salt and pepper and add 30–45ml/ 2–3 tbsp water, then cover and cook for a few minutes more. Uncover and cook until the liquid has reduced. Set aside off the heat.

4 Melt half the rest of the butter with 15ml/1 tbsp of the remaining oil in a heavy-based saucepan. Add the onion and fry for 3–4 minutes, until softened but not browned.

5 Add the long grain rice and bay leaf and cook, stirring constantly, until the rice looks translucent and the grains are coated with oil.

6 Pour in half the wine and half the stock. Season with 2.5ml/½ tsp salt and bring to the boil. Stir, then cover and cook very gently for 15 minutes, or until the liquid is absorbed and the rice is cooked and tender.

7 Reheat the carrots and leeks gently, then stir them into the long grain rice with the wild rice. Add seasoning to taste, if necessary.

8 Meanwhile, pour the remaining wine and stock into a small saucepan and boil rapidly until reduced by half.

COOK'S TIP
Choose fresh, rather than frozen, scallops as the frozen ones tend to exude water on cooking. Scallops need only the briefest cooking at high heat, just until they turn opaque and brown on each side, so have the pan very hot. Although some people avoid eating the orange-coloured coral, it is delicious and many people consider it to be the best bit.

9 Heat a heavy frying pan over a high heat. Add the remaining butter and oil. Sear the scallops for 1–2 minutes each side, then set aside and keep warm.

10 Pour the reduced stock into the pan and heat until bubbling, then add the cream and boil until thickened. Season with lemon juice, salt and pepper. Stir in the chives and scallops.

11 Stir the chervil into the rice and pile it on to plates. Arrange the scallops on top and spoon the sauce over the rice.

CHINESE-STYLE STEAMED FISH

THIS IS A CLASSIC CHINESE WAY OF COOKING WHOLE FISH, WITH GARLIC, SPRING ONIONS, GINGER AND BLACK BEANS. THE FISH MAKES A SPLENDID CENTREPIECE FOR A CHINESE MEAL OR IT CAN BE SERVED MORE SIMPLY, WITH BOILED RICE AND SOME STIR-FRIED CHINESE GREENS.

SERVES FOUR TO SIX

INGREDIENTS

2 sea bass, grey mullet or trout, each
  weighing about 675–800g/1½–1¾lb
25ml/1½ tbsp salted black beans
2.5ml/½ tsp sugar
30ml/2 tbsp finely shredded fresh
  root ginger
4 garlic cloves, thinly sliced
30ml/2 tbsp Chinese rice wine or
  dry sherry
30ml/2 tbsp light soy sauce
4–6 spring onions, finely shredded or
  sliced diagonally
45ml/3 tbsp groundnut oil
10ml/2 tsp sesame oil

1 Wash the fish inside and out under cold running water, then pat them dry on kitchen paper. Using a sharp knife, slash 3–4 deep cross shapes on each side of each fish.

2 Mash half the black beans with the sugar in a small bowl and then stir in the remaining whole beans.

3 Place a little ginger and garlic inside the cavity of each fish and then lay them on a plate or dish that will fit inside a large steamer. Rub the bean mixture into the fish, especially into the slashes, then scatter the remaining ginger and garlic over the top. Cover and chill for 30 minutes.

4 Place the steamer over a pan of boiling water. Sprinkle the rice wine or sherry and half the soy sauce over the fish and steam them for 15–20 minutes, or until just cooked.

5 Sprinkle with the remaining soy sauce and scatter the spring onions over the fish.

6 In a small saucepan, heat the groundnut oil until smoking, then trickle it over the spring onions. Sprinkle with the sesame oil and serve immediately.

SEAFOOD LAKSA

A LAKSA IS A MALAYSIAN STEW OF FISH, POULTRY, MEAT OR VEGETABLES WITH NOODLES. AUTHENTIC LAKSAS ARE OFTEN VERY HOT, AND COOLED BY THE COCONUT MILK AND THE NOODLES. IF YOU WOULD PREFER A SPICY VERSION, ADD A LITTLE CHILLI POWDER INSTEAD OF SOME OF THE PAPRIKA.

SERVES FOUR TO FIVE

INGREDIENTS

    3 medium-hot fresh red
      chillies, seeded
    4–5 garlic cloves
    5ml/1 tsp mild paprika
    10ml/2 tsp fermented shrimp
      paste (*trassi*)
    25ml/1½ tbsp chopped fresh root
      ginger or galangal
    250g/9oz small red shallots
    25g/1oz fresh coriander (preferably
      with roots)
    45ml/3 tbsp groundnut oil
    5ml/1 tsp fennel seeds, crushed
    2 fennel bulbs, cut into thin wedges
    600ml/1 pint/2½ cups fish stock
    300g/11oz thin vermicelli
      rice noodles
    450ml/¾ pint/scant 2 cups
      coconut milk
    juice of 1–2 limes
    30–45ml/2–3 tbsp Thai fish sauce
      (*nam pla*)
    450g/1lb firm white fish fillet, such
      as monkfish, halibut or snapper
    450g/1lb large raw prawns (about
      20), shelled and deveined
    small bunch of fresh holy basil or
      ordinary basil
    2 spring onions, thinly sliced

1 Process the chillies, garlic, paprika, shrimp paste, ginger or galangal and 2 shallots to a paste in a food processor, blender or spice grinder. Remove the roots and stems from the coriander and add them to the paste; chop and reserve the coriander leaves. Add 15ml/1 tbsp of the oil to the paste and process again until fairly smooth.

2 Heat the remaining oil in a large saucepan. Add the remaining shallots, the fennel seeds and fennel wedges. Cook until lightly browned, then add 45ml/3 tbsp of the paste and stir-fry for about 1–2 minutes. Pour in the fish stock and bring to the boil. Reduce the heat and simmer for 8–10 minutes.

3 Meanwhile, cook the vermicelli rice noodles according to the packet instructions. Drain and set aside.

4 Add the coconut milk and the juice of 1 lime to the pan of shallots. Stir in 30ml/2 tbsp of the fish sauce. Bring to a simmer and taste, adding a little more spice paste, lime juice or fish sauce as necessary.

5 Cut the fish into chunks and add to the pan. Cook for 2–3 minutes, then add the prawns and cook until they turn pink. Chop most of the basil and add to the pan with the reserved coriander.

6 Divide the noodles among 4–5 wide bowls, then ladle in the stew. Sprinkle with spring onions and the remaining whole basil leaves. Serve immediately.

We add onions to marinades, to stews and casseroles, to roasts and braises, and we cook them in countless ways to accompany simply grilled meat or poultry. Certain classics stand out: lamb studded with garlic, steak topped with deep-fried onions or the Cantonese mixture of garlic, black beans and spring onions with beef. Imagine liver without onions, Thai curries without garlic, or sausages and mash without onion gravy. In fact, it is hard to think of many meat and poultry recipes in which onions aren't an essential ingredient.

Meat and Poultry

GIGOT BOULANGÈRE

Lamb cooked in the style of the baker's wife (la boulangère) is a classic of French provincial cooking. One of the best-known and best-loved pairings of lamb and garlic, this is a trouble-free and delicious choice for Sunday lunch.

4 Pour in the hot stock and add a little hot water, if necessary, to bring the liquid to just below the level of the potatoes. Dot with the remaining butter, cover them with foil and cook in the oven for 40 minutes. Increase the oven temperature to 200°C/400°F/Gas 6.

SERVES SIX

INGREDIENTS
50g/2oz/¼ cup butter, plus extra
  for greasing
4–6 garlic cloves
2 yellow onions, thinly sliced
12–18 small fresh thyme or
  rosemary sprigs
2 fresh bay leaves
1.8kg/4lb red potatoes, thinly sliced
450ml/¾ pint/scant 2 cups hot lamb
  or vegetable stock
2kg/4½lb leg of lamb
30ml/2 tbsp olive oil
salt and ground black pepper

1 Preheat the oven to 190°C/375°F/ Gas 5. Use a little butter to grease a large ovenproof dish, about 6cm/2½in deep. Finely chop half the garlic and sprinkle a little over the prepared dish.

2 Fry the onions in 25g/1oz/2 tbsp of the butter for 5–8 minutes, until softened. Roughly chop half the thyme or rosemary and crush the bay leaves.

3 Arrange a layer of potatoes in the dish, season and sprinkle with half the remaining chopped garlic, rosemary or thyme, 1 bay leaf and the onions. Add the remaining potatoes, chopped garlic and herbs.

5 Meanwhile, cut the rest of the garlic into slivers. Make slits all over the lamb with a narrow, sharp knife and insert slivers of garlic and sprigs of thyme or rosemary into the slits. Season the lamb well with salt and pepper.

6 Uncover the potatoes and scatter a few rosemary or thyme sprigs over them. Rest a roasting rack or ovenproof cooling rack over the dish and place the lamb on it. Rub the olive oil over the meat, then return the dish to the oven. Cook, turning the lamb once or twice, for 1½–1¾ hours, depending on how well done you prefer lamb. Leave the lamb to rest for 20 minutes in a warm place (in the switched-off oven, for example) before carving.

LAMB BURGERS WITH RED ONION AND TOMATO RELISH

A SHARP-SWEET RED ONION RELISH WORKS WELL WITH BURGERS BASED ON MIDDLE-EASTERN STYLE LAMB. SERVE WITH PITTA BREAD AND TABBOULEH OR WITH CHIPS AND A CRISP GREEN SALAD.

SERVES FOUR

INGREDIENTS

25g/1oz/3 tbsp bulgur wheat
500g/1¼lb lean minced lamb
1 small red onion, finely chopped
2 garlic cloves, finely chopped
1 green chilli, seeded and
  finely chopped
5ml/1 tsp ground toasted
  cumin seeds
2.5ml/½ tsp ground sumac
15g/½oz chopped fresh flat
  leaf parsley
30ml/2 tbsp chopped fresh mint
olive oil, for frying
salt and ground black pepper
For the relish
2 red peppers, halved and seeded
2 red onions, cut into 5mm/¼in
  thick slices
75–90ml/5–6 tbsp extra virgin olive oil
350g/12oz cherry tomatoes, chopped
½–1 fresh red or green chilli, seeded
  and finely chopped (optional)
30ml/2 tbsp chopped fresh mint
30ml/2 tbsp chopped fresh parsley
15ml/1 tbsp chopped fresh oregano
  or marjoram
2.5–5ml/½–1 tsp each ground toasted
  cumin seeds
2.5–5ml/½–1 tsp sumac
juice of ½ lemon
caster sugar, to taste

1 Pour 150ml/¼ pint/⅔ cup hot water over the bulgur wheat in a bowl and leave to stand for 15 minutes, then drain in a sieve and squeeze out the excess moisture.

2 Place the bulgur in a bowl and add the minced lamb, onion, garlic, chilli, cumin, sumac, parsley and mint. Mix the ingredients thoroughly together by hand, then season with 5ml/1 tsp salt and plenty of black pepper and mix again. Form the mixture into 8 small burgers and set aside while you make the relish.

3 Grill the peppers, skin side up, until the skin chars and blisters. Place in a bowl, cover and leave to stand for 10 minutes. Peel off the skin, dice the peppers finely and place in a bowl.

4 Brush the onions with 15ml/1 tbsp oil and grill for 5 minutes on each side, until browned. Cool, then chop.

5 Add the onions, tomatoes, chilli to taste, the mint, parsley, oregano or marjoram and 2.5ml/½ tsp each of the cumin and sumac to the peppers. Stir in 60ml/4 tbsp of the remaining oil and 15ml/1 tbsp of the lemon juice. Season with salt, pepper and sugar and allow to stand for 20–30 minutes.

6 Heat a heavy frying pan or a ridged, cast-iron grill pan over a high heat and grease lightly with olive oil. Cook the burgers for about 5–6 minutes on each side, or until just cooked at the centre.

7 While the burgers are cooking, taste the relish and adjust the seasoning, adding more salt, pepper, sugar, oil, chilli, cumin, sumac and lemon juice to taste. Serve the burgers immediately as they are cooked, with the relish.

LAMB STEW ^{WITH} BABY ONIONS AND NEW POTATOES

THIS FRESH LEMON-SEASONED STEW IS FINISHED WITH AN ITALIAN MIXTURE OF CHOPPED GARLIC, PARSLEY AND LEMON RIND KNOWN AS GREMOLATA, THE TRADITIONAL TOPPING FOR OSSO BUCCO.

SERVES SIX

INGREDIENTS

1kg/2¼lb boneless shoulder of lamb,
  trimmed of fat and cut into 5cm/
  2in cubes
1 garlic clove, finely chopped
finely grated rind of ½ lemon and
  juice of 1 lemon
90ml/6 tbsp olive oil
45ml/3 tbsp plain flour
1 large onion, sliced
5 anchovy fillets in olive oil, drained
2.5ml/½ tsp caster sugar
300ml/½ pint/1¼ cups fruity
  white wine
475ml/16fl oz/2 cups lamb stock or
  half stock and half water
1 fresh bay leaf
fresh thyme sprig
fresh parsley sprig
500g/1¼lb small new potatoes
250g/9oz shallots, peeled but
  left whole
45ml/3 tbsp double cream (optional)
salt and ground black pepper
For the gremolata
  1 garlic clove, finely chopped
  finely shredded rind of ½ lemon
  45ml/3 tbsp chopped fresh flat
    leaf parsley

1 Mix the lamb with the garlic and the rind and juice of ½ lemon. Season with pepper and mix in 15ml/1 tbsp olive oil, then leave to marinate for 12–24 hours.

2 Drain the lamb, reserving the marinade, and pat the lamb dry with kitchen paper. Preheat the oven to 180°C/350°F/Gas 4.

COOK'S TIP

A mezzaluna (double-handled, half-moon shaped, curved chopping blade) makes a very good job of chopping gremolata ingredients. If using a food processor or electric chopper, take care not to overprocess the mixture as it is easy to mince the ingredients to a paste.

3 Heat 30ml/2 tbsp olive oil in a large, heavy-based frying pan. Season the flour with salt and pepper and toss the lamb in it to coat, shaking off any excess. Seal the lamb on all sides in the hot oil. Do this in batches, transferring each batch of lamb to an ovenproof saucepan or flameproof casserole as you brown it. You may need to add an extra 15ml/1 tbsp olive oil to the pan.

4 Reduce the heat, add another 15ml/1 tbsp oil to the pan and cook the onion gently over a very low heat, stirring frequently, for 10 minutes, until softened and golden but not browned. Add the anchovies and caster sugar and cook, mashing the anchovies into the soft onion with a wooden spoon.

5 Add the reserved marinade, increase the heat a little and cook for about 1–2 minutes, then pour in the wine and stock or stock and water, and bring to the boil. Simmer gently for about 5 minutes, then pour over the lamb.

6 Tie the bay leaf, thyme and parsley together and add to the lamb. Season with salt and pepper, then cover tightly and cook in the oven for 1 hour. Stir the potatoes into the stew and cook for a further 20 minutes.

7 Meanwhile, to make the gremolata, chop all the ingredients together finely. Place in a dish, cover and set aside.

8 Heat the remaining oil in a frying pan and brown the shallots on all sides, then stir them into the lamb. Cover and cook for a further 30–40 minutes, until the lamb is tender. Transfer the lamb and vegetables to a dish and keep warm. Discard the herbs.

9 Boil the cooking juices to reduce and concentrate them, then add the cream, if using, and simmer for 2–3 minutes. Adjust the seasoning, adding a little lemon juice to taste. Pour this sauce over the lamb, scatter the gremolata on top and serve immediately.

LAMB SMOTHERED IN ONIONS AND NORTH AFRICAN SPICES

THIS IS A WONDERFUL WAY OF COOKING A LEG OR SHOULDER OF LAMB, BY FIRST MARINATING IT IN YOGURT WITH NORTH AFRICAN SPICES, THEN COVERING WITH SLICED ONIONS AND POT-ROASTING. SERVE A COUSCOUS PILAFF AND YOGURT FLAVOURED WITH GARLIC AS ACCOMPANIMENTS.

SERVES SIX

INGREDIENTS
2kg/4½lb leg or shoulder of lamb
30ml/2 tbsp olive oil
2 large onions, halved and
   thinly sliced
3 fresh bay leaves
300ml/½ pint/1¼ cups water
500g/1¼lb prepared butternut or
   onion squash, peeled, seeded and
   cut into thick chunks or wedges
2–3 green or red peppers, seeded
   and cut into thick slices
chopped fresh coriander, to serve
For the spice paste
15ml/1 tbsp cumin seeds
15ml/1 tbsp coriander seeds
2.5cm/1in piece cinnamon stick
7.5ml/1½ tsp paprika
good pinch of saffron strands
1 green chilli, seeded and chopped
2 garlic cloves, chopped
15g/½oz fresh coriander, chopped
30ml/2 tbsp fresh mint, chopped
45ml/3 tbsp extra virgin olive oil
grated rind and juice of 1 lemon
250ml/8fl oz/1 cup plain yogurt
salt and ground black pepper

1 First prepare the spice paste. Set 5ml/1 tsp each of the cumin and coriander seeds aside and toast the remainder separately in a small dry pan until they are aromatic. Take care not to overcook the spices or cook them too quickly or they will taste bitter.

2 Grind the toasted spices with the cinnamon in a spice or coffee grinder. Then process them with all the paste ingredients, apart from the yogurt, in a food processor or blender to make a paste. Season with salt and pepper.

3 Use a sharp knife to make deep slits all over the lamb, then rub the spice paste all over, forcing it into the slits. Place the lamb in a roasting tin and rub the yogurt all over. Cover and marinate for several hours, preferably overnight, turning once or twice.

4 Preheat the oven to 180°C/350°F/ Gas 4. Scrape the marinade off the meat and reserve. Heat a large roasting tin and brown the lamb all over. Remove it and set aside. Add the oil and cook the onions for 6–8 minutes, until softened. Coarsely grind the reserved coriander and cumin seeds, add to the onions and cook for 2–3 minutes. Transfer the onions to a plate.

5 Add the marinade to the tin with the bay leaves and water. Bring to the boil. Return the lamb to the tin and turn it in the liquid. Cover with the onions, then cover the dish tightly with foil and cook in the oven for 1¾–2 hours, until tender. Baste the lamb occasionally and add a little more water if the dish seems dry. Remove the lamb and onions, cover and keep warm. Increase the oven temperature to 200°C/400°F/Gas 6.

6 Add the squash and peppers to the tin and toss in the lamb juices. Roast, uncovered, for 30–35 minutes, stirring once or twice, until the squash is tender. Return the lamb for the last 15 minutes.

7 Transfer the lamb and vegetables to a warmed serving dish and scatter with the fresh coriander. Serve immediately, cut into thick slices.

GARLIC AND CHILLI MARINATED BEEF WITH CORN-CRUSTED ONION RINGS

FRUITY, SMOKY AND MILD MEXICAN CHILLIES COMBINE WELL WITH GARLIC IN THIS MARINADE FOR GRILLED STEAK. POLENTA MAKES A CRISP COATING FOR THE ACCOMPANYING FRIED ONION RINGS.

SERVES FOUR

INGREDIENTS
  20g/¾oz large mild dried red chillies
    (such as *mulato* or *pasilla*)
  2 garlic cloves, plain or smoked,
    finely chopped
  5ml/1 tsp ground toasted
    cumin seeds
  5ml/1 tsp dried oregano
  60ml/4 tbsp olive oil
  4 × 175–225g/6–8oz beef steaks
    (rump or rib-eye)
  salt and ground black pepper
For the onion rings
  2 onions, sliced into rings
  250ml/8fl oz/1 cup milk
  75g/3oz/¾ cup coarse
    cornmeal (polenta)
  2.5ml/½ tsp dried red
    chilli flakes
  5ml/1 tsp ground toasted
    cumin seeds
  5ml/1 tsp dried oregano
  vegetable oil, for deep-frying

1 Cut the stalks from the chillies and discard the seeds. Toast the chillies in a dry frying pan for 2–4 minutes, until they give off their aroma. Place the chillies in a bowl, cover with warm water and leave to soak for 20–30 minutes. Drain and reserve the water.

2 Process the chillies to a paste with the garlic, cumin, oregano and oil in a food processor. Add a little soaking water, if needed. Season with pepper.

3 Wash and dry the steaks, rub the chilli paste all over them and leave to marinate for up to 12 hours.

4 For the onion rings, soak the onions in the milk for 30 minutes. Mix the cornmeal, chilli, cumin and oregano and season with salt and pepper.

5 Heat the oil for deep-frying to 160–180°C/325–350°F, or until a cube of day-old bread turns brown in about a minute.

6 Drain the onion rings and dip each one into the cornmeal mixture, coating it thoroughly. Fry for 2–4 minutes, until browned and crisp. Do not overcrowd the pan, but cook in batches. Lift the onion rings out of the pan with a slotted spoon and drain on kitchen paper.

7 Heat a barbecue or cast-iron grill pan. Season the steaks with salt and grill for about 4 minutes on each side for a medium result; reduce or increase this time according to how rare or well done you like steak. Serve the steaks with the onion rings.

STIR-FRIED BEEF AND MUSHROOMS WITH GARLIC, BLACK BEANS AND SPRING ONIONS

THE COMBINATION OF GARLIC AND SALTED BLACK BEANS IS A CLASSIC CANTONESE SEASONING FOR BEEF. SERVE RICE AND SIMPLE BRAISED CHINESE GREENS AS ACCOMPANIMENTS.

SERVES FOUR

INGREDIENTS
30ml/2 tbsp soy sauce
30ml/2 tbsp Chinese rice wine or
    dry sherry
10ml/2 tsp cornflour
10ml/2 tsp sesame oil
450g/1lb fillet or rump steak,
    trimmed of fat
12 dried shiitake mushrooms
    (Chinese black mushrooms)
25ml/1½ tbsp salted black beans
5ml/1 tsp caster sugar
120ml/4fl oz/½ cup groundnut oil
4 garlic cloves, thinly sliced
2.5cm/1in piece fresh root ginger,
    cut into fine strips
200g/7oz open cap
    mushrooms, sliced
1 bunch spring onions,
    sliced diagonally
1 fresh red chilli, seeded and
    finely shredded
salt and ground black pepper

1 In a bowl large enough to hold the meat, mix half the soy sauce, half the rice wine or sherry, half the cornflour and all the sesame oil with 15ml/1 tbsp cold water until smooth. Add a good pinch of salt and pepper.

2 Cut the beef into very thin slices, no more than 5mm/¼in thick. Add the slices to the cornflour mixture and rub the mixture into the beef with your fingers. Set aside for 30 minutes.

3 Pour boiling water over the dried mushrooms and soak for 25 minutes. Drain, reserving 45ml/3 tbsp of the soaking water. Remove and discard the hard stalks and cut the caps in half.

4 Using a fork mash the black beans with the caster sugar in a small bowl. Stir the remaining cornflour, soy sauce and rice wine or sherry together in another small bowl.

5 Heat the oil in a wok until very hot, then stir-fry the beef for 30–45 seconds, until just brown. Use a draining spoon to transfer it to a plate. Pour off some oil to leave about 45ml/3 tbsp in the wok.

6 Add the garlic and ginger, stir-fry for 1 minute, then add the shiitake and fresh mushrooms and stir-fry for 2 minutes. Set aside a few tablespoons of the green part of the spring onions, then add the rest to the wok. Stir, add the mashed black beans and stir-fry for another 1–2 minutes.

7 Stir the beef back into the mixture in the wok, then add 45ml/3 tbsp of the shiitake soaking water. Let the mixture bubble. Stir the cornflour mixture to mix it well, pour it into the wok, stirring, and simmer until the sauce thickens. Sprinkle the chilli and reserved spring onions over the beef and serve.

BEEF CARBONADE

THIS RICH, DARK STEW OF BEEF COOKED SLOWLY WITH LOTS OF ONIONS, GARLIC AND BEER IS A CLASSIC CASSEROLE FROM THE NORTH OF FRANCE AND NEIGHBOURING BELGIUM.

3 Reduce the heat and return the onions to the pan. Add the garlic, cook briefly, then add the beer or ale, water and sugar. Tie the thyme and bay leaf together and add to the pan with the celery. Bring to the boil, stirring, then season with salt and pepper.

4 Pour the sauce over the beef and mix well. Cover tightly, then place in the oven for 2½ hours. Check the beef once or twice to make sure that it is not too dry, adding a little water, if necessary. Test for tenderness, allowing an extra 30–40 minutes' cooking if necessary.

SERVES SIX

INGREDIENTS
   45ml/3 tbsp vegetable oil or
      beef dripping
   3 onions, sliced
   45ml/3 tbsp plain flour
   2.5ml/½ tsp mustard powder
   1kg/2¼lb stewing beef (shin or
      chuck), cut into large cubes
   2–3 garlic cloves, finely chopped
   300ml/½ pint/1¼ cups dark beer or ale
   150ml/¼ pint/⅔ cup water
   5ml/1 tsp dark brown sugar
   1 fresh thyme sprig
   1 fresh bay leaf
   1 piece celery stick
   salt and ground black pepper
For the topping
   50g/2oz/¼ cup butter
   1 garlic clove, crushed
   15ml/1 tbsp Dijon mustard
   45ml/3 tbsp chopped fresh parsley
   6–12 slices baguette or ficelle loaf

1 Preheat the oven to 160°C/325°F/ Gas 3. Heat 30ml/2 tbsp of the oil or dripping in a frying pan and cook the onions over a low heat until softened. Remove from the pan and set aside.

2 Meanwhile, mix together the flour and mustard and season. Toss the beef in the flour. Add the remaining oil or dripping to the pan and heat over a high heat. Brown the beef all over, then transfer it to a casserole.

5 To make the topping, cream the butter with the garlic, mustard and 30ml/2 tbsp of the parsley. Spread the butter thickly over the bread. Increase the oven temperature to 190°C/375°F/ Gas 5. Taste and season the casserole, then arrange the bread slices, buttered side uppermost, on top. Bake for 20–25 minutes, until the bread is browned and crisp. Scatter the remaining parsley over the top and serve immediately.

CALF'S LIVER WITH SLOW-COOKED ONIONS, MARSALA AND SAGE

LIVER AND ONIONS ARE AN INTERNATIONAL FAVOURITE, FROM BRITISH LIVER WITH ONION GRAVY TO THE FAMOUS VENETIAN DISH OF FEGATO ALLA VENEZIANA. INSPIRED BY ITALIAN COOKING, THIS DISH IS GOOD SERVED WITH POLENTA, EITHER SOFT OR SET AND GRILLED.

SERVES FOUR

INGREDIENTS
   45ml/3 tbsp olive oil, plus extra for
      shallow frying
   25g/1oz/2 tbsp butter
   500g/1¼lb mild onions,
      thinly sliced
   small bunch of fresh sage leaves
   30ml/2 tbsp chopped fresh parsley,
      plus a little extra to garnish
   2.5ml/½ tsp caster sugar
   15ml/1 tbsp balsamic vinegar
   30ml/2 tbsp plain flour
   675g/1½lb calf's liver,
      thinly sliced
   150ml/¼ pint/⅔ cup Marsala
   salt and ground black pepper

1 Heat half the oil with half the butter in a large, wide, heavy-based saucepan and cook the onions, covered, over a very gentle heat for 30 minutes. Stir once or twice.

2 Chop 5 of the sage leaves and add them to the pan with the parsley, a pinch of salt, the sugar and balsamic vinegar. Cook, uncovered and stirring frequently, until very tender and golden. Taste for seasoning and add salt and pepper as necessary.

3 Heat a shallow layer of olive oil in a frying pan and fry the remaining sage leaves for 15–30 seconds, then drain them on kitchen paper.

4 Heat the remaining butter and oil together in a frying pan over a high heat. Season the flour, then dip the liver in it and fry it quickly for about 2 minutes on each side until browned, but still pink in the middle. Use a draining spoon to transfer the liver to warm plates and keep warm.

5 Immediately add the Marsala to the pan and let it bubble fiercely until reduced to a few tablespoons of sticky glaze. Distribute the onions over the liver and spoon over the Marsala juices. Scatter with the fried sage leaves and extra parsley and serve immediately.

VARIATION
Chicken liver and onion bruschetta Cook the onions as above, replacing the sage with 5ml/1 tsp chopped thyme. Fry 400g/14oz trimmed chicken livers in 25g/1oz/2 tbsp butter and 15ml/1 tbsp oil until browned but still pink in the centre. Flame the chicken livers with 45ml/3 tbsp cognac, and add 150g/ 5oz seeded, skinned grapes (optional). Heat the grapes through, then toss into the cooked onions. Heap on to thick slices of toasted country bread rubbed with oil and garlic or on to slices of grilled polenta. Serve sprinkled with chopped fresh parsley.

BAKED STUFFED ONIONS
WITH TOMATO SAUCE

THESE ARE IDEAL COMFORT FOOD FOR SUPPER ON COLD WINTER EVENINGS. SERVE WITH BUTTERED CABBAGE AND RICE OR THICK SLICES OF BREAD TO MOP UP THE SAUCE.

SERVES EIGHT

INGREDIENTS
  8 onions, each about 8.5cm/3½in
    in diameter, peeled but left whole
  60ml/4 tbsp olive oil
  2.5ml/½ tsp ground allspice
  50g/2oz pancetta or bacon, chopped
  250g/9oz minced pork
  115g/4oz/2 cups fresh breadcrumbs
  45ml/3 tbsp chopped fresh parsley
  15ml/1 tbsp chopped fresh oregano
  1.5ml/½ tsp ground cinnamon
  75ml/5 tbsp water
  25g/1oz/2 tbsp butter
For the tomato sauce
  30ml/2 tbsp olive oil
  1 garlic clove, finely chopped
  2.5ml/½ tsp ground allspice
  400g/14oz can chopped tomatoes
  small piece of cinnamon stick
  1 fresh bay leaf
  30ml/2 tbsp chopped fresh oregano
  30ml/2 tbsp double cream
  1.5–2.5ml/¼–½ tsp harissa or other
    chilli paste
  pinch of brown sugar (optional)
  salt and ground black pepper

1 Place the onions in a large saucepan, pour in water to cover and bring to the boil. Reduce the heat and simmer for 10–15 minutes. Drain and cool.

2 Cut a small cap off the top of each onion, then use a small, sharp knife and a teaspoon to hollow out the centres, leaving a shell of 2–3 layers.

3 Stand the onion shells in a large ovenproof dish and patch any holes in their bases with pieces of onion. Chop the flesh removed from the centres and set aside 45ml/3 tbsp for the sauce. Heat 30ml/2 tbsp of the oil in a frying pan and cook the chopped onion over a low heat until just beginning to brown. Add the allspice and cook for a little longer. Remove and set aside.

4 Fry the pancetta or bacon in the pan until the fat melts, then add the pork and fry until it is beginning to brown. Preheat the oven to 190°C/375°F/Gas 5.

5 Place 75g/3oz/1½ cups of the breadcrumbs in a bowl and add the cooked onions, pork, half the parsley, the oregano and the ground cinnamon. Season well and mix to form a stuffing.

6 Fill the onions with the stuffing. Spoon the water around the onions and dot the butter on top of them. Cover with foil and bake for 30 minutes.

7 To make the sauce, heat the oil and cook the reserved onion and the garlic until soft and just beginning to brown. Add the allspice and fry for 2 minutes, then add the tomatoes, cinnamon stick, bay leaf and oregano. Cook, uncovered, for 15–20 minutes.

8 Remove the cinnamon and bay leaf. Process the sauce in a blender or food processor until smooth. Add 45–60ml/ 3–4 tbsp water to thin to a pouring consistency. Add the cream with seasoning, harissa and sugar to taste.

9 Pour the sauce around the onions and use it to baste them. Cover the dish and bake for 20–25 minutes, then uncover and baste again. Mix together the remaining breadcrumbs and parsley. Scatter the crumbs over the onions, then drizzle with the remaining 30ml/2 tbsp of oil. Return the dish to the oven and bake for 15–20 minutes, until the topping is browned and crisp. Serve immediately.

BRAISED PORK CHOPS WITH ONION AND MUSTARD SAUCE

THE PIQUANT SAUCE ADDS PUNCH AND EXTRA FLAVOUR TO THIS SIMPLE SUPPER DISH. SERVE IT WITH CELERIAC AND POTATO MASH AND A GREEN VEGETABLE, SUCH AS BROCCOLI OR CABBAGE.

SERVES FOUR

INGREDIENTS

4 pork loin chops, at least
  2cm/¾in thick
30ml/2 tbsp plain flour
45ml/3 tbsp olive oil
2 Spanish onions, thinly sliced
2 garlic cloves, finely chopped
250ml/8fl oz/1 cup dry cider
150ml/¼ pint/⅔ cup vegetable,
  chicken or pork stock
generous pinch of brown sugar
2 fresh bay leaves
6 fresh thyme sprigs
2 strips lemon rind
120ml/4fl oz/½ cup double cream
30–45ml/2–3 tbsp wholegrain
  mustard
30ml/2 tbsp chopped fresh parsley
salt and ground black pepper

1 Preheat the oven to 200°C/400°F/Gas 6. Trim the chops of excess fat. Season the flour with salt and pepper and use to coat the chops. Heat 30ml/2 tbsp of the oil in a frying pan and brown the chops on both sides, then transfer them to an ovenproof dish.

2 Add the remaining oil to the pan and cook the onions over a fairly gentle heat until they soften and begin to brown at the edges. Add the garlic and cook for 2 minutes more.

3 Stir in any left-over flour, then gradually stir in the cider and stock. Season well with salt and pepper and add the brown sugar, bay leaves, thyme sprigs and lemon rind. Bring the sauce to the boil, stirring constantly, then pour over the chops.

4 Cover and cook in the oven for 20 minutes. Reduce the heat to 180°C/350°F/Gas 4 and continue cooking for another 30–40 minutes. Remove the foil for the last 10 minutes of the cooking time. Remove the chops from the dish and keep warm, covered with foil.

5 Tip the remaining contents of the dish into a saucepan or, if the dish is flameproof, place it over a direct heat. Discard the herbs and lemon rind, then bring to the boil.

6 Add the cream and continue to boil, stirring constantly. Taste for seasoning, adding a pinch more sugar if necessary. Finally, stir in the mustard to taste and pour the sauce over the braised chops. Sprinkle with the chopped parsley and serve immediately.

VARIATION
For a less rich sauce, omit the cream and purée the sauce in a blender. Reheat, thinning with a little extra stock if necessary, then adjust the seasoning and add mustard to taste. This will produce a sharper tasting sauce that will need less mustard.

ROAST PORK WITH SAGE AND ONION STUFFING

*SAGE AND ONION MAKE A CLASSIC STUFFING FOR ROAST PORK, DUCK AND TURKEY, WITH THE SAGE
COUNTERACTING THE FATTINESS OF THE RICH MEATS. SERVE WITH APPLE SAUCE AND ROAST POTATOES.*

SERVES SIX TO EIGHT

INGREDIENTS
  1.3–1.6kg/3–3½lb boneless loin of pork
  60ml/4 tbsp fine, dry breadcrumbs
  10ml/2 tsp chopped fresh sage
  25ml/1½ tbsp plain flour
  300ml/½ pint/1¼ cups cider
  150ml/¼ pint/⅔ cup water
  5–10ml/1–2 tsp crab apple or
    redcurrant jelly
  salt and ground black pepper
  sprigs of thyme, to garnish
For the stuffing
  25g/1oz/2 tbsp butter
  50g/2oz bacon, finely chopped
  2 large onions, finely chopped
  75g/3oz/1½ cups fresh
    white breadcrumbs
  30ml/2 tbsp chopped fresh sage
  5ml/1 tsp chopped fresh thyme
  10ml/2 tsp finely grated lemon rind
  1 small egg, beaten

1 Preheat the oven to 220°C/425°F/
Gas 7. Make the stuffing first. Melt the
butter in a heavy-based pan and fry the
bacon until it begins to brown, then add
the onions and cook gently until they
soften, but do not allow to brown. Mix
with the breadcrumbs, sage, thyme,
lemon rind and egg, then season well
with salt and pepper.

2 Cut the rind off the joint of pork in
one piece and score it well. Cooking the
rind separately makes crisper crackling
than leaving it on the pork.

3 Place the pork fat-side down and
season. Add a layer of stuffing, then
roll up and tie neatly.

4 Lay the rind over the pork and rub in
5ml/1 tsp salt. Roast for 2–2½ hours,
basting with the pork fat once or twice.
Reduce the temperature to 190°C/375°F/
Gas 5 after 20 minutes. Shape the
remaining stuffing into balls and add to
the roasting tin for the last 30 minutes.

5 Remove the rind from the pork.
Increase the oven temperature to
220°C/425°F/Gas 7 and roast the rind
for a further 20–25 minutes, until crisp.

6 Mix the dry breadcrumbs and sage
and press them into the fat. Cook the
pork for 10 minutes, then cover and set
aside in a warm place for 15–20 minutes.

7 Remove all but 30–45ml/2–3 tbsp of
the fat from the roasting tin and place it
on the hob to make gravy. Stir in the
flour, followed by the cider and water.
Bring to the boil and then cook gently
for 10 minutes. Strain the gravy into a
clean pan, add the crab apple or
redcurrant jelly, and cook for another
5 minutes. Adjust the seasoning.

8 Serve the pork cut into thick slices and
the crisp crackling cut into strips with the
cider gravy, garnished with thyme.

PORK CASSEROLE ᵂᴵᵀᴴ ONIONS, CHILLI ᴬᴺᴰ DRIED FRUIT

INSPIRED BY SOUTH AMERICAN COOKING, A MOLE — PASTE — OF CHILLI, SHALLOTS AND NUTS IS ADDED TO THIS CASSEROLE OF PORK AND ONIONS. PART OF THE MOLE IS ADDED AT THE END OF COOKING TO RETAIN ITS FRESH FLAVOUR. SERVE WITH RICE AND A GREEN SALAD.

SERVES SIX

INGREDIENTS
   25ml/1½ tbsp plain flour
   1kg/2¼lb shoulder or leg of pork,
      cut into 5cm/2in cubes
   45–60ml/3–4 tbsp olive oil
   2 large onions, chopped
   2 garlic cloves, finely chopped
   600ml/1 pint/2½ cups fruity
      white wine
   105ml/7 tbsp water
   115g/4oz ready-to-eat prunes
   115g/4oz ready-to-eat
      dried apricots
   grated rind and juice of
      1 small orange
   pinch of muscovado sugar (optional)
   30ml/2 tbsp chopped fresh parsley
   ½–1 fresh green chilli, seeded and
      finely chopped (optional)
   salt and ground black pepper
For the mole
   3 *ancho* chillies and 2 *pasilla* chillies
      (or other varieties of large, medium-
      hot dried red chillies)
   30ml/2 tbsp olive oil
   2 shallots, chopped
   2 garlic cloves, chopped
   1 fresh green chilli, seeded
      and chopped
   10ml/2 tsp ground coriander
   5ml/1 tsp mild Spanish paprika
      or *pimentón*
   50g/2oz/½ cup blanched
      almonds, toasted
   15ml/1 tbsp chopped fresh oregano
      or 2.5ml/½ tsp dried oregano

1 Make the mole paste first. Toast the dried chillies in a dry frying pan over a low heat for 1–2 minutes, until they are aromatic, then soak them in warm water for 30 minutes.

2 Drain the chillies, reserving the soaking water, and discard their stalks and seeds. Preheat the oven to 160°C/325°F/Gas 3.

3 Heat the oil in a small frying pan and fry the shallots, garlic, fresh green chilli and ground coriander over a very low heat for 5 minutes.

4 Transfer the shallot mixture to a food processor or blender and add the drained chillies, paprika or *pimentón*, almonds and oregano. Process the mixture, adding 45–60ml/3–4 tbsp of the chilli soaking liquid to make a workable paste.

5 Season the flour with salt and black pepper, then use to coat the pork. Heat 45ml/3 tbsp of the olive oil in a large, heavy-based frying pan and fry the pork, stirring frequently, until sealed on all sides. Transfer the pork cubes to a flameproof casserole.

6 If necessary, add the remaining oil to the frying pan and cook the onions and garlic gently for 8–10 minutes, stirring occasionally.

7 Add the wine and water to the frying pan. Cook for 2 minutes. Stir in half the mole paste, bring back to the boil and bubble for a few seconds before pouring over the pork.

8 Season lightly with salt and pepper and stir to mix, then cover and cook in the oven for 1½ hours.

9 Increase the oven temperature to 180°C/350°F/Gas 4. Stir in the prunes, apricots and orange juice. Test the seasoning, adding the muscovado sugar if necessary, cover and cook for another 30–45 minutes.

10 Place the casserole over a direct heat and stir in the remaining mole paste. Simmer, stirring once or twice, for 5 minutes. Serve sprinkled with the orange rind, chopped parsley and fresh chilli, if using.

LEEKS BAKED WITH HAM, CREAM AND MINT

CHOOSE LEEKS THAT ARE NOT TOO THICK FOR THIS VERY EASY BUT DELICIOUS SUPPER DISH.
SERVE GOOD BREAD TO MOP UP THE SAUCE AND A GREEN SALAD TO REFRESH THE PALATE.

SERVES FOUR

INGREDIENTS

8–12 slender leeks
8–12 large, medium-thick slices
  Parma or Serrano ham
15g/½oz/1 tbsp butter
75g/3oz/1 cup freshly grated
  Parmesan cheese
250ml/8fl oz/1 cup double cream
15ml/1 tbsp chopped fresh mint
pinch of cayenne pepper
45ml/3 tbsp fine white breadcrumbs
salt and ground black pepper

1 Trim the leeks so that they are all the same size. Bring a large saucepan of lightly salted water to the boil, add the leeks and cook for 5–8 minutes. Test the leeks with the tip of a sharp knife to check if they are cooked. Drain, reserving 60ml/4 tbsp of the cooking water. Squeeze the excess water out of the leeks. Preheat the oven to 190°C/375°F/Gas 5.

VARIATIONS

• Arrange the leeks on a bed of 350g/12oz ripe tomatoes, peeled, seeded and finely chopped.
• Wrap the cooked leeks in fried, but not crisp, bacon. Then pour over a cheese sauce made with equal quantities of the reserved cooking water and milk. Season the sauce to taste with Dijon mustard, grated Cheddar cheese and a little nutmeg. Scatter with freshly grated Parmesan and fine white breadcrumbs and bake as above.
• Wrap 8 raw, slender leeks in slices of pancetta or prosciutto, then fry gently in 25g/1oz/2 tbsp butter for 5 minutes. Add 90ml/6 tbsp white wine and some sprigs of thyme and season to taste with salt and pepper. Cover and cook very gently for 15–20 minutes, until the leeks are cooked. Remove the leeks from the pan, increase the heat and add 60ml/4 tbsp double cream, then bubble to make a sauce. Adjust the seasoning and pour over the leeks. Sprinkle with a little chopped parsley before serving.

2 Wrap each leek in a slice of ham. Butter an ovenproof gratin dish just large enough to take the leeks in one layer and arrange the leeks in it. Season to taste with salt and pepper and scatter half the grated Parmesan cheese over the leeks.

3 Mix the cream, cooking water and mint. Season with salt, pepper and cayenne and pour over the leeks. Scatter the breadcrumbs and the remaining Parmesan on top. Bake for 30–35 minutes, until bubbling and browned. Serve immediately.

BOILED BACON WITH ONION AND CAPER SAUCE

ONIONS AND CAPERS MAKE A PIQUANT SAUCE THAT IS TRADITIONAL WITH BOILED MUTTON, BUT IT IS ALSO DELICIOUS WITH BOILED BACON OR GAMMON. SERVE WITH SMALL NEW POTATOES, SAUTÉED WITH BUTTER AND A LITTLE GARLIC, AND BROAD BEANS TO MAKE A SPLENDID MEAL.

SERVES SIX

INGREDIENTS
   1.8–2kg/4–4½lb gammon or bacon
   joint, soaked if necessary
   4 cloves
   1 onion, quartered
   1 large carrot, sliced
   1 celery stick
   1 fresh bay leaf
   fresh thyme sprig
   30ml/2 tbsp Dijon mustard
   45–60ml/3–4 tbsp demerara sugar
For the sauce
   50g/2oz/¼ cup butter
   225g/8oz onions, chopped
   25g/1oz/¼ cup plain flour
   250ml/8fl oz/1 cup milk
   1 fresh bay leaf
   30ml/2 tbsp small salted capers,
   rinsed and roughly chopped
   30ml/2 tbsp chopped fresh
   parsley (optional)
   15–30ml/1–2 tbsp Dijon mustard
   salt and ground black pepper

1 Place the joint in a large saucepan and cover with cold water. Bring to the boil and simmer for 5 minutes. Drain, rinse, then return the meat to the pan and cover with fresh water. Stick the cloves into the onion and add to the pan with the carrot. Tie the celery, bay leaf and thyme together and add to the pan. Bring to the boil, then part-cover and simmer very gently for 25 minutes per 450g/1lb.

2 Preheat the oven 200°C/400°F/ Gas 6. Drain the gammon or bacon, reserving 475ml/16fl oz/2 cups of the cooking liquid. Place the joint in a roasting tin and strip off and discard the skin. Spread the mustard over the fat and press the sugar all over the joint.

3 Cook in the oven for 20–25 minutes, until glazed and browned. Keep warm, covered in foil, until ready to serve.

4 Start making the sauce just before the joint has finished boiling. Melt 40g/1½oz/3 tbsp of the butter in a saucepan and cook the onions very gently, half-covered, for 20 minutes, until soft and yellow but not browned. Stir occasionally.

5 Stir in the flour and cook, stirring constantly, for 2–3 minutes. Gradually stir in 300ml/½ pint/1¼ cups of the hot reserved cooking liquid. Cook until the sauce is thick and smooth, then gradually stir in the milk. Add the bay leaf and cook very gently for 20–25 minutes, stirring frequently.

6 Gradually stir in a little more of the reserved cooking liquid to make a sauce of pouring consistency and cook for a further 5 minutes. Remove the bay leaf. Stir in the chopped capers and parsley, if using. Add 15ml/1 tbsp mustard, then taste for seasoning. Add salt, pepper and more mustard to taste. Stir in the remaining butter and serve immediately with the sliced meat.

VEAL IN A WHEAT BEER SAUCE WITH ONIONS AND CARROTS

WHEAT BEERS ARE MADE IN BAVARIA, BELGIUM AND NORTHERN FRANCE, WHERE THEY ARE KNOWN AS BIÈRES BLANCHES OR WHITE BEERS. THE SLIGHT BITTERNESS THAT THE BEER GIVES THE SAUCE IN THIS DELECTABLE STEW IS MATCHED BY THE SWEETNESS OF THE CARAMELIZED ONIONS AND CARROTS.

SERVES FOUR

INGREDIENTS
  45ml/3 tbsp plain flour
  900g/2lb boned shoulder or leg of
    veal, cut into 5cm/2in cubes
  65g/2½oz/5 tbsp butter
  3 shallots, finely chopped
  1 celery stick
  fresh parsley sprig
  2 fresh bay leaves
  5ml/1 tsp caster sugar, plus a
    good pinch
  200ml/7fl oz/scant 1 cup wheat beer
  450ml/¾ pint/scant 2 cups
    veal stock
  20–25 large silverskin onions or
    small pickling onions
  450g/1lb carrots, thickly sliced
  2 large egg yolks
  105ml/7 tbsp double cream
  a little lemon juice (optional)
  30ml/2 tbsp chopped fresh parsley
  salt and ground black pepper

1 Season the flour and dust the veal in it. Heat 25g/1oz/2 tbsp of the butter in a deep, lidded frying pan, add the veal and quickly seal it on all sides. The veal should be golden but not dark brown. Use a draining spoon to remove the veal from the pan and set aside.

2 Reduce the heat, add another 15g/½oz/1 tbsp butter to the pan and cook the shallots gently for 5–6 minutes, until soft and yellow.

3 Replace the veal. Tie the celery, parsley and 1 bay leaf together in a bundle, then add them to the pan with a good pinch of caster sugar. Increase the heat, pour in the beer and allow to bubble briefly before pouring in the stock. Season, bring to the boil, then cover and simmer gently, stirring once or twice, for 40–50 minutes, or until the veal is cooked and tender.

4 Meanwhile, melt the remaining butter in another frying pan and add the onions, then fry them over a low heat until golden all over. Use a draining spoon to remove the onions from the pan and set aside.

5 Add the carrots and turn to coat them in the butter remaining from the onions. Stir in 5ml/1 tsp caster sugar, a pinch of salt, the remaining bay leaf and enough water to cover the carrots. Bring to the boil and cook, uncovered, for 10–12 minutes.

6 Return the onions to the pan with the carrots and continue to cook until all but a few tablespoons of the liquid has evaporated and the onions and carrots are tender and slightly caramelized. Keep warm.

7 Use a draining spoon to transfer the veal to a bowl and discard the celery and herb bundle.

8 Beat the egg yolks and cream together in another bowl, then beat in a ladleful of the hot, but not boiling, carrot liquid. Return this mixture to the pan and cook over a very low heat without boiling, stirring constantly, until the sauce has thickened a little.

9 Add the veal to the sauce, add the onions and carrots and reheat slightly until thoroughly warmed through. Taste and adjust the seasoning, adding a little lemon juice, if necessary, then serve immediately, sprinkled with the parsley.

CHICKEN WITH FORTY CLOVES OF GARLIC

THIS DISH DOES NOT HAVE TO BE MATHEMATICALLY EXACT, SO DO NOT WORRY IF YOU HAVE 35 OR EVEN 50 CLOVES OF GARLIC — THE IMPORTANT THING IS THAT THERE SHOULD BE LOTS. THE SMELL THAT EMANATES FROM THE OVEN AS THE CHICKEN AND GARLIC COOK IS INDESCRIBABLY DELICIOUS.

SERVES FOUR TO FIVE

INGREDIENTS
  5–6 whole heads of garlic
  15g/½oz/1 tbsp butter
  45ml/3 tbsp olive oil
  1.8–2kg/4–4½lb chicken
  150g/5oz/1¼ cups plain flour,
    plus 5ml/1 tsp
  75ml/5 tbsp white port, Pineau
    de Charentes or other white,
    fortified wine
  2–3 fresh tarragon or rosemary sprigs
  30ml/2 tbsp crème fraîche (optional)
  few drops of lemon juice (optional)
  salt and ground black pepper

1 Separate 3 of the heads of garlic into cloves and peel them. Remove the first layer of papery skin from the remaining heads of garlic and cut off the tops to expose the cloves, if you like, or leave them whole. Preheat the oven to 180°C/350°F/Gas 4.

2 Heat the butter and 15ml/1 tbsp of the olive oil in a flameproof casserole that is just large enough to take the chicken and garlic. Add the chicken and cook over a medium heat, turning frequently, for 10–15 minutes, until it is browned all over.

3 Sprinkle in 5ml/1 tsp flour and cook for 1 minute. Add the port or wine. Tuck in the whole heads of garlic and the peeled cloves with the herb sprigs. Pour over the remaining oil and season to taste with salt and pepper.

4 Mix the main batch of flour with sufficient water to make a firm dough. Roll it out into a long sausage and press it around the rim of the casserole, then press on the lid, folding the dough up and over it to create a tight seal. Cook in the oven for 1½ hours.

5 To serve, lift off the lid to break the seal and remove the chicken and whole garlic to a serving platter and keep warm. Remove and discard the herb sprigs, then place the casserole on the hob and whisk to combine the garlic cloves with the juices. Add the crème fraîche, if using, and a little lemon juice to taste. Process the sauce in a food processor or blender or press through a sieve if a smoother result is required. Serve the garlic purée with the chicken.

CHICKEN BAKED WITH SHALLOTS, GARLIC AND FENNEL

THIS IS A VERY SIMPLE AND DELICIOUS WAY TO COOK CHICKEN. IF YOU HAVE TIME, LEAVE THE CHICKEN TO MARINATE FOR A FEW HOURS FOR THE BEST FLAVOUR.

SERVES FOUR

INGREDIENTS

1.6–1.8kg/3½–4lb chicken, cut into 8 pieces or 8 chicken joints
250g/9oz shallots, peeled
1 head garlic, separated into cloves and peeled
60ml/4 tbsp extra virgin olive oil
45ml/3 tbsp tarragon vinegar
45ml/3 tbsp white wine or vermouth (optional)
5ml/1 tsp fennel seeds, crushed
2 bulbs fennel, cut into wedges, feathery tops reserved
150ml/¼ pint/⅔ cup double cream
5ml/1 tsp redcurrant jelly
15ml/1 tbsp tarragon mustard
caster sugar (optional)
30ml/2 tbsp chopped fresh flat leaf parsley
salt and ground black pepper

1 Place the chicken pieces, shallots and all but one of the garlic cloves in a flameproof dish or roasting tin. Add the oil, vinegar, wine or vermouth, if using, and fennel seeds. Season with pepper, then set aside to marinate for 2–3 hours.

2 Preheat the oven to 190°C/375°F/ Gas 5. Add the fennel to the chicken, season with salt and stir to mix.

3 Cook the chicken in the oven for 50–60 minutes, stirring once or twice. The chicken juices should run clear, not pink, when the thick thigh meat is pierced with a skewer.

4 Transfer the chicken and vegetables to a serving dish and keep them warm. Skim off some of the fat and bring the cooking juices to the boil, then pour in the cream. Stir, scraping up all the delicious juices. Whisk in the redcurrant jelly followed by the mustard. Check the seasoning, adding a little sugar if liked.

5 Chop the remaining garlic clove with the feathery fennel tops and mix with the parsley. Pour the sauce over the chicken and scatter the chopped garlic and herb mixture over the top. Serve immediately.

COOK'S TIPS
• If possible, use the fresh new season's garlic for this dish, as it is plump, moist and full of flavour. Purple-skinned garlic is considered by many cooks to have the best flavour.
• The cut surfaces of fennel quickly discolour, so do not prepare it much in advance of using it. If you must prepare it beforehand, then put the wedges into a bowl of cold water acidulated with a little lemon juice.

COQ AU VIN

THIS IS A FAMOUS BURGUNDIAN RECIPE THAT IS GARNISHED WITH LITTLE ONIONS AND MUSHROOMS. IT WAS THE HEIGHT OF FASHION IN THE 1960s AND IT IS BACK IN VOGUE AGAIN.

SERVES FOUR

INGREDIENTS
1 celery stick
1 fresh bay leaf
fresh thyme sprig
1 bottle full-bodied red wine (Shiraz
   or Zinfandel would be good)
600ml/1 pint/2½ cups good
   chicken stock
50g/2oz/¼ cup butter
30ml/2 tbsp olive oil
24 small pickling onions
115g/4oz piece of bacon or
   unsmoked pancetta, cut
   into lardons
45ml/3 tbsp plain flour
2.25kg/5lb chicken, jointed
   into 8 pieces
45ml/3 tbsp cognac
2 garlic cloves, chopped
15ml/1 tbsp tomato purée
piece of fresh pork skin, about
   15cm/6in square (optional)
250g/9oz button mushrooms
30ml/2 tbsp chopped fresh parsley
salt and ground black pepper
croûtons, to garnish (optional)

1 Tie the celery, bay leaf and thyme together in a bundle and place in a saucepan. Pour in the wine and stock and simmer, uncovered, for 15 minutes.

2 Melt 15g/½oz/1 tbsp of the butter with half the olive oil in a heavy-based frying pan and brown 16 of the onions all over. Use a draining spoon to transfer the onions to a plate.

3 Add the bacon or pancetta and cook until browned, then set aside.

COOK'S TIP
For a really good flavour, complete the casserole up to the end of step 5, then cool and leave in the fridge overnight. Next day, skim off the excess fat from the top of the casserole and reheat gently on the hob for about 20 minutes before finishing steps 6–11.

4 Meanwhile, season 30ml/2 tbsp of the flour with salt and pepper. Dust the chicken joints in the seasoned flour and fry them in the fat remaining in the pan over a medium heat, turning frequently, for about 10 minutes, or until golden brown all over.

5 Pour in the cognac and carefully set it alight using a long match or taper. When the flames have died down, remove the chicken from the pan and set aside.

6 Chop the remaining onions. Add another 15g/½oz/1 tbsp of the butter to the frying pan and fry the chopped onions with the garlic over a medium heat, stirring frequently, for 5 minutes, until softened and just turning brown. Preheat the oven to 190°C/375°F/Gas 5.

7 Add the wine and stock mixture, with the herb bundle, and stir in the tomato purée. Lower the heat, then simmer gently, stirring frequently, for about 20 minutes. Taste and adjust the seasoning, if necessary.

8 Place the pork skin, if using, rind side down in a flameproof casserole, then add the chicken pieces and bacon or pancetta. Pour in the sauce (with the bundle of herbs). Cover and place in the oven. Reduce the temperature to 160°C/325°F/Gas 3 immediately and cook for 1½ hours. Add the whole browned onions and cook for a further 30 minutes.

9 Meanwhile, fry the mushrooms in another 15g/½oz/1 tbsp butter and the remaining oil until browned. Set them aside. Mix the remaining butter and flour to make a paste (known in French as beurre manié).

10 Using a slotted spoon, transfer the chicken and onions to a serving plate. Discard the pork skin from the casserole and heat the cooking juices on the hob until simmering. Add the beurre manié in small lumps, whisking to blend the paste into the sauce as it melts. Continue adding small pieces of paste, allowing each to melt completely before adding the next, until the simmering sauce is thickened to taste. (You may not need to use all the beurre manié.)

11 Add the mushrooms and cook for a few minutes. Pour the sauce over the chicken and sprinkle with chopped parsley. Garnish with croûtons, if using, and serve immediately.

GUINEA FOWL AND SPRING VEGETABLE STEW

MILD, SWEET LEEKS ARE EXCELLENT IN THIS LIGHT STEW OF GUINEA FOWL AND SPRING VEGETABLES.
CHICKEN OR RABBIT JOINTS CAN BE USED INSTEAD OF GUINEA FOWL.

SERVES FOUR

INGREDIENTS

45ml/3 tbsp olive oil
115g/4oz pancetta, cut into lardons
30ml/2 tbsp plain flour
2 × 1.2–1.6kg/2½–3½lb guinea fowl,
  each jointed in 4 portions
1 onion, chopped
1 head of garlic, separated into
  cloves and peeled
1 bottle dry white wine
fresh thyme sprig
1 fresh bay leaf
a few parsley stalks
250g/9oz baby carrots
250g/9oz baby turnips
6 slender leeks, cut into 7.5cm/
  3in lengths
250g/9oz shelled peas
15ml/1 tbsp French herb mustard
15g/½oz flat leaf parsley, chopped
15ml/1 tbsp chopped fresh mint
salt and ground black pepper

1 Heat 30ml/2 tbsp of the oil in a large frying pan and cook the pancetta over a medium heat until lightly browned, stirring occasionally. Remove the pancetta from the pan and set aside.

2 Season the flour with salt and pepper and toss the guinea fowl portions in it. Fry in the oil remaining in the pan until browned on all sides. Transfer to a flameproof casserole. Preheat the oven to 180°C/350°F/Gas 4.

3 Add the remaining oil to the pan and cook the onion gently until soft. Add the garlic and fry for 3–4 minutes, then stir in the pancetta and wine.

4 Tie the thyme, bay leaf and parsley into a bundle and add to the pan. Bring to the boil, then simmer gently for 3–4 minutes. Pour over the guinea fowl and add seasoning. Cover and cook in the oven for 40 minutes.

5 Add the baby carrots and turnips to the casserole and cook, covered, for another 30 minutes, or until the vegetables are just tender.

6 Stir in the leeks and cook for a further 15–20 minutes, or until all the vegetables are fully cooked.

7 Meanwhile, blanch the peas in boiling water for 2 minutes, then drain. Transfer the guinea fowl and vegetables to a warmed serving dish. Place the casserole on the hob and boil the juices vigorously over a high heat until they are reduced by about half.

8 Stir in the peas and cook gently for 2–3 minutes, then stir in the mustard and adjust the seasoning. Stir in most of the parsley and the mint. Pour this sauce over the guinea fowl or return the joints and vegetables to the casserole. Scatter the remaining parsley over the top and serve immediately.

CHICKEN FAJITAS WITH GRILLED ONIONS

GRILLED MARINATED CHICKEN AND ONIONS, SERVED WITH SOFT TORTILLAS, SALSA, GUACAMOLE AND SOURED CREAM MAKES A CLASSIC TEX-MEX MEAL AND IS A GOOD CHOICE FOR AN INFORMAL SUPPER.

SERVES SIX

INGREDIENTS

   finely grated rind of 1 lime and the
     juice of 2 limes
   120ml/4fl oz/½ cup olive oil
   1 garlic clove, finely chopped
   2.5ml/½ tsp dried oregano
   good pinch of dried red chilli flakes
   5ml/1 tsp coriander seeds, crushed
   6 boneless chicken breasts
   3 Spanish onions, thickly sliced
   2 large red, yellow or orange peppers,
     seeded and cut into strips
   30ml/2 tbsp chopped fresh coriander
   salt and ground black pepper
For the salsa
   450g/1lb tomatoes, peeled, seeded
     and chopped
   2 garlic cloves, finely chopped
   1 small red onion, finely chopped
   1–2 green chillies, seeded and
     finely chopped
   finely grated rind of ½ lime
   30ml/2 tbsp chopped fresh coriander
   pinch of caster sugar
   2.5–5ml/½–1 tsp ground roasted
     cumin seeds
To serve
   12–18 soft flour tortillas
   guacamole
   120ml/4fl oz/½ cup soured cream
   crisp lettuce leaves
   coriander sprigs
   lime wedges

1 In an ovenproof dish, combine the lime rind and juice, 75ml/5 tbsp of the oil, the garlic, oregano, chilli flakes and coriander seeds and season with salt and pepper. Slash the skin on the chicken breasts several times and turn them in the mixture, then cover and set aside to marinate for several hours.

2 To make the salsa, combine the tomatoes, garlic, onion, chillies, lime rind and crushed coriander. Season to taste with salt, pepper, caster sugar and cumin. Set aside for 30 minutes, then taste and adjust the seasoning, adding more cumin and sugar, if necessary.

3 Heat the grill. Thread the onion slices on to a skewer or place them on a grill rack. Brush with 15ml/1 tbsp of the remaining oil and season. Grill until softened and slightly charred in places. Preheat the oven to 200°C/400°F/Gas 6.

4 Cook the chicken breasts in their marinade, covered, in the oven for 20 minutes. Remove, then grill the chicken for 8–10 minutes, until browned and fully cooked.

5 Meanwhile, heat the remaining oil in a large frying pan and cook the peppers for about 10 minutes, until softened and browned in places. Add the grilled onions and fry briskly for 2–3 minutes.

6 Add the chicken cooking juices and fry over a high heat, stirring frequently, until the liquid evaporates. Stir in the chopped coriander.

7 Reheat the tortillas following the instructions on the packet. Using a sharp knife, cut the grilled chicken into strips and transfer to a serving dish. Place the onion and pepper mixture and the salsa in separate dishes.

8 Serve the dishes of chicken, onions and peppers and salsa with the tortillas, guacamole, soured cream, lettuce and coriander for people to help themselves. Serve lime wedges so that the juice can be squeezed over to taste.

Apart from those vegetarians whose religious beliefs forbid the eating of alliums, onions are an essential part of meat-free cookery around the globe. From the strongest garlic to the mildest chives, all the members of the onion family are delicious with eggs, cheese and dairy foods. Classic dishes such as French onion tart, Spanish tortilla or Italian risotto would be unimaginable without onions. Here is a selection of meat-free dishes that shows just how versatile onions really are.

Vegetarian
Main Courses

ONION TART

NO BOOK ON ONION COOKERY WOULD BE COMPLETE WITHOUT A RECIPE FOR THIS CLASSIC TART FROM ALSACE IN EASTERN FRANCE. TRADITIONALLY SERVED IN SMALL SLICES AS A FIRST COURSE, IT ALSO MAKES A DELICIOUS MAIN COURSE WHEN SERVED WARM AND ACCOMPANIED BY A GREEN SALAD.

SERVES FOUR TO SIX

INGREDIENTS
175g/6oz/1½ cups plain flour
75g/3oz/6 tbsp butter, chilled
30–45ml/2–3 tbsp iced water
For the filling
50g/2oz/¼ cup butter
900g/2lb Spanish onions,
 thinly sliced
1 egg plus 2 egg yolks
250ml/8fl oz/1 cup double cream
1.5ml/¼ tsp freshly grated
 nutmeg
salt and ground black pepper

VARIATIONS
There are endless variations on this classic tart: try adding chopped fresh herbs such as thyme. The tart is also delicious made with cheese pastry; add 50g/2oz/⅔ cup grated Parmesan to the flour.

1 Process the flour, a pinch of salt and the chilled butter or butter and lard in a food processor until reduced to fine crumbs. Add the iced water and process briefly to form a dough. Wrap in clear film and chill for 40 minutes.

2 Melt the butter in a large saucepan and add the onions and a pinch of salt. Turn them in the butter. Cover and cook very gently, stirring frequently, for 30–40 minutes. Cool slightly.

3 Preheat the oven to 190°C/375°F/ Gas 5. Roll out the dough thinly and use to line a 23–25cm/9–10in loose-based flan tin. Line with foil or baking parchment and baking beans, then bake blind for 10 minutes.

4 Remove the foil or parchment and baking beans, and bake for another 4–5 minutes, until the pastry is lightly cooked to a pale brown colour (blonde is a good description). Reduce the oven temperature to 180°C/350°F/Gas 4.

5 Beat the egg, egg yolks and cream together. Season with salt, lots of black pepper and the grated nutmeg. Place half the onions in the pastry shell and add half the egg mixture. Add the remaining onions, then pour in as much of the remaining custard as you can.

6 Place on a baking sheet and bake on the middle shelf for 40–50 minutes, or until the custard is risen, browned and set in the centre. Serve warm rather than piping hot.

RED ONION TART <u>WITH</u> A CORNMEAL CRUST

RED ONIONS ARE WONDERFULLY MILD AND SWEET WHEN COOKED AND THEY GO WELL WITH FONTINA CHEESE AND THYME IN THIS TART. CORNMEAL GIVES THE PASTRY A CRUMBLY TEXTURE TO CONTRAST WITH THE JUICINESS OF THE ONION FILLING. A TOMATO AND BASIL SALAD IS GOOD WITH THE TART.

SERVES FIVE TO SIX

INGREDIENTS
    60ml/4 tbsp olive oil
    1kg/2¼lb red onions, thinly sliced
    2–3 garlic cloves, thinly sliced
    5ml/1 tsp chopped fresh thyme, plus
      a few whole sprigs
    5ml/1 tsp dark brown sugar
    10ml/2 tsp sherry vinegar
    225g/8oz fontina cheese,
      thinly sliced
    salt and ground black pepper
For the pastry
    115g/4oz/1 cup plain flour
    75g/3oz/¾ cup fine yellow cornmeal
    5ml/1 tsp dark brown sugar
    5ml/1 tsp chopped fresh thyme
    90g/3½oz/7 tbsp butter
    1 egg yolk
    30–45ml/2–3 tbsp iced water

1 To make the pastry, sift the plain flour and cornmeal into a bowl with 5ml/1 tsp salt. Add plenty of black pepper and stir in the sugar and thyme. Rub in the butter until the mixture looks like breadcrumbs. Beat the egg yolk with 30ml/2 tbsp iced water and use to bind the pastry, adding another 15ml/1 tbsp iced water, if necessary. Gather the dough into a ball with your fingertips, wrap in clear film and chill it for 30–40 minutes.

2 Heat 45ml/3 tbsp of the oil in a large, deep frying pan and add the onions. Cover and cook slowly, stirring occasionally, for 20–30 minutes. They should collapse but not brown.

3 Add the garlic and chopped thyme, then cook, stirring occasionally, for another 10 minutes. Increase the heat slightly, then add the sugar and sherry vinegar. Cook, uncovered, for another 5–6 minutes, until the onions start to caramelize slightly. Season to taste with salt and pepper. Cool.

4 Preheat the oven to 190°C/375°F/ Gas 5. Roll out the pastry thinly and use to line a 25cm/10in loose-based metal flan tin.

5 Prick the pastry all over with a fork and support the sides with foil. Bake for 12–15 minutes, until lightly coloured.

6 Remove the foil and spread the caramelized onions evenly over the base of the pastry case. Add the slices of fontina and sprigs of thyme and season with pepper. Drizzle over the remaining oil, then bake for 15–20 minutes, until the filling is piping hot and the cheese is beginning to bubble. Garnish the tart with thyme and serve immediately.

LEEK AND ROQUEFORT TART WITH WALNUT PASTRY

MILD LEEKS GO EXCEPTIONALLY WELL WITH THE SALTY FLAVOUR OF THE ROQUEFORT CHEESE, AND THE NUTTINESS OF THE PASTRY MARRIES THE INGREDIENTS PERFECTLY IN THIS TART. SERVE THE TART WARM WITH A PEPPERY GREEN SALAD OF ROCKET, MIZUNA OR WATERCRESS.

SERVES FOUR TO SIX

INGREDIENTS
- 25g/1oz/2 tbsp butter
- 450g/1lb leeks (trimmed weight), sliced
- 175g/6oz Roquefort cheese, sliced
- 2 large eggs
- 250ml/8fl oz/1 cup double cream
- 10ml/2 tsp chopped fresh tarragon
- salt and ground black pepper

For the pastry
- 175g/6oz/1½ cups plain flour
- 5ml/1 tsp dark brown sugar
- 50g/2oz/¼ cup butter
- 75g/3oz walnuts, ground
- 15ml/1 tbsp lemon juice
- 30ml/2 tbsp iced water

1 First make the pastry. Sift the flour and 2.5ml/½ tsp salt into a bowl. Add some black pepper and the sugar. Rub in the butter until the mixture looks like breadcrumbs, then stir in the ground walnuts. Bind with the lemon juice and iced water. Gather into a ball, wrap in clear film and chill for 30–40 minutes.

2 Preheat the oven to 190°C/375°F/Gas 5. Roll out the pastry and use to line a 21–23cm/8½–9in loose-based metal flan tin.

COOK'S TIP
Grind walnuts in a small food processor or clean coffee mill with a little of the pastry flour.

3 Protect the sides of the pastry with foil, prick the base with a fork and bake for 15 minutes. Remove the foil and bake for a further 5–10 minutes, until just firm to the touch. Reduce the oven temperature to 180°C/350°F/Gas 4.

4 Meanwhile, to make the filling, melt the butter in a pan, add the leeks, cover and cook for 10 minutes. Season and cook for a further 10 minutes. Cool.

5 Spoon the leeks into the pastry case and arrange the slices of Roquefort on top. Beat the eggs with the cream and season with pepper (the cheese will probably be sufficiently salty). Beat in the tarragon and carefully pour the mixture into the tart.

6 Bake the tart on the centre shelf of the oven for 30–40 minutes, until the filling has risen and browned and become firm to a gentle touch. Allow to cool for 10 minutes before serving.

SHALLOT AND GARLIC TARTE TATIN WITH PARMESAN PASTRY

SAVOURY VERSIONS OF THE FAMOUS APPLE TARTE TATIN HAVE BEEN POPULAR FOR SOME YEARS. HERE, SHALLOTS ARE CARAMELIZED IN BUTTER, SUGAR AND VINEGAR BEFORE BEING BAKED BENEATH A LAYER OF PARMESAN PASTRY. THIS IS DELICIOUS SERVED WITH A PEAR, CHEESE AND WATERCRESS SALAD.

2 Melt the butter in a 23–25cm/9–10in round heavy tin or skillet that will go in the oven. Add the shallots and garlic, and cook until lightly browned all over.

3 Scatter the sugar over the top and increase the heat a little. Cook until the sugar begins to caramelize, then turn the shallots and garlic in the buttery juices. Add the vinegar, water, thyme and seasoning. Cook, part-covered, for 5–8 minutes, until the garlic cloves are just tender. Cool.

SERVES FOUR TO SIX

INGREDIENTS
    300g/11oz puff pastry, thawed
      if frozen
    50g/2oz/¼ cup butter
    75g/3oz/1 cup freshly grated
      Parmesan cheese
For the topping
    40g/1½oz/3 tbsp butter
    500g/1¼lb shallots
    12–16 large garlic cloves, peeled but
      left whole
    15ml/1 tbsp golden caster sugar
    15ml/1 tbsp balsamic or
      sherry vinegar
    45ml/3 tbsp water
    5ml/1 tsp chopped fresh thyme, plus
     a few extra sprigs (optional)
    salt and ground black pepper

1 Roll out the pastry into a rectangle. Spread the butter over it, leaving a 2.5cm/1in border. Scatter the Parmesan on top. Fold the bottom third of the pastry up to cover the middle and the top third down. Seal the edges, give a quarter turn and roll out to a rectangle, then fold as before. Chill for 30 minutes.

4 Preheat the oven to 190°C/375°F/ Gas 5. Roll out the pastry to the diameter of the tin or skillet and lay it over the shallots and garlic. Prick the pastry with a sharp knife, then bake for 25–35 minutes, or until the pastry is risen and golden. Set aside to cool for 5–10 minutes, then invert the tart on to a serving platter. Scatter with a few thyme sprigs, if you like, and serve.

POTATO AND LEEK FILO PIE

THIS FILO PASTRY PIE MAKES AN ATTRACTIVE AND UNUSUAL CENTREPIECE FOR A VEGETARIAN BUFFET.
SERVE IT COOL, WITH A CHOICE OF SALADS.

SERVES EIGHT

INGREDIENTS
    800g/1¾lb new potatoes, sliced
    400g/14oz leeks (trimmed weight)
    75g/3oz/6 tbsp butter
    15g/½oz parsley, finely chopped
    60ml/4 tbsp chopped mixed fresh
        herbs (such as chervil, chives, a
        little tarragon and basil)
    12 sheets filo pastry
    150g/5oz white Cheshire,
        Lancashire or Cantal
        cheese, sliced
    2 garlic cloves, finely chopped
    250ml/8fl oz/1 cup
        double cream
    2 large egg yolks
    salt and ground black pepper

1 Preheat the oven to 190°C/375°F/
Gas 5. Cook the potatoes in boiling,
lightly salted water for 3–4 minutes,
then drain and set aside.

2 Thinly slice the leeks. Melt 25g/1oz/
2 tbsp of the butter in a frying pan and
fry the leeks gently, stirring occasionally,
until softened. Remove from the heat,
season with pepper and stir in half the
parsley and half the mixed herbs.

3 Melt the remaining butter. Line a
23cm/9in loose-based metal cake tin
with 6–7 sheets of filo pastry, brushing
each layer with butter. Let the edges
of the pastry overhang the tin.

4 Layer the potatoes, leeks and cheese
in the tin, scattering a few herbs and
the garlic between the layers. Season.

5 Flip the overhanging pastry over the
filling and cover with 2 sheets of filo,
tucking in the sides to fit and brushing
with melted butter as before. Cover
the pie loosely with foil and bake for
35 minutes. (Keep the remaining pastry
covered with a polythene bag and a
damp cloth.)

6 Meanwhile beat the cream, egg yolks
and remaining herbs together. Make a
hole in the centre of the pie and
gradually pour in the eggs and cream.

7 Arrange the remaining pastry on top,
teasing it into swirls and folds, then
brush with melted butter. Reduce the
oven temperature to 180°C/350°F/
Gas 4 and bake the pie for another
25–30 minutes, until the top is golden
and crisp. Allow to cool before serving.

POTATO AND ONION TORTILLA WITH BROAD BEANS

THE CLASSIC TORTILLA OR SPANISH OMELETTE INCLUDES NOTHING MORE THAN ONIONS, POTATO, EGGS AND OLIVE OIL. ADDING CHOPPED HERBS AND A FEW SKINNED BROAD BEANS MAKES THIS A VERY SUMMERY DISH TO ENJOY AT LUNCH, OR CUT IT INTO SMALL PIECES AND SERVE AS A SPANISH TAPAS.

SERVES TWO

INGREDIENTS
 45ml/3 tbsp olive oil
 2 Spanish onions, thinly sliced
 300g/11oz waxy potatoes, cut into
   1cm/½in dice
 250g/9oz/1¾ cups shelled
   broad beans
 5ml/1 tsp chopped fresh thyme or
   summer savory
 6 large eggs
 45ml/3 tbsp mixed snipped chives
   and chopped flat leaf parsley
 salt and ground black pepper

1 Heat 30ml/2 tbsp of the oil in a 23cm/9in deep non-stick frying pan. Add the onions and potatoes and stir to coat. Cover and cook gently, stirring frequently, for 20–25 minutes until the potatoes are cooked and the onions collapsed. Do not let the mixture brown.

2 Meanwhile, cook the beans in boiling salted water for 5 minutes. Drain well and set aside to cool.

3 When the beans are cool enough to handle, peel off the grey outer skins. Add the beans to the frying pan, together with the thyme or summer savory and season with salt and pepper to taste. Stir well to mix and cook for a further 2–3 minutes.

4 Beat the eggs with salt and pepper to taste and the mixed herbs, then pour over the potatoes and onions and increase the heat slightly. Cook gently until the egg on the bottom sets and browns, gently pulling the omelette away from the sides of the pan and tilting it to allow the uncooked egg to run underneath.

5 Invert the tortilla on to a plate. Add the remaining oil to the pan and heat until hot. Slip the tortilla back into the pan, uncooked side down, and cook for another 3–5 minutes to allow the underneath to brown. Slide the tortilla out on to a plate. Divide as wished, and serve warm rather than piping hot.

FRITTATA WITH LEEK, RED PEPPER AND SPINACH

APART FROM THE FACT THAT ITALIAN FRITTATA DOES NOT USUALLY CONTAIN POTATO AND IS GENERALLY SLIGHTLY SOFTER IN TEXTURE, IT IS NOT HUGELY DIFFERENT FROM SPANISH TORTILLA. THIS COMBINATION OF SWEET LEEK, RED PEPPER AND SPINACH IS DELICIOUS WITH THE EGG.

SERVES THREE TO FOUR

INGREDIENTS
30ml/2 tbsp olive oil
1 large red pepper, seeded and diced
2.5–5ml/½–1 tsp ground
   toasted cumin
3 leeks (about 450g/1lb),
   thinly sliced
150g/5oz small spinach leaves
45ml/3 tbsp pine nuts, toasted
5 large eggs
15ml/1 tbsp chopped fresh basil
15ml/1 tbsp chopped fresh flat
   leaf parsley
salt and ground black pepper
watercress, to garnish
50g/2oz Parmesan cheese, grated,
   to serve (optional)

1 Heat a frying pan and add the oil. Add the red pepper and cook over a medium heat, stirring occasionally, for 6–8 minutes, until soft and beginning to brown. Add 2.5ml/½ tsp of the cumin and cook for another 1–2 minutes.

2 Stir in the leeks, then part cover the pan and cook gently for about 5 minutes, until the leeks have softened and collapsed. Season with salt and ground black pepper.

3 Add the spinach and cover. Allow the spinach to wilt in the steam for 3–4 minutes, then stir to mix it into the vegetables, adding the pine nuts.

4 Beat the eggs with salt, pepper, the remaining cumin, basil and parsley. Add to the pan and cook over a gentle heat until the bottom of the omelette sets and turns golden brown. Pull the edges of the omelette away from the sides of the pan as it cooks and tilt the pan so that the uncooked egg runs underneath.

5 Preheat the grill. Flash the frittata under the hot grill to set the egg on top, but do not let it become too brown. Cut the frittata into wedges and serve warm, garnished with watercress and sprinkled with Parmesan, if using.

VARIATION
A delicious way to serve frittata is to pack it into a slightly hollowed-out loaf and then drizzle it with a little extra virgin olive oil. Wrap tightly in clear film and leave to stand for 1–2 hours before cutting into thick slices. A frittata-filled loaf is ideal picnic fare.

PEPPERS FILLED WITH SPICED VEGETABLES

INDIAN SPICES SEASON THE POTATO AND AUBERGINE STUFFING IN THESE COLOURFUL BAKED PEPPERS.
THEY ARE GOOD WITH PLAIN RICE AND A LENTIL DHAL. ALTERNATIVELY, SERVE THEM WITH A SALAD,
INDIAN BREADS AND A CUCUMBER OR MINT AND YOGURT RAITA.

SERVES SIX

INGREDIENTS

    6 large evenly shaped red or
      yellow peppers
    500g/1¼lb waxy potatoes
    1 small onion, chopped
    4–5 garlic cloves, chopped
    5cm/2in piece fresh root
      ginger, chopped
    1–2 fresh green chillies, seeded
      and chopped
    105ml/7 tbsp water
    90–105ml/6–7 tbsp groundnut oil
    1 aubergine, cut into 1cm/
      ½in dice
    10ml/2 tsp cumin seeds
    5ml/1 tsp kalonji seeds
    2.5ml/½ tsp ground turmeric
    5ml/1 tsp ground coriander
    5ml/1 tsp ground toasted
      cumin seeds
    pinch of cayenne pepper
    about 30ml/2 tbsp lemon juice
    salt and ground black pepper
    30ml/2 tbsp chopped fresh coriander,
      to garnish

3 Cook the potatoes in boiling, salted water for 10–12 minutes, until just tender. Drain, cool and peel, then cut into 1cm/½in dice.

4 Put the onion, garlic, ginger and green chillies in a food processor or blender with 60ml/4 tbsp of the water and process to a purée.

5 Heat 45ml/3 tbsp of the oil in a large, deep frying pan and cook the aubergine, stirring occasionally, until browned on all sides. Remove from the pan and set aside. Add another 30ml/2 tbsp of the oil to the pan and cook the potatoes until lightly browned. Remove from the pan and set aside.

6 If necessary, add another 15ml/1 tbsp oil to the pan, then add the cumin and kalonji seeds. Fry briefly until the seeds darken, then add the turmeric, coriander and ground cumin. Cook for 15 seconds. Stir in the onion and garlic purée and fry, scraping the pan with a spatula, until it begins to brown.

7 Return the potatoes and aubergines to the pan, season with salt, pepper and 1–2 pinches of cayenne. Add the remaining water and 15ml/1 tbsp lemon juice and then cook, stirring, until the liquid evaporates. Preheat the oven to 190°C/375°F/Gas 5.

8 Fill the peppers with the potato mixture and place on a lightly greased baking tray. Brush the peppers with a little oil and bake for 30–35 minutes, until the peppers are cooked. Allow to cool a little, then sprinkle with a little more lemon juice, garnish with the coriander and serve.

COOK'S TIP

Kalonji, or nigella as it is sometimes known, is a tiny black seed. It is widely used in Indian cookery, especially sprinkled over breads or in potato dishes. It has a mild, slightly nutty flavour and is best toasted for a few seconds in a dry frying pan over a medium heat. This helps to bring out its flavour.

1 Cut the tops off the red or yellow peppers then remove and discard the seeds. Cut a thin slice off the base of the peppers, if necessary, to make them stand upright.

2 Bring a large saucepan of lightly salted water to the boil. Add the peppers and cook for 5–6 minutes. Drain and leave the peppers upside down in a colander.

POTATO AND ONION CAKES WITH BEETROOT RELISH

THESE IRRESISTIBLE PANCAKES ARE BASED ON TRADITIONAL LATKE, GRATED POTATO CAKES. THEY ARE ESPECIALLY DELICIOUS WITH A SWEET-SHARP BEETROOT RELISH AND SOURED CREAM.

SERVES FOUR

INGREDIENTS

500g/1¼lb potatoes (such as King
   Edward, Estima or Desirée)
1 small Bramley cooking apple,
   peeled, cored and coarsely grated
1 small onion, finely chopped
50g/2oz/½ cup plain flour
2 large eggs, beaten
30ml/2 tbsp snipped chives
vegetable oil, for shallow frying
salt and ground black pepper
250ml/8fl oz/1 cup soured cream
   or crème fraîche
fresh dill sprigs and fresh chives
   or chive flowers, to garnish
For the beetroot relish
250g/9oz beetroot, cooked
   and peeled
1 large dessert apple, cored and
   finely diced
15ml/1 tbsp finely chopped red onion
15–30ml/1–2 tbsp tarragon vinegar
15ml/1 tbsp chopped fresh dill
15–30ml/1–2 tbsp light olive oil
pinch of caster sugar (optional)

1 To make the relish, finely dice the beetroot, then mix it with the apple and onion. Add 15ml/1 tbsp of the vinegar, the dill and 15ml/1 tbsp of the oil. Season, adding more vinegar and oil, and a pinch of caster sugar to taste.

2 Coarsely grate the potatoes, then rinse, drain and dry them on a clean dish towel.

3 Mix the potatoes, apple and onion in a bowl. Stir in the flour, eggs and chives. Season and mix again.

4 Heat about 5mm/¼in depth of oil in a frying pan and fry spoonfuls of the mixture. Flatten them to make pancakes 7.5–10cm/3–4in across and cook for 3–4 minutes on each side, until browned. Drain on kitchen paper and keep warm until the mixture is used up.

5 Serve a stack of pancakes – there should be about 16–20 in total – with spoonfuls of soured cream or crème fraîche, and beetroot relish. Garnish with dill sprigs and chives or chive flowers and grind black pepper on top just before serving.

VARIATION
To make a leek and potato cake, melt 25g/1oz/2 tbsp butter in a saucepan, add 400g/14oz thinly sliced leeks and cook until tender. Season well. Coarsely grate 500g/1¼lb peeled potatoes, then season. Melt another 25g/1oz/2 tbsp butter in a medium frying pan and add a layer of half the potatoes. Cover with the leeks, then add the remaining potatoes, pressing down with a spatula to form a cake. Cook for 20–25 minutes over a low heat until the potatoes are browned, then turn over and cook for 15–20 minutes until the potatoes are browned.

GRILLED POLENTA <u>WITH</u> CARAMELIZED ONIONS, RADICCHIO <u>AND</u> TALEGGIO CHEESE

SLICES OF GRILLED POLENTA, ONE OF THE STAPLES OF NORTH ITALIAN COOKING, ARE TASTY TOPPED WITH SLOWLY CARAMELIZED ONIONS AND BUBBLING TALEGGIO CHEESE, ALSO FROM NORTH ITALY.

SERVES FOUR

INGREDIENTS
900ml/1½ pints/3¾ cups water
5ml/1 tsp salt
150g/5oz/generous 1 cup polenta
  or cornmeal
50g/2oz/⅔ cup freshly grated
  Parmesan cheese
5ml/1 tsp chopped fresh thyme
90ml/6 tbsp olive oil
675g/1½lb onions, halved and sliced
2 garlic cloves, chopped
a few fresh thyme sprigs
5ml/1 tsp brown sugar
15–30ml/1–2 tbsp balsamic vinegar
2 heads radicchio, cut into thick
  slices or wedges
225g/8oz Taleggio cheese, sliced
salt and ground black pepper

1 In a large saucepan, bring the water to the boil and add the salt. Adjust the heat so that it simmers. Stirring all the time, add the polenta in a steady stream, then bring to the boil. Cook over a very low heat, stirring frequently, for 30–40 minutes, until thick and smooth.

2 Beat in the Parmesan and chopped thyme, then turn on to a work surface or tray. Spread evenly, then leave to cool.

3 Heat 30ml/2 tbsp of the oil in a frying pan over a moderate heat. Add the onions and stir to coat in the oil, then cover and cook over a very low heat for 15 minutes, stirring occasionally.

4 Add the garlic and most of the thyme sprigs and cook, uncovered, for another 10 minutes, or until light brown.

5 Add the sugar, 15ml/1 tbsp of the vinegar and salt and pepper. Cook for another 5–10 minutes, until soft and well-browned. Taste and add more vinegar and seasoning as necessary.

6 Preheat the grill. Cut the polenta into thick slices and brush with a little of the remaining oil, then grill until crusty and lightly browned.

7 Turn over the polenta and add the radicchio to the grill rack or pan. Season the radicchio and brush with a little oil. Grill for about 5 minutes, until the polenta and radicchio are browned. Drizzle a little vinegar over the radicchio.

8 Heap the onions on to the polenta. Scatter the cheese and a few sprigs of thyme over both polenta and radicchio. Grill until the cheese is bubbling. Season with pepper and serve immediately.

PANCAKES WITH LEEK, CHICORY AND SQUASH STUFFING

SERVE A CHUNKY HOME-MADE TOMATO SAUCE AND A CRISP GREEN SALAD WITH THESE DELICIOUS, MELT-IN-THE-MOUTH STUFFED PANCAKES.

SERVES FOUR

INGREDIENTS
115g/4oz/1 cup plain flour
50g/2oz/½ cup yellow cornmeal
2.5ml/½ tsp salt
2.5ml/½ tsp chilli powder
2 large eggs
450ml/¾ pint/scant 2 cups milk
25g/1oz/2 tbsp butter, melted
vegetable oil, for greasing
For the filling
30ml/2 tbsp olive oil
450g/1lb butternut squash (peeled
   weight), seeded and diced
large pinch of dried red chilli flakes
2 large leeks, thickly sliced
2.5ml/½ tsp chopped fresh thyme
3 chicory heads, thickly sliced
115g/4oz full-flavoured goat's
   cheese, cut into cubes
90g/3½oz walnuts, roughly chopped
30ml/2 tbsp chopped fresh flat
   leaf parsley
25g/1oz Parmesan cheese, grated
45ml/3 tbsp melted butter or olive oil
salt and ground black pepper

2 When ready to cook the pancakes, whisk the melted butter into the batter. Heat a lightly greased or oiled 18cm/7in heavy-based frying pan or crêpe pan. Pour about 60ml/4 tbsp batter into the pan and cook for 2–3 minutes, until set and lightly browned underneath. Turn and cook the pancake on the second side for 2–3 minutes. Lightly grease the pan after every second pancake.

3 To make the filling, heat the oil in a large frying pan. Add the squash and cook, stirring frequently, for 10 minutes, until almost tender. Add the chilli flakes and cook, stirring, for 1–2 minutes. Stir in the leeks and thyme and cook for another 4–5 minutes.

5 Preheat the oven to 200°C/400°F/ Gas 6. Lightly grease an ovenproof dish. Spoon 30–45ml/2–3 tbsp filling on to each pancake. Roll or fold each pancake to enclose the filling, then place in the prepared dish.

6 Scatter the Parmesan over the pancakes and drizzle about 45ml/3 tbsp melted butter or olive oil over. Bake for 10–15 minutes, until the cheese is bubbling and the pancakes are piping hot. Serve immediately.

1 Sift the flour, cornmeal, salt and chilli powder into a bowl and make a well in the centre. Add the eggs and a little milk. Whisk the eggs and milk, gradually incorporating the dry ingredients and adding more milk as the mixture comes together. You may not need all the milk – add enough to make a batter similar to thick cream.

4 Add the chicory and cook, stirring frequently, for another 4–5 minutes, until the leeks are cooked and the chicory is hot, but still has some bite to its texture. Cool slightly, then stir in the cheese, walnuts and parsley. Season the mixture well.

ONIONS STUFFED WITH GOAT'S CHEESE AND SUN-DRIED TOMATOES

ROASTED ONIONS AND GOAT'S CHEESE ARE A WINNING COMBINATION. THESE STUFFED ONIONS MAKE AN EXCELLENT MAIN COURSE WHEN SERVED WITH A RICE OR CRACKED WHEAT PILAFF.

SERVES FOUR

INGREDIENTS

   4 large onions
   150g/5oz goat's cheese, crumbled
      or cubed
   50g/2oz fresh breadcrumbs
   8 sun-dried tomatoes in olive oil,
      drained and chopped
   1–2 garlic cloves, finely chopped
   2.5ml/½ tsp chopped fresh thyme
   30ml/2 tbsp chopped fresh parsley
   1 small egg, beaten
   45ml/3 tbsp pine nuts, toasted
   30ml/2 tbsp olive oil (use oil from
      the tomatoes)
   salt and ground black pepper

1 Bring a large pan of lightly salted water to the boil. Add the whole onions in their skins and boil for 10 minutes. Drain and cool, then cut each onion in half horizontally and peel.

2 Using a teaspoon, remove the centre of each onion, leaving a thick shell. Reserve the flesh and place the shells in an oiled baking dish. Preheat the oven to 190°C/375°F/Gas 5.

3 Chop the scooped-out onion flesh and place in a bowl. Add the goat's cheese, breadcrumbs, sun-dried tomatoes, garlic, thyme, parsley and egg. Mix well, then season with salt and pepper and add the toasted pine nuts.

4 Divide the stuffing among the onions and cover with foil. Bake for about 25 minutes. Uncover, drizzle with the oil and cook for another 30–40 minutes, until bubbling and well cooked. Baste occasionally during cooking.

VARIATIONS
• Use feta cheese in place of the goat's cheese and substitute chopped mint, currants and pitted black olives for the other flavourings.
• Stuff the onions with spinach and rice mixed with some smoked mozzarella and toasted almonds instead of the goat's cheese and sun-dried tomato mixture.
• Use red and yellow peppers preserved in olive oil instead of sun-dried tomatoes.
• Substitute 175g/6oz Roquefort or Gorgonzola for the goat's cheese, omit the sun-dried tomatoes and pine nuts, and add 75g/3oz chopped walnuts and 115g/4oz chopped celery, cooked until soft with the chopped onion in 25ml/1½ tbsp olive oil.

ROASTED GARLIC AND GOAT'S CHEESE SOUFFLÉ

THE MELLOW FLAVOUR OF ROASTED GARLIC PERVADES THIS SIMPLE SOUFFLÉ. BALANCE THE RICH SOUFFLÉ WITH A CRISP GREEN SALAD, INCLUDING PEPPERY LEAVES, SUCH AS MIZUNA AND WATERCRESS.

5 Cook the sauce very gently for 10 minutes, stirring frequently. Season with salt, pepper and a pinch of cayenne. Cool slightly. Preheat the oven to 200°C/400°F/Gas 6.

6 Beat in the egg yolks one at a time. Then beat in the goat's cheese, all but 15ml/1 tbsp of the Parmesan and the chopped thyme. Use the remaining butter to grease 1 large soufflé dish (1 litre/1¾ pints/4 cups) or 4 large ramekins (about 250ml/8fl oz/1 cup).

7 Whisk the egg whites and cream of tartar in a scrupulously clean bowl until firm, but not dry. Stir 45ml/3 tbsp of the whites into the sauce, then gently, but thoroughly, fold in the remainder.

8 Pour the mixture into the prepared dish or dishes. Run a knife around the edge of each dish, pushing the mixture away from the rim. Scatter with the reserved Parmesan.

9 Place the dish or dishes on a baking sheet and cook for 25–30 minutes for a large soufflé or 20 minutes for small soufflés. The mixture should be risen and firm to a light touch in the centre; it should not wobble excessively when given a light push. Serve immediately.

SERVES THREE TO FOUR

INGREDIENTS
2 large heads of garlic (choose heads with plump cloves)
3 fresh thyme sprigs
15ml/1 tbsp olive oil
250ml/8fl oz/1 cup milk
1 fresh bay leaf
2 × 1cm/½in thick onion slices
2 cloves
50g/2oz/¼ cup butter
40g/1½oz/⅓ cup plain flour, sifted
cayenne pepper
3 eggs, separated, plus 1 egg white
150g/5oz goat's cheese, crumbled
50g/2oz/⅔ cup freshly grated Parmesan cheese
2.5–5ml/½–1 tsp chopped fresh thyme
2.5ml/½ tsp cream of tartar
salt and ground black pepper

1 Preheat the oven to 180°C/350°F/Gas 4. Place the garlic and thyme sprigs on a piece of foil. Sprinkle with the oil and close the foil around the garlic, then bake for about 1 hour, until the garlic is soft. Leave to cool.

2 Squeeze the garlic out of its skin. Discard the thyme and garlic skins, then purée the garlic flesh with the oil.

3 Meanwhile, place the milk, bay leaf, onion slices and cloves in a small saucepan. Bring to the boil, then remove from the heat. Cover and leave to stand for 30 minutes.

4 Melt 40g/1½oz/3 tbsp of the butter in another saucepan. Stir in the flour and cook gently for 2 minutes, stirring. Reheat and strain the milk, then gradually stir it into the flour and butter.

ROASTED GARLIC AND AUBERGINE CUSTARDS WITH RED PEPPER DRESSING

THESE ELEGANT LITTLE MOULDS MAKE A RATHER SPLENDID MAIN COURSE FOR A SPECIAL DINNER.
SERVE GOOD BREAD AND STEAMED BROCCOLI AS ACCOMPANIMENTS.

SERVES SIX

INGREDIENTS

2 large heads of garlic
6–7 fresh thyme sprigs
60ml/4 tbsp extra virgin olive oil,
   plus extra for greasing
350g/12oz aubergines, cut into
   1cm/½in dice
2 large red peppers, halved
   and seeded
pinch of saffron strands
300ml/½ pint/1¼ cups
   whipping cream
2 large eggs
pinch of caster sugar
30ml/2 tbsp shredded fresh
   basil leaves
salt and ground black pepper

For the dressing

90ml/6 tbsp extra virgin oil
15–25ml/1–1½ tbsp balsamic vinegar
pinch of caster sugar
115g/4oz tomatoes, peeled, seeded
   and finely diced
½ small red onion, finely chopped
generous pinch of ground toasted
   cumin seeds
handful of fresh basil leaves

1 Preheat the oven to 190°C/375°F/
Gas 5. Place the garlic on a piece of foil
with the thyme and sprinkle with 15ml/
1 tbsp of the oil. Wrap the foil around
the garlic and cook for 35–45 minutes,
or until the garlic is soft. Cool slightly.
Reduce the oven temperature to 180°C/
350°F/Gas 4.

2 Meanwhile, heat the remaining olive
oil in a heavy-based saucepan. Add
the diced aubergines and fry over a
moderate heat, stirring frequently, for
5–8 minutes, until they are browned
and cooked.

3 Grill the peppers, skin sides
uppermost, until they are black. Place
the peppers in a bowl, cover and leave
for 10 minutes.

4 When the peppers are cool enough to
handle, peel and dice them. Soak the
saffron in 15ml/1 tbsp hot water for
10 minutes.

5 Unwrap the roasted garlic and pop
it out of its skin into a blender or food
processor. Discard the thyme sprigs.
Add the oil from cooking, the cream
and eggs to the garlic. Process until
smooth. Add the soaked saffron with its
liquid and season well with salt, pepper
and a pinch of sugar. Stir in half the
diced red pepper and the basil.

6 Lightly grease 6 large ovenproof
ramekins (about 200–250ml/7–8fl oz/
1 cup capacity) and line the base of
each with a circle of non-stick baking
parchment. Grease the parchment.

COOK'S TIP
It is important that the custards cook at
an even temperature throughout and are
surround by a water bath or they may
crack, spoiling their appearance.

7 Divide the aubergines among the
dishes. Pour the egg mixture into
the ramekins, then place them in a
roasting tin. Cover each dish with foil
and make a little hole in the centre of
the foil to allow steam to escape. Pour
hot water into the tin to come halfway
up the outsides of the ramekins. Bake
for 25–30 minutes, until the custards
are just set in the centre.

8 Make the dressing while the custards
are cooking. Whisk the oil and vinegar
with salt, pepper and a pinch of
sugar. Stir in the tomatoes, red onion,
remaining red pepper and cumin.
Set aside some basil leaves for
garnishing, then chop the rest and
add to the dressing.

9 Leave the custards to cool for about
5 minutes, then turn them out on to
warmed serving plates. Spoon the
dressing around the custards and
garnish each with the reserved fresh
basil leaves.

LEEK ROULADE with CHEESE, WALNUT and SWEET PEPPER FILLING

THIS ROULADE IS SURPRISINGLY EASY TO PREPARE AND IT MAKES A GOOD MAIN COURSE, SERVED WITH HOME-MADE TOMATO SAUCE. IT IS ALSO EXCELLENT AS PART OF A BUFFET.

SERVES FOUR TO SIX

INGREDIENTS
butter or oil, for greasing
30ml/2 tbsp fine dry
  white breadcrumbs
75g/3oz/1 cup finely grated
  Parmesan cheese
50g/2oz/¼ cup butter
2 leeks, thinly sliced
40g/1½oz/⅓ cup plain flour
250ml/8fl oz/1 cup milk
5ml/1 tsp Dijon mustard
1.5ml/¼ tsp freshly grated nutmeg
2 large eggs, separated, plus
  1 egg white
2.5ml/½ tsp cream of tartar
salt and ground black pepper
rocket and balsamic dressing,
  to serve

For the filling
2 large red peppers
350g/12oz/1½ cups ricotta cheese,
  curd cheese or soft goat's cheese
  (or a mixture)
90g/3½oz chopped walnuts
4 spring onions, finely chopped
15g/½oz fresh basil leaves

1 Grease and line a 30 × 23cm/ 12 × 9in Swiss roll tin with baking parchment, then sprinkle with the breadcrumbs and 30ml/2 tbsp of the grated Parmesan. Preheat the oven to 190°C/375°F/Gas 5.

2 Melt the butter in a saucepan and fry the leeks for 5 minutes, until softened.

3 Stir in the flour and cook over a low heat, stirring constantly, for 2 minutes, then gradually stir in the milk. Cook for 3–4 minutes, stirring constantly to make a thick sauce.

4 Stir in the mustard and nutmeg and season with salt and plenty of pepper. Reserve 30–45ml/2–3 tbsp of the remaining Parmesan, then stir the rest into the sauce. Cool slightly.

5 Beat the egg yolks into the sauce. In a scrupulously clean bowl, whisk the egg whites and cream of tartar until stiff. Stir 2–3 spoonfuls of the egg white into the leek mixture, then carefully fold in the remaining egg white.

6 Pour the mixture into the tin and gently level it out using a spatula. Bake for 15–18 minutes, until risen and just firm to a light touch in the centre. If the roulade is to be served hot, increase the oven temperature to 200°C/400°F/Gas 6 after removing the roulade.

7 Meanwhile, heat the grill. Halve and seed the peppers, then grill them, skin sides uppermost, until black. Place in a bowl, cover and leave for 10 minutes. Peel off the skin and cut into strips.

8 Beat the cheese with the walnuts and spring onions. Chop half the basil and beat it into the mixture. Season to taste.

9 Place a large sheet of baking parchment on the work surface and scatter with the remaining Parmesan. Turn out the roulade on to it. Strip off the lining paper and allow the roulade to cool slightly. Spread the cheese mixture over it and top with the red pepper strips. Tear the remaining basil leaves and sprinkle them over the top.

10 Using the paper as a guide, roll up the roulade and roll it on to a serving platter. If serving hot, roll the roulade on to a baking sheet, cover with a tent of foil and bake for 15–20 minutes. Serve with rocket and drizzle with dressing.

THREE ALLIUM RISOTTO
WITH FRIZZLED ONIONS AND PARMESAN

GENTLY COOKING CHOPPED ONION IN BUTTER IS THE FIRST STEP IN MAKING ALL CLASSIC RISOTTOS. IN THIS RECIPE, GARLIC AND CHIVES ARE ALSO ADDED AND A FINAL SPRINKLING OF CRISP FRIED ONIONS BRING A DELICIOUS CHANGE OF TEXTURE TO THE COOKED DISH.

SERVES FOUR

INGREDIENTS

75g/3oz/6 tbsp butter
15ml/1 tbsp olive oil, plus extra
1 onion, finely chopped
4 garlic cloves, finely chopped
350g/12oz/1¾ cups risotto rice
150ml/¼ pint/⅔ cup dry white wine
pinch of saffron strands (12 strands)
about 1.2 litres/2 pints/5 cups hot
   vegetable stock
1 large yellow onion, thinly sliced
15g/½oz chives, snipped, plus extra
   to garnish
75g/3oz/1 cup grated Parmesan
   cheese, plus more to taste
salt and ground black pepper

1 Melt half the butter with the oil in a large deep frying pan or heavy-based saucepan. Add the onion with a pinch of salt and cook over a very low heat, stirring frequently, for 10–15 minutes, until softened and just turning golden. Do not allow the onion to brown.

2 Add the garlic and rice and cook, stirring constantly, for 3–4 minutes, until the rice is coated and looks translucent. Season with a little salt and black pepper.

3 Pour in the wine and stir in the saffron with a ladleful of hot stock. Cook slowly, stirring frequently, until the liquid is absorbed.

4 Continue cooking for 18–20 minutes, adding 1–2 ladlefuls of stock at a time, until the rice is swollen and tender outside, but still *al dente* on the inside. Keep the heat low and stir frequently. The finished risotto should be moist, but not like soup.

5 Separate the slices of yellow onion into rings while the risotto is cooking. Heat a shallow layer of oil in a frying pan. Cook the onion rings slowly at first until soft, then increase the heat and fry briskly until they are brown and crisp. Drain on kitchen paper.

6 Beat the chives, the remaining butter and half the Parmesan into the risotto until it looks creamy. Taste and add seasoning, if necessary.

7 Serve the risotto in warm serving bowls, topped with the crisp onions and chives. Add more grated Parmesan to taste at the table.

BARLEY RISOTTO <u>WITH</u> ROASTED SQUASH <u>AND</u> LEEKS

THIS IS MORE LIKE A PILAFF, MADE WITH SLIGHTLY CHEWY, NUTTY-FLAVOURED PEARL BARLEY, THAN A CLASSIC RISOTTO. SWEET LEEKS AND ROASTED SQUASH ARE SUPERB WITH THIS EARTHY GRAIN.

3 Heat half the butter with the remaining oil in a large frying pan. Cook the leeks and garlic gently for 5 minutes. Add the mushrooms and remaining thyme, then cook until the liquid from the mushrooms evaporates and they begin to fry.

4 Stir in the carrots and cook for 2 minutes, then add the barley and most of the stock. Season well and part-cover the pan. Cook for a further 5 minutes. Pour in the remaining stock if the mixture seems dry.

5 Stir in the parsley, the remaining butter and half the Pecorino. Then stir in the squash. Add seasoning to taste and serve immediately, sprinkled with the toasted pumpkin seeds or walnuts and the remaining Pecorino.

SERVES FOUR TO FIVE

INGREDIENTS
200g/7oz/1 cup pearl barley
1 butternut squash, peeled, seeded and cut into chunks
10ml/2 tsp chopped fresh thyme
60ml/4 tbsp olive oil
25g/1oz/2 tbsp butter
4 leeks, cut into fairly thick diagonal slices
2 garlic cloves, finely chopped
175g/6oz chestnut mushrooms, sliced
2 carrots, coarsely grated
about 120ml/4fl oz/½ cup vegetable stock
30ml/2 tbsp chopped fresh flat leaf parsley
50g/2oz Pecorino cheese, grated or shaved
45ml/3 tbsp pumpkin seeds, toasted, or chopped walnuts
salt and ground black pepper

1 Rinse the barley, then cook it in simmering water, keeping the saucepan part-covered, for 35–45 minutes, or until tender. Drain. Preheat the oven to 200°C/400°F/Gas 6.

2 Place the squash in a roasting tin with half the thyme. Season with pepper and toss with half the oil. Roast, stirring once, for 30–35 minutes, until tender and beginning to brown.

PASTA WITH GARLIC AND CHILLI

THIS IS THE SIMPLEST OF PASTA DISHES AND ONE OF THE BEST. MINT AND OREGANO GIVE VERY DIFFERENT RESULTS, BOTH GOOD. THERE IS NO NEED TO SERVE GRATED PARMESAN WITH THIS DISH — INSTEAD, LET THE CLEAR FLAVOUR OF THE GARLIC AND OLIVE OIL SING OUT.

SERVES THREE TO FOUR

INGREDIENTS

400g/14oz dried spaghetti
105ml/7 tbsp extra virgin olive oil,
 plus more to taste
1.5ml/¼ tsp dried red chilli flakes or
 2 small whole dried red chillies
6 large garlic cloves, finely chopped
15ml/1 tbsp chopped fresh mint
 or oregano
15g/½ oz chopped fresh flat
 leaf parsley
salt and ground black pepper

1 Cook the spaghetti in boiling lightly salted water for 9–11 minutes, or according to the packet instructions, until just tender.

2 Meanwhile, warm the oil in a large frying pan or saucepan over a very gentle heat. Add the chilli flakes or whole chillies and cook very gently for 2–3 minutes.

COOK'S TIP
If you use fresh spaghetti, cook for only 2–3 minutes in boiling salted water.

3 Add the garlic to the pan. Keep the heat very low, so that the garlic barely bubbles and does not brown, then cook, shaking the pan occasionally, for about 2 minutes. Remove the pan from the heat and cool a little, then add the fresh mint or oregano.

4 Drain the pasta, then immediately add it to the oil and garlic mixture, with the parsley. Toss thoroughly. Season with freshly ground black pepper and transfer to warmed serving bowls. Serve immediately, offering more olive oil at the table.

VARIATION
Cook 250g/9oz broccoli florets in boiling salted water for 4 minutes. Add to the chilli oil and gently fry for 5–8 minutes.

PASTA <u>WITH</u> SLOWLY COOKED ONIONS, CABBAGE, PARMESAN <u>AND</u> PINE NUTS

THIS IS AN UNUSUAL, BUT QUITE DELICIOUS, WAY OF SERVING PASTA. CAVOLO NERO, TUSCAN BLACK CABBAGE, IS A CLOSE RELATIVE OF CURLY KALE, WITH LONG LEAVES AND A SPICY FLAVOUR.

SERVES FOUR

INGREDIENTS
    25g/1oz/2 tbsp butter
    15ml/1 tbsp extra virgin olive oil,
        plus more for drizzling (optional)
    500g/1¼lb Spanish onions, halved
        and thinly sliced
    5–10ml/1–2 tsp balsamic vinegar
    400–500g/14oz–20oz cavolo nero,
        spring greens, kale or Brussels
        sprout tops, shredded
    400–500g/14–20oz dried pasta (such
        as penne or fusilli)
    75g/3oz/1 cup freshly grated
        Parmesan cheese
    50g/2oz/½ cup pine nuts, toasted
    salt and ground black pepper

VARIATION
To make a delicious pilaff, cook 250g/
9oz/1¼ cups brown basmati rice and use
in place of the pasta.

1 Heat the butter and olive oil together in a large saucepan. Stir in the onions, cover and cook very gently, stirring occasionally, for about 20 minutes, until very soft.

2 Uncover, and continue to cook gently, until the onions have turned golden yellow. Add the balsamic vinegar and season well, then cook for a further 1–2 minutes. Set aside.

3 Blanch the cavolo nero, spring greens, kale or Brussels sprout tops in boiling, lightly salted water for about 3 minutes. Drain well and add to the onions, then cook over a low heat for 3–4 minutes.

4 Cook the pasta in boiling, lightly salted water for 8–12 minutes, or according to the packet instructions, until just tender. Drain, then add to the pan of onions and greens and toss thoroughly to mix.

5 Season well with salt and pepper and stir in half the Parmesan. Transfer the pasta to warmed plates. Scatter the pine nuts and more Parmesan on top and serve immediately, offering more olive oil for drizzling over to taste.

PASTA WITH PESTO, POTATOES AND GREEN BEANS

THIS IS ONE OF THE TRADITIONAL WAYS TO SERVE PESTO IN LIGURIA. ALTHOUGH THE COMBINATION OF PASTA AND POTATOES MAY SEEM ODD, IT IS DELICIOUS WITH THE RICH PESTO SAUCE.

SERVES FOUR

INGREDIENTS
  50g/2oz/½ cup pine nuts
  2 large garlic cloves, chopped
  90g/3½oz fresh basil leaves, plus a
    few extra leaves
  90ml/6 tbsp extra virgin olive oil (use
    a mild Ligurian or French oil)
  50g/2oz/⅔ cup freshly grated
    Parmesan cheese
  40g/1½oz/½ cup freshly grated
    Pecorino cheese
For the pasta mixture
  275g/10oz waxy potatoes, thickly
    sliced or cut into 1cm/½in cubes
  200g/7oz fine green beans
  350g/12oz dried trenette, linguine,
    tagliatelle or tagliarini
  salt and ground black pepper
To serve
  extra virgin olive oil
  pine nuts, toasted
  Parmesan cheese, grated

1 Toast the pine nuts in a dry frying pan until golden. (Watch them carefully or they will burn.) Place in a mortar with the garlic and a pinch of salt, and crush with a pestle. Add the basil and continue pounding the mixture. Gradually add a little oil as you work the mixture to form a paste. Then work the Parmesan and Pecorino with the remaining oil. (Alternatively, blend the pine nuts, garlic, basil and oil in a food processor, then stir in the cheeses.)

2 Bring a pan of lightly salted water to the boil and add the potatoes. Cook for 10–12 minutes, until tender. Add the green beans to the pan for the last 5–6 minutes of cooking.

3 Meanwhile, cook the pasta in boiling salted water for 8–12 minutes, or according to the packet instructions, until just tender. Times vary according to the pasta shapes. Try to time the cooking so that both pasta and potatoes are ready at the same time.

4 Drain the pasta and potatoes and beans. Place in a large, warmed bowl and toss with two-thirds of the pesto. Season with black pepper and scatter extra basil leaves over the top.

5 Serve immediately with the rest of the pesto, extra olive oil, pine nuts and grated Parmesan.

COOK'S TIP
To freeze pesto, make it without the cheeses, then freeze. To use, remove the pesto from the freezer and leave to thaw, then simply stir in the cheeses. If you plan to freeze pesto for more than a few weeks, omit the garlic as well and stir it in with the cheeses on thawing as the flavour of garlic can change during prolonged freezing.

CHEESE AND LEEK SAUSAGES WITH TOMATO, GARLIC AND CHILLI SAUCE

THESE ARE BASED ON THE WELSH SPECIALITY OF GLAMORGAN SAUSAGES, WHICH ARE TRADITIONALLY MADE USING WHITE OR WHOLEMEAL BREADCRUMBS ALONE. HOWEVER, ADDING A LITTLE MASHED POTATO LIGHTENS THE SAUSAGES AND MAKES THEM MUCH EASIER TO HANDLE.

SERVES FOUR

INGREDIENTS
25g/1oz/2 tbsp butter
175g/6oz leeks, finely chopped
90ml/6 tbsp cold mashed potato
115g/4oz/2 cups fresh white or
   wholemeal breadcrumbs
150g/5oz/1¼ cups grated Caerphilly,
   Lancashire or Cantal cheese
30ml/2 tbsp chopped fresh parsley
5ml/1 tsp chopped fresh sage
   or marjoram
2 large eggs, beaten
cayenne pepper
65g/2½oz/1 cup dry white
   breadcrumbs
oil for shallow frying
For the sauce
30ml/2 tbsp olive oil
2 garlic cloves, thinly sliced
1 fresh red chilli, seeded and finely
   chopped, or a good pinch of dried
   red chilli flakes
1 small onion, finely chopped
500g/1¼lb tomatoes, peeled, seeded
   and chopped
few fresh thyme sprigs
10ml/2 tsp balsamic vinegar or red
   wine vinegar
pinch of light muscovado sugar
15–30ml/1–2 tbsp chopped fresh
   marjoram or oregano
salt and ground black pepper

1 Melt the butter and fry the leeks for 4–5 minutes, until softened but not browned. Mix with the mashed potato, fresh breadcrumbs, cheese, parsley and sage or marjoram. Add sufficient beaten egg (about two-thirds of the quantity) to bind the mixture. Season well and add a good pinch of cayenne.

COOK'S TIP
These sausages are also delicious served with garlic mayonnaise or confit of slow-cooked onions.

2 Shape the mixture into 12 sausage shapes. Dip in the remaining egg, then coat with the dry breadcrumbs. Chill the coated sausages.

3 To make the sauce, heat the oil over a low heat in a pan, add the garlic, chilli and onion and cook for 3–4 minutes. Add the tomatoes, thyme and vinegar. Season with salt, pepper and sugar.

4 Cook the sauce for 40–50 minutes, until much reduced. Remove the thyme and purée the sauce in a blender. Reheat with the marjoram or oregano, then adjust the seasoning, adding more sugar, if necessary.

5 Fry the sausages in shallow oil until golden brown on all sides. Drain on kitchen paper and serve with the sauce.

VEGETABLE STEW WITH ROASTED TOMATO AND GARLIC SAUCE

THIS LIGHTLY SPICED STEW MAKES A PERFECT MATCH FOR COUSCOUS, ENRICHED WITH A LITTLE BUTTER OR OLIVE OIL. ADD SOME CHOPPED FRESH CORIANDER AND A HANDFUL EACH OF RAISINS AND TOASTED PINE NUTS TO THE COUSCOUS TO MAKE IT EXTRA SPECIAL.

SERVES SIX

INGREDIENTS

    45ml/3 tbsp olive oil
    250g/9oz small pickling onions
      or shallots
    1 large onion, chopped
    2 garlic cloves, chopped
    5ml/1 tsp cumin seeds
    5ml/1 tsp ground coriander seeds
    5ml/1 tsp paprika
    5cm/2in piece cinnamon stick
    2 fresh bay leaves
    300–450ml/½–¾ pint/
      1¼–scant 2 cups good
      vegetable stock
    good pinch of saffron strands
    450g/1lb carrots, thickly sliced
    2 green peppers, seeded and
      thickly sliced
    115g/4oz ready-to-eat dried apricots,
      halved if large
    5–7.5ml/1–1½ tsp ground toasted
      cumin seeds
    450g/1lb squash, peeled, seeded
      and cut into chunks
    pinch of sugar, to taste
    25g/1oz/2 tbsp butter (optional)
    salt and ground black pepper
    45ml/3 tbsp fresh coriander leaves,
      to garnish
For the roasted tomato and garlic sauce
    1kg/2¼lb tomatoes, halved
    5ml/1 tsp sugar
    45ml/3 tbsp olive oil
    1–2 fresh red chillies, seeded
      and chopped
    2–3 garlic cloves, chopped
    5ml/1 tsp fresh thyme leaves

VARIATION
Other vegetables could be used. A mixture of aubergine and potato is good. Fry the cubed aubergine with the shallots until brown and cook the potatoes as you would the squash. Allow 2 medium aubergines and about 500g/1¼lb small potatoes. Omit the carrots and apricots.

1 Preheat the oven to 180°C/350°F/Gas 4. First make the sauce. Place the tomatoes, cut sides uppermost, in a roasting tin. Season well with salt and pepper and sprinkle the sugar over the top, then drizzle with the olive oil. Roast for 30 minutes.

2 Scatter the chillies, garlic and thyme over the tomatoes, stir to mix and roast for another 30–45 minutes, until the tomatoes are collapsed but still a little juicy. Cool, then process in a food processor or blender to make a thick sauce. Sieve to remove the seeds.

3 Heat 30ml/2 tbsp of the oil in a large, wide saucepan or deep frying pan and cook the pickling onions or shallots until browned all over. Remove from the pan and set aside. Add the chopped onion to the pan and cook over a low heat for 5–7 minutes, until softened. Stir in the garlic and cumin seeds and cook for a further 3–4 minutes.

4 Add the ground coriander seeds, paprika, cinnamon stick and bay leaves. Cook, stirring constantly, for another 2 minutes, then mix in the vegetable stock, saffron, carrots and green peppers. Season well, cover and simmer gently for 10 minutes.

5 Stir in the apricots, 5ml/1 tsp of the ground toasted cumin, the browned onions or shallots and the squash. Stir in the tomato sauce.

6 Cover the pan and cook for a further 5 minutes. Uncover the pan and continue to cook, stirring occasionally, for 10–15 minutes, until the vegetables are all fully cooked.

7 Adjust the seasoning, adding a little more cumin and a pinch of sugar to taste. Remove and discard the cinnamon stick. Stir in the butter, if using, and serve scattered with the fresh coriander leaves.

AUBERGINE <u>AND</u> SWEET POTATO STEW WITH GARLIC <u>AND</u> COCONUT MILK

INSPIRED BY THAI COOKING, THIS AUBERGINE AND SWEET POTATO STEW COOKED IN A COCONUT SAUCE IS SCENTED WITH FRAGRANT LEMON GRASS, GINGER AND LOTS OF GARLIC.

SERVES SIX

INGREDIENTS

60ml/4 tbsp groundnut oil
400g/14oz baby aubergines, halved,
  or 2 standard aubergines, cut
  into chunks
225g/8oz Thai red shallots or other
  small shallots or pickling onions
5ml/1 tsp fennel seeds,
  lightly crushed
4–5 garlic cloves, thinly sliced
25ml/1½ tbsp finely chopped fresh
  root ginger
475ml/16fl oz/2 cups vegetable stock
2 stems lemon grass, outer layers
  discarded, finely chopped or minced
15g/½oz fresh coriander, stalks and
  leaves chopped separately
3 kaffir lime leaves, lightly bruised
2–3 small red chillies
45–60ml/3–4 tbsp Thai green
  curry paste
675g/1½lb sweet potatoes, peeled
  and cut into thick chunks
400ml/14fl oz/1⅔ cups coconut milk
2.5–5ml/½–1 tsp light
  muscovado sugar
250g/9oz mushrooms, thickly sliced
juice of 1 lime, to taste
salt and ground black pepper
18 fresh Thai basil leaves or ordinary
  basil, to serve

1 Heat half the oil in a wide saucepan or deep, lidded frying pan. Add the aubergines and cook over a medium heat, stirring occasionally, until lightly browned on all sides. Remove from the pan and set aside.

2 Slice 4–5 of the shallots and set aside. Fry the remaining whole shallots in the oil remaining in the pan, adding a little more oil if necessary, until lightly browned. Set aside with the aubergines. Add the remaining oil to the pan and cook the sliced shallots, fennel seeds, garlic and ginger very gently until soft but not browned.

3 Add the vegetable stock, lemon grass, chopped coriander stalks and any roots, lime leaves and whole chillies. Cover and simmer over a low heat for 5 minutes.

4 Stir in 30ml/2 tbsp of the curry paste and the sweet potatoes. Simmer gently for about 10 minutes, then return the aubergines and browned shallots to the pan and cook for a further 5 minutes.

5 Stir in the coconut milk and the sugar. Season to taste, then stir in the mushrooms and simmer for 5 minutes, or until all the vegetables are cooked.

6 Stir in more curry paste and lime juice to taste, followed by the chopped coriander leaves. Adjust the seasoning and ladle the vegetables into warmed bowls. Scatter basil leaves over the vegetables and serve.

PARSNIPS AND CHICK-PEAS IN GARLIC, ONION, CHILLI AND GINGER PASTE

THE SWEET FLAVOUR OF PARSNIPS GOES VERY WELL WITH THE SPICES IN THIS INDIAN-STYLE VEGETABLE STEW. OFFER INDIAN BREADS TO MOP UP THE DELICIOUS SAUCE.

SERVES FOUR

INGREDIENTS

200g/7oz dried chick-peas,
  soaked overnight in cold water,
  then drained
7 garlic cloves, finely chopped
1 small onion, chopped
5cm/2in piece fresh root
  ginger, chopped
2 green chillies, seeded and
  finely chopped
450ml/¾ pint/scant 2 cups plus
  75ml/5 tbsp water
60ml/4 tbsp groundnut oil
5ml/1 tsp cumin seeds
10ml/2 tsp ground coriander seeds
5ml/1 tsp ground turmeric
2.5–5ml/½–1 tsp chilli powder or
  mild paprika
50g/2oz cashew nuts, toasted
  and ground
250g/9oz tomatoes, peeled
  and chopped
900g/2lb parsnips, cut
  into chunks
5ml/1 tsp ground roasted
  cumin seeds
juice of 1 lime, to taste
salt and ground black pepper
To serve
  fresh coriander leaves
  a few cashew nuts, toasted

1 Put the soaked chick-peas in a saucepan, cover with cold water and bring to the boil. Boil vigorously for 10 minutes, then reduce the heat so that the water boils steadily and cook for 1–1½ hours, or until the chick-peas are tender. (The cooking time depends on how long the chick-peas have been stored.) Drain.

2 Set 10ml/2 tsp of the garlic aside, then place the remainder in a food processor or blender with the onion, ginger and half the chillies. Add the 75ml/5 tbsp water and process to make a smooth paste.

3 Heat the oil in a large, deep, frying pan and cook the cumin seeds for 30 seconds. Stir in the coriander seeds, turmeric, chilli powder or paprika and the ground cashew nuts. Add the ginger and chilli paste and cook, stirring frequently, until the water begins to evaporate. Add the tomatoes and stir-fry until the mixture begins to turn red-brown in colour.

4 Mix in the chick-peas and parsnips with the main batch of water, 5ml/1 tsp salt and plenty of black pepper. Bring to the boil, stir, then simmer, uncovered, for 15–20 minutes, until the parsnips are completely tender.

5 Reduce the liquid, if necessary, by boiling fiercely until the sauce is thick. Add the ground roasted cumin with more salt and/or lime juice to taste. Stir in the reserved garlic and green chilli, and cook for a further 1–2 minutes. Scatter the fresh coriander leaves and toasted cashew nuts over and serve straight away.

COOK'S TIP
Do not add salt to the water when cooking dried chick-peas, as this will toughen them.

We often forget that onions are vegetables in their own right, but the recipes in this section show how essential they really are. Foods such as bread and rice are particularly good with onions, garlic, leeks and chives. Onions roast beautifully and are wonderful cooked with other vegetables, adding a delicious caramelized sweetness. Whether it's a panful of caramelized shallots, a pile of onion rings or a heap of chive-flavoured rice, alliums are essential for adding savour to a whole host of meals.

Side Dishes

CARAMELIZED SHALLOTS

THESE SHALLOTS ARE GOOD WITH GRILLED OR BRAISED POULTRY OR MEAT, ESPECIALLY TURKEY, PORK, VEAL AND BEEF. THEY ARE ALSO EXCELLENT MIXED WITH OTHER BRAISED OR ROASTED VEGETABLES, SUCH AS CHESTNUTS, CARROTS OR CHUNKS OF BUTTERNUT SQUASH.

SERVES FOUR TO SIX

INGREDIENTS

50g/2oz/¼ cup butter or 60ml/4 tbsp
  olive oil
500g/1¼lb shallots or small onions,
  peeled with root ends intact
15ml/1 tbsp golden caster sugar
30ml/2 tbsp red or white wine or port
150ml/¼ pint/⅔ cup rich veal,
  chicken or beef stock or water
2–3 fresh bay leaves and/or 2–3 fresh
  thyme sprigs
salt and ground black pepper
chopped fresh parsley,
  to garnish (optional)

1 Heat the butter or oil in a large frying pan and add the shallots or onions in a single layer. Fry gently, turning occasionally, until lightly browned.

2 Sprinkle the sugar over the shallots and cook gently, turning the shallots in the juices, until the sugar begins to caramelize. Add the wine or port and let the mixture bubble for 4–5 minutes.

3 Add the stock, seasoning and herbs. Cover and cook for 5 minutes, then remove the lid and cook until the liquid evaporates and the shallots are tender and glazed. Adjust the seasoning and sprinkle with the parsley, if liked.

VARIATION
Shallots with chestnuts and pancetta
Cook the shallots in butter or bacon fat with 90g/3½oz pancetta, cut into thick strips. Use water or ham stock in place of the wine or port. Toss in 250–350g/9–12oz part-cooked chestnuts in step 3. Cook for 5–10 minutes, then serve sprinkled with chopped flat leaf parsley.

JERUSALEM ARTICHOKES WITH GARLIC, SHALLOTS AND BACON

THE SLIGHTLY SMOKY AND EARTHY FLAVOUR OF JERUSALEM ARTICHOKES IS EXCELLENT WITH SHALLOTS AND SMOKED BACON. THESE ARE GOOD WITH CHICKEN, ROAST COD OR MONKFISH, OR PORK.

3 Season with salt and black pepper to taste and stir in the water. Cover and cook for a further 8–10 minutes, shaking the pan occasionally.

4 Uncover the pan, increase the heat and cook for 5–6 minutes, until all the moisture has evaporated and the artichokes are tender.

SERVES FOUR

INGREDIENTS

50g/2oz/¼ cup butter
115g/4oz smoked bacon or pancetta, chopped
800g/1¾lb Jerusalem artichokes, peeled
8–12 garlic cloves, peeled
115g/4oz shallots, chopped
75ml/5 tbsp water
30ml/2 tbsp olive oil
25g/1oz/½ cup fresh white breadcrumbs
30–45ml/2–3 tbsp chopped fresh parsley
salt and ground black pepper

1 Melt half the butter in a heavy-based frying pan and cook the chopped bacon or pancetta until brown and beginning to crisp. Remove half the bacon or pancetta from the pan and set aside.

2 Add the artichokes, garlic and shallots, and cook, stirring frequently, until the artichokes and garlic begin to brown slightly.

COOK'S TIP

Do not peel the artichokes too far in advance as they discolour quickly on exposure to air. If necessary, drop them into a bowl of acidulated water.

5 In another frying pan, melt the remaining butter in the olive oil. Add the white breadcrumbs and fry over a moderate heat, stirring frequently, until crisp and golden. Stir in the chopped parsley and the reserved cooked bacon or pancetta.

6 Combine the artichokes with the breadcrumb mixture, mixing well. Adjust the seasoning, if necessary, then turn into a warmed serving dish. Serve immediately.

CHAMP

THIS TRADITIONAL IRISH DISH OF POTATOES, GREEN OR SPRING ONIONS, AND BUTTERMILK OR CREAMY MILK, IS ENRICHED WITH A WICKEDLY INDULGENT AMOUNT OF GOOD BUTTER.

SERVES FOUR

INGREDIENTS

1kg/2¼lb boiling potatoes,
   cut into chunks
250ml/8fl oz/1 cup milk
1 bunch spring onions,
   thinly sliced, plus extra
   to garnish
115g/4oz/½ cup slightly
   salted butter
60ml/4 tbsp buttermilk or
   crème fraîche
salt and ground black pepper

1 Boil the potatoes in lightly salted water for 20–25 minutes, until tender. Drain and mash with a fork until smooth.

2 Place the milk, spring onions and half the butter in a small saucepan and set over a low heat until just simmering. Cook for 2–3 minutes, until the butter has melted and the spring onions have softened.

3 Beat the milk mixture into the mashed potato using a wooden spoon. Beat in the buttermilk or crème fraîche until the mixture is light and fluffy. Reheat gently, adding salt and pepper to taste.

4 Turn the potato into a warmed serving dish and make a well in the centre with a spoon. Place the remaining butter in the well and let it melt. Serve immediately, sprinkled with extra spring onion.

VARIATIONS
• **Colcannon** This is another Irish speciality. Follow the main recipe, using half the butter. Cook about 500g/1¼lb finely shredded green cabbage or kale in a little water until just tender, drain thoroughly and then beat into the creamed potato. This is delicious with sausages and grilled ham or bacon. It may also be fried in butter and then browned lightly under the grill.
• **Clapshot** To make this Scottish dish, halve the quantity of potato and replace with an equal weight (or slightly more) of swede. Use less butter and omit the cream, then season with black pepper and plenty of freshly grated nutmeg. Traditionally, a chopped onion would be cooked with the potatoes and swede.

FENNEL, POTATO AND GARLIC MASH

THIS FLAVOURSOME MASH OF POTATO, FENNEL AND GARLIC GOES PARTICULARLY WELL WITH FISH OR CHICKEN. IT IS ALSO EXTREMELY DELICIOUS WITH ROAST PORK.

SERVES FOUR

INGREDIENTS
    1 head of garlic, separated
      into cloves
    800g/1¾lb boiling potatoes, cut
      into chunks
    2 large fennel bulbs
    65g/2½oz/5 tbsp butter or 90ml/
      6 tbsp extra virgin olive oil
    120–150ml/4–5fl oz/½–⅔ cup milk
      or single cream
    freshly grated nutmeg
    salt and ground black pepper

1 If using a food mill to mash the potato, leave the garlic unpeeled, otherwise peel it. Boil the garlic with the potatoes in salted water for 20 minutes.

2 Meanwhile, trim and roughly chop the fennel, reserving any feathery tops. Chop the tops and set them aside. Heat 25g/1oz/2 tbsp of the butter or 30ml/ 2 tbsp of the oil in a heavy-based saucepan. Add the fennel, cover and cook over a low heat for 20–30 minutes, until soft but not browned.

3 Drain and mash the potatoes and garlic. Purée the fennel in a food mill or blender and beat it into the potato with the remaining butter or olive oil.

COOK'S TIP
A food mill is good for mashing potatoes as it ensures a smooth texture. Never mash potatoes in a food processor or blender as this releases the starch, giving a result that resembles wallpaper paste.

4 Warm the milk or cream and beat sufficient into the potato and fennel to make a creamy, light mixture. Season to taste and add a little grated nutmeg.

5 Reheat gently, then beat in any chopped fennel tops. Transfer to a warmed dish and serve immediately.

VARIATIONS
• For a stronger garlic flavour, use 30–45ml/2–3 tbsp roasted garlic purée.
• To give a stronger fennel flavour, cook 2.5–5ml/½–1 tsp ground fennel seeds with the fennel.
• For a slightly less rich mash, substitute hot stock for some or all of the milk or cream. Mash made with fish stock is particularly good with grilled fish or as a topping for fish pie.

SWEET-SOUR ROASTED ONIONS

THESE ONIONS ARE DELICIOUS WITH ROAST PORK OR LAMB OR SERVED WITH A CRACKED WHEAT PILAFF.

SERVES FOUR

INGREDIENTS
    4 large onions
    60ml/4 tbsp olive oil
    10ml/2 tsp crushed coriander seeds
    15ml/1 tbsp honey
    30ml/2 tbsp pomegranate molasses
    15ml/1 tbsp sherry vinegar
    salt and ground black pepper

COOK'S TIP
Pomegranate molasses is made by
boiling down the juice of the fruit to
produce a thick, sticky liquid with a
wonderful sweet-sour taste. It is available
from Middle Eastern food shops and
some large supermarkets. There is no
suitable substitute.

1 Cut the onions into wedges, leaving
them attached at the root end. Preheat
the oven to 200°C/400°F/Gas 6. Place the
onion wedges, olive oil and crushed
coriander in a roasting tin and mix
thoroughly with your hands. Season to
taste, then roast for 20 minutes.

2 Mix the honey, pomegranate
molasses and vinegar with 15ml/1 tbsp
water. Drizzle this mixture over the
onions and stir to mix. Reduce the oven
temperature to 180°C/350°F/Gas 4 and
cook for another 20–30 minutes, until
well browned. Serve immediately.

ROASTED RED ONIONS WITH CRUMBLY CHEESE AND SUN-DRIED TOMATO BUTTER

*ONIONS ROAST TO A WONDERFUL SWEET CREAMINESS WHEN COOKED IN THEIR SKINS. THEY NEED
BUTTER, LOTS OF BLACK PEPPER AND SALTY FOOD TO SET OFF THEIR SWEETNESS.*

SERVES SIX

INGREDIENTS
    6 even-sized red onions, unpeeled
    175–225g/6–8oz crumbly cheese
        (such as Lancashire, Caerphilly or
        Cheshire), thinly sliced
    a few snipped chives
    salt and ground black pepper
For the sun-dried tomato butter
    115g/4oz butter, softened
    65g/2½oz sun-dried tomatoes in olive
        oil, drained and finely chopped
    30ml/2 tbsp chopped fresh basil
        or parsley

VARIATIONS
• Use goat's cheese instead of
Lancashire, Caerphilly or Cheshire.
• Fry fresh white breadcrumbs in butter
with a little garlic until crisp and then
mix with lots of chopped fresh parsley.
Scatter the crisp crumb mixture over the
onions before serving.

1 Preheat the oven to 180°C/350°F/
Gas 4. Put the unpeeled onions in a
roasting tin and roast for 1¼–1½ hours,
until they are tender and feel soft when
lightly squeezed.

2 Meanwhile, prepare the sun-dried
tomato butter. Cream the butter and
then beat in the tomatoes and basil or
parsley. Season to taste with salt and
pepper and shape into a roll, then wrap
in foil and chill.

3 Slit the tops of the onions and open
them up. Season with plenty of black
pepper and add chunks of the sun-
dried tomato butter. Scatter the cheese
and chives over the top and eat
immediately, mashing the butter and
cheese into the soft, sweet onion.

COOK'S TIP
Sun-dried tomatoes are easiest to chop
if you snip them into tiny pieces with a
sharp pair of kitchen scissors.

POTATO, ONION AND GARLIC GRATIN

THIS IS A SIMPLE BUT DELICIOUS WAY OF COOKING POTATOES AND ONIONS TOGETHER. CHOOSE STOCK TO COMPLEMENT THE MAIN DISH THAT IT IS ACCOMPANYING. ALTERNATIVELY, USE WATER AND ADD SOME BACON TO GIVE FLAVOUR. THE GRATIN ALSO MAKES A GOOD BASE ON WHICH TO BAKE FISH.

SERVES FOUR TO SIX

INGREDIENTS

40g/1½oz/3 tbsp butter or bacon fat
  or 45ml/3 tbsp olive oil
2–4 garlic cloves, finely chopped
900g/2lb waxy potatoes, thinly sliced
450g/1lb onions, thinly sliced
450ml/¾ pint/scant 2 cups fish,
  chicken, beef or lamb stock
salt and ground black pepper

VARIATIONS
• Layer 175g/6oz thinly sliced cheese with the potatoes. About 15–20 minutes before the end of cooking time, sprinkle the gratin with another 50g/2oz/½ cup grated cheese, dot with more butter and finish baking. This version is also good made with leeks.
• For a simple topping, crumble 165g/5½oz soft goat's cheese on the gratin 15 minutes before the end of cooking.

1 Use half the butter, bacon fat or oil to grease a 1.5 litre/2½ pint/6¼ cup gratin dish. Preheat the oven to 180°C/350°F/Gas 4.

2 Sprinkle a little of the chopped garlic over the base of the dish and then layer the potatoes and onions in the dish, seasoning each layer with a little salt and pepper and adding the remaining garlic. Finish with a layer of overlapping potato slices on top.

3 Bring the stock to the boil in a saucepan and pour it over the gratin. Dot the top with the remaining butter or bacon fat cut into small pieces, or drizzle the remaining olive oil over the top. Cover tightly with foil and bake for 1½ hours.

4 Increase the oven temperature to 200°C/400°F/Gas 6. Uncover the gratin and then cook for a further 35–50 minutes, until the potatoes are completely cooked and the top layer is browned and crusty. Serve immediately.

LEEK, SQUASH AND TOMATO GRATIN

THIS AUTUMNAL GRATIN COMPLEMENTS ROAST OR GRILLED LAMB OR CHICKEN. OR SERVE IT AS A SIMPLE SUPPER DISH ACCOMPANIED BY A GREEN SALAD AND GOOD BREAD.

4 Heat the cream in a small saucepan with the chilli and garlic. Bring to the boil, then stir in the mint and pour over the gratin, thoroughly scraping the contents out of the pan.

SERVES FOUR TO SIX

INGREDIENTS
  450g/1lb peeled and seeded squash,
    cut into 1cm/½in slices
  60ml/4 tbsp olive oil
  450g/1lb leeks, cut into thick,
    diagonal slices
  675g/1½lb tomatoes, peeled and
    thickly sliced
  2.5ml/½ tsp ground toasted cumin seeds
  450ml/¾ pint/scant 2 cups single cream
  1 fresh red chilli, seeded and
    thinly sliced
  1 garlic clove, finely chopped
  15ml/1 tbsp chopped fresh mint
  30ml/2 tbsp chopped fresh parsley
  60ml/4 tbsp fine white breadcrumbs
  salt and ground black pepper

1 Steam the squash over boiling salted water for 10 minutes.

2 Heat half the oil in a frying pan and cook the leeks gently for 5–6 minutes until lightly coloured. Try to keep the slices intact. Preheat the oven to 190°C/375°F/Gas 5.

3 Layer the squash, leeks and tomatoes in a 2 litre/3½ pint/8¾ cup gratin dish, arranging them in rows. Season with salt, pepper and cumin.

5 Bake for 50–55 minutes, or until the gratin is bubbling and the vegetables are tender. Scatter the parsley and breadcrumbs on top and drizzle over the remaining oil. Then bake for another 15–20 minutes until the breadcrumbs are browned and crisp. Serve immediately.

CABBAGE WITH ONIONS, BACON AND GARLIC

SERVE THIS QUICK, EASY AND FLAVOURSOME DISH WITH GOOSE, TURKEY OR PORK, OR TRY IT WITH SAUSAGES OR CHOPS AND CREAMY MASHED POTATOES.

SERVES FOUR

INGREDIENTS
25g/1oz/2 tbsp butter or bacon fat or
   pork fat, or 30ml/2 tbsp olive oil
115g/4oz bacon or pancetta, chopped
1 onion, halved and thinly sliced
5ml/1 tsp caraway seeds or cumin
   seeds (optional)
2 garlic cloves, finely chopped
1 green cabbage (such as Savoy
   cabbage), thick stalks removed and
   leaves shredded
105ml/7 tbsp water
salt and ground black pepper

1 Melt the butter or fat or heat the oil in a large frying pan over a gentle heat. Cook the bacon or pancetta and onion gently, until the onion is soft.

2 Increase the heat slightly to medium-low and scatter over the caraway seeds or cumin seeds, if using, then cook, stirring occasionally, until the onion begins to brown.

3 Add the chopped garlic and stir-fry for 2 minutes.

4 Add the cabbage and turn it in the juices to coat, then stir in 5ml/1 tsp salt and the water. Cover tightly and cook over a high heat for 5–6 minutes, stirring once. The cabbage should be tender, but still retain a little crispness. Season to taste with black pepper and serve immediately.

DEEP-FRIED ONION RINGS

THESE ARE A POPULAR ACCOMPANIMENT FOR GRILLED MEATS, ESPECIALLY STEAKS AND BURGERS. THEY ALSO PROVIDE A CRISP CONTRAST WHEN SERVED WITH SLICED HARD-BOILED EGGS IN ONION SAUCE.

SERVES FOUR

INGREDIENTS
2 Spanish onions, thickly sliced
1 large egg white, lightly beaten
60ml/4 tbsp plain flour
groundnut oil for deep-frying
salt and ground black pepper

1 Separate the onion slices into rings. Dip them into the egg white.

2 Season the flour with salt and pepper, then dip the onion rings into it, one at a time, until evenly coated, shaking off any excess.

3 Heat the oil for deep-frying to 190°C/375°F, or until a cube of day-old bread browns in 30–40 seconds. Fry the onion rings for 3–4 minutes, until browned and crisp. Drain on kitchen paper and serve immediately.

VARIATIONS
• For corn-crusted onion rings, soak red onion rings in milk for about 30 minutes. Drain, then dip into coarse cornmeal (polenta), mixed with a pinch each of dried red chilli flakes, paprika and ground toasted cumin seeds. Deep-fry.
• For spicy onion rings, mix 90ml/6 tbsp chick-pea flour (besan or gram flour) with 2.5ml/½ tsp each of ground cumin, ground coriander, chilli powder and garam masala. Season and add 1 chopped green chilli and 30ml/2 tbsp chopped fresh coriander. Mix with 45–60ml/3–4 tbsp cold water to make a fairly thick batter. Dip the onion rings into the batter, then deep-fry until crisp.
• For onion tempura, beat 2 egg yolks with 150ml/¼ pint/⅔ cup iced sparkling water. Lightly mix in 115g/4oz sifted self-raising flour and a pinch of salt, leaving the batter lumpy. Dip onion rings into the batter and deep-fry.

POTATOES BAKED WITH FENNEL, ONIONS, GARLIC AND SAFFRON

POTATOES, FENNEL AND ONIONS INFUSED WITH GARLIC, SAFFRON AND SPICES MAKE A SOPHISTICATED AND ATTRACTIVE ACCOMPANIMENT FOR FISH OR CHICKEN OR AN EGG-BASED MAIN-COURSE DISH.

SERVES FOUR TO SIX

INGREDIENTS

500g/1¼lb small waxy potatoes,
  cut into chunks or wedges
good pinch of saffron strands
  (12–15 strands)
1 head of garlic, separated
  into cloves
12 small red or yellow onions,
  peeled but left whole
3 fennel bulbs, cut into wedges,
  feathery tops reserved
4–6 fresh bay leaves
6–9 fresh thyme sprigs
175ml/6fl oz/¾ cup fish, chicken
  or vegetable stock
30ml/2 tbsp sherry vinegar
2.5ml/½ tsp sugar
5ml/1 tsp fennel seeds,
  lightly crushed
2.5ml/½ tsp paprika
45ml/3 tbsp olive oil
salt and ground black pepper

1 Boil the potatoes in salted water for 8–10 minutes. Drain. Preheat the oven to 190°C/375°F/Gas 5. Soak the saffron in 30ml/2 tbsp warm water for 10 minutes.

2 Peel and finely chop 2 garlic cloves. Place the potatoes, onions, unpeeled garlic cloves, fennel wedges, bay leaves and thyme sprigs in a roasting dish.

3 Mix together the stock, saffron and its soaking liquid, vinegar and sugar, then pour over the vegetables. Stir in the fennel seeds, paprika, garlic and oil, and season with salt and pepper.

4 Cook in the oven for 1–1¼ hours, stirring occasionally, until the vegetables are tender. Chop the reserved fennel, sprinkle over the vegetables and serve.

ROASTED SWEET POTATOES, ONIONS AND BEETROOT IN COCONUT AND GINGER PASTE

SWEET POTATOES AND BEETROOT TAKE ON A WONDERFUL SWEETNESS WHEN ROASTED, AND THEY ARE DELICIOUS WITH THE SAVOURY ONIONS AND AROMATIC COCONUT, GINGER AND GARLIC PASTE.

SERVES FOUR

INGREDIENTS
  30ml/2 tbsp groundnut oil or
    mild olive oil
  450g/1lb sweet potatoes, peeled and
    cut into thick strips or chunks
  4 beetroot, cooked, peeled and cut
    into wedges
  450g/1lb small red or yellow
    onions, halved
  5ml/1 tsp coriander seeds,
    lightly crushed
  3–4 small whole fresh red chillies
  salt and ground black pepper
  chopped fresh coriander, to garnish
For the paste
  2 large garlic cloves, chopped
  1 2 green chillies, seeded
    and chopped
  15ml/1 tbsp chopped fresh
    root ginger
  45ml/3 tbsp chopped fresh coriander
  75ml/5 tbsp coconut milk
  30ml/2 tbsp groundnut oil or
    mild olive oil
  grated rind of ½ lime
  2.5ml/½ tsp light muscovado sugar

1 First make the paste. Process the garlic, chillies, ginger, coriander and coconut milk in a food processor, blender or coffee grinder.

2 Turn the paste into a small bowl and beat in the oil, lime rind and muscovado sugar. Preheat the oven to 200°C/400°F/Gas 6.

3 Heat the oil in a roasting tin in the oven for 5 minutes. Add the sweet potatoes, beetroot, onions and coriander seeds, tossing them in the hot oil. Roast for 10 minutes.

4 Stir in the paste and the whole red chillies. Season well with salt and pepper, and toss the vegetables to coat them thoroughly with the paste.

5 Roast the vegetables for a further 25–35 minutes, or until the sweet potatoes and onions are fully cooked and tender. Stir 2–3 times to prevent the paste from sticking to the tin. Serve immediately, sprinkled with a little chopped fresh coriander.

COOK'S TIP
Orange-fleshed sweet potatoes look more attractive than white-fleshed ones in this dish – and they are more nutritious.

GUACAMOLE

THIS DISH HAS ALMOST BECOME A CLICHÉ OF TEX-MEX COOKING, USUALLY SERVED AS A FIRST COURSE WITH BREAD OR CORN CHIPS FOR DIPPING. CAREFULLY SEASONED, IT IS A GREAT ACCOMPANIMENT FOR SIMPLE GRILLED FISH, POULTRY OR MEAT, ESPECIALLY STEAK.

SERVES FOUR

INGREDIENTS

2 large ripe avocados
1 small red onion, very
   finely chopped
1 red or green chilli, seeded and very
   finely chopped
½–1 garlic clove, crushed with a
   little salt (optional)
finely shredded rind of ½ lime and
   juice of 1–1½ limes
pinch of caster sugar
225g/8oz tomatoes, seeded
   and chopped
30ml/2 tbsp roughly chopped
   fresh coriander
2.5–5ml/½–1 tsp ground toasted
   cumin seeds
15ml/1 tbsp olive oil
15–30ml/1–2 tbsp soured
   cream (optional)
salt and ground black pepper
lime wedges, dipped in sea salt, and
   fresh coriander sprigs, to garnish

1 Halve, stone and peel the avocados. Set one half aside and roughly mash the remainder in a bowl using a fork.

COOK'S TIP
Leaving some of the avocado in chunks adds a slightly different texture, but if you prefer, mash all the avocado together. Hard avocados will soften in a few seconds in a microwave. Check frequently until you get the softness you like.

2 Add the onion, chilli, garlic (if using), lime rind, juice of 1 lime, sugar, tomatoes and coriander. Add ground cumin, seasoning and more lime juice to taste. Stir in the olive oil.

3 Dice the remaining avocado and stir into the guacamole, then cover and leave to stand for 15 minutes so that the flavour develops. Stir in the soured cream, if using. Serve immediately with lime wedges, dipped in sea salt, and coriander sprigs.

LENTIL DHAL WITH ROASTED GARLIC AND WHOLE SPICES

THIS SPICY LENTIL DHAL MAKES A SUSTAINING AND COMFORTING MEAL WHEN SERVED WITH RICE OR INDIAN BREADS AND ANY DRY-SPICED DISH, PARTICULARLY A CAULIFLOWER OR POTATO DISH.

SERVES FOUR TO SIX

INGREDIENTS
  40g/1½oz/3 tbsp butter or ghee
  1 onion, chopped
  2 green chillies, seeded and chopped
  15ml/1 tbsp chopped fresh
    root ginger
  225g/8oz/1 cup yellow or red lentils
  900ml/1½ pints/3¾ cups water
  45ml/3 tbsp roasted garlic purée
  5ml/1 tsp ground cumin
  5ml/1 tsp ground coriander
  200g/7oz tomatoes, peeled and diced
  a little lemon juice
  salt and ground black pepper
  30–45ml/3–4 tbsp coriander sprigs
    and fried onion and garlic slices,
    to garnish
For the whole spice mix
  30ml/2 tbsp peanut oil
  4–5 shallots, sliced
  2 garlic cloves, thinly sliced
  15g/½oz/1 tbsp butter or ghee
  5ml/1 tsp cumin seeds
  5ml/1 tsp mustard seeds
  3–4 small dried red chillies
  8–10 fresh curry leaves

1 Melt the butter or ghee in a large saucepan and cook the onion, chillies and ginger for 10 minutes, until golden.

2 Stir in the lentils and water, then bring to the boil, then reduce the heat and part-cover the pan. Simmer, stirring occasionally, for 50–60 minutes, until similar to a very thick soup.

3 Stir in the roasted garlic purée, cumin and ground coriander, then season with salt and pepper to taste. Cook for a further 10–15 minutes, uncovered, stirring frequently.

4 Stir in the tomatoes and then adjust the seasoning, adding a little lemon juice to taste.

5 To make the whole spice mix, heat the oil in a small, heavy-based pan. Add the shallots and fry over a medium heat, stirring occasionally, until crisp and browned. Add the garlic and cook, stirring frequently, until the garlic colours slightly. Use a draining spoon to remove the shallot mixture from the pan and set aside.

6 Melt the butter or ghee in the same pan. Add the cumin and mustard seeds and fry until the mustard seeds pop. Stir in the chillies, curry leaves and the shallot mixture, then immediately swirl the mixture into the cooked dhal. Garnish with coriander, onions and garlic and serve.

SAFFRON RICE WITH ONION AND CARDAMOM

THIS DELIGHTFULLY FRAGRANT, BUTTERY PILAFF IS WONDERFUL WITH BOTH INDIAN AND MIDDLE-EASTERN DISHES, ESPECIALLY ONES FEATURING SEAFOOD, CHICKEN OR LAMB.

SERVES FOUR

INGREDIENTS

350g/12oz/generous 1½ cups
  basmati rice
good pinch of saffron strands
  (about 15 strands)
25g/1oz/2 tbsp butter
1 onion, finely chopped
6 green cardamom pods,
  lightly crushed
5ml/1 tsp salt
2–3 fresh bay leaves
600ml/1 pint/2½ cups well-flavoured
  chicken or vegetable stock
  or water

1 Put the rice into a sieve and rinse well under cold running water. Tip it into a bowl, add cold water to cover and set aside to soak for 30–40 minutes. Drain in the sieve.

2 Toast the saffron strands in a dry pan over a low heat for 1–2 minutes, then place in a small bowl and add 30ml/2 tbsp warm water. Leave to soak for 10–15 minutes.

3 Melt the butter in a heavy saucepan, then cook the onion with the cardamoms very gently for 8–10 minutes, until soft and buttery yellow.

4 Add the drained rice and stir to coat the grains. Add the salt and bay leaves, followed by the stock and saffron with its liquid. Bring to the boil, stir, then reduce the heat to very low and cover tightly. Cook for 10–12 minutes, until the rice has absorbed all the liquid.

5 Lay a clean, folded dish towel over the pan under the lid and press on the lid to wedge it firmly in place. Leave to stand for 10–15 minutes.

6 Fluff up the grains of rice with a fork. Turn into a warmed serving dish and serve immediately.

COOK'S TIP
After boiling, when all the liquid has been absorbed, basmati rice is set aside to finish cooking in its own heat and become tender. Wedging a folded dish towel under the pan lid ensures the heat is not lost and the steam is absorbed.

GARLIC CHIVE RICE WITH MUSHROOMS

RICE IS READILY INFUSED WITH THE PUNGENT AROMA AND FLAVOUR OF GARLIC CHIVES, CREATING A DISH WITH AN EXCELLENT FLAVOUR. SERVE WITH VEGETARIAN DISHES, FISH OR CHICKEN.

3 Add the rice to the onions and fry over a low heat, stirring frequently, for 4–5 minutes. Pour in the stock mixture, then stir in 5ml/1 tsp salt and a good grinding of black pepper. Bring to the boil, stir and reduce the heat to very low. Cover tightly and cook for 15–20 minutes, until the rice has absorbed all the liquid.

4 Lay a clean, folded dish towel over the pan under the lid and press on the lid to wedge it firmly in place. Leave to stand for 10 minutes, allowing the towel to absorb the steam while the rice becomes completely tender.

5 Meanwhile, heat the remaining oil in a frying pan and cook the mushrooms for 5–6 minutes, until tender and browned. Add the remaining chives and cook for another 1–2 minutes.

6 Stir the mushrooms and chopped coriander leaves into the rice. Adjust the seasoning, transfer to a warmed serving dish and serve immediately, scattered with the cashew nuts.

SERVES FOUR

INGREDIENTS

350g/12oz/generous 1½ cups
   long grain rice
60ml/4 tbsp groundnut oil
1 small onion, finely chopped
2 green chillies, seeded and
   finely chopped
25g/1oz garlic chives, chopped
15g/½oz fresh coriander
600ml/1 pint/2½ cups vegetable or
   mushroom stock
5ml/1 tsp salt
250g/9oz mixed mushrooms,
   thickly sliced
50g/2oz cashew nuts, fried in 15ml/
   1 tbsp oil until golden brown
ground black pepper

1 Wash and drain the rice. Heat half the oil in a saucepan and cook the onion and chillies over a gentle heat, stirring occasionally, for 10–12 minutes, until soft but not browned.

2 Set half the garlic chives aside. Cut the stalks off the coriander and set the leaves aside. Purée the remaining chives and the coriander stalks with the stock in a blender or food processor.

COOK'S TIP

Wild mushrooms are often expensive, but they do have distinctive flavours. Mixing them with cultivated mushrooms is an economical way of using them. Look for oyster mushrooms, ceps, chanterelles, morels, and horse mushrooms.

ONION, PARMESAN AND OLIVE BREAD

THIS BREAD IS GOOD FOR SANDWICHES OR CUT INTO THICK SLICES AND DIPPED IN OLIVE OIL THEN EATEN AS A SNACK. IT IS REALLY EXCELLENT WHEN TOASTED – FOR EXAMPLE, MAKING A WONDERFUL BASE FOR BRUSCHETTA OR DELICIOUS CROÛTONS FOR TOSSING INTO SALAD.

MAKES ONE LARGE OR TWO SMALL LOAVES

INGREDIENTS
  350g/12oz/3 cups unbleached
    strong plain flour, plus a little extra
  115g/4oz/1 cup yellow cornmeal,
    plus a little extra
  rounded 5ml/1 tsp salt
  15g/½oz fresh yeast or 10ml/2 tsp
    active dried yeast
  5ml/1 tsp muscovado sugar
  270ml/9fl oz/generous 1 cup
    warm water
  5ml/1 tsp chopped fresh thyme
  30ml/2 tbsp olive oil, plus a little
    extra for greasing
  1 onion, finely chopped
  75g/3oz/1 cup freshly grated
    Parmesan cheese
  90g/3½oz/scant 1 cup stoned
    black olives, halved

1 Mix the flour, cornmeal and salt in a warmed bowl. If using fresh yeast, cream it with the sugar and gradually stir in 120ml/4fl oz/½ cup of the warm water. If using dried yeast, stir the sugar into the water and then sprinkle the dried yeast over the surface. Leave in a warm place for 10 minutes, until frothy.

2 Make a well in the centre of the dry ingredients and pour in the yeast liquid and a further 150ml/¼ pint/⅔ cup of the remaining warm water.

3 Add the chopped fresh thyme and 15ml/1 tbsp of the olive oil and mix thoroughly with a wooden spoon, gradually drawing in the dry ingredients until they are fully incorporated. Add a dash more warm water, if necessary, to make a soft, but not sticky, dough.

4 Knead the dough on a lightly floured work surface for 5 minutes, until smooth and elastic. Place in a clean, lightly oiled bowl and place in a polythene bag or cover with oiled clear film. Set aside to rise in a warm, not hot place for 1–2 hours or until well risen.

5 Meanwhile, heat the remaining olive oil in a heavy-based frying pan. Add the onion and cook over fairly gentle heat, stirring occasionally, for 8 minutes, until softened, but not at all browned. Set aside to cool.

6 Brush a baking sheet with olive oil. Turn out the dough on to a floured work surface. Gently knead in the onions, followed by the Parmesan and olives.

7 Shape the dough into one or two rough oval loaves. Sprinkle a little cornmeal on the work surface and roll the bread in it, then place on the prepared baking sheet. Make several slits across the top.

8 Slip the baking sheet into the polythene bag or cover with oiled clear film and leave to rise in a warm place for about 1 hour, or until well risen. Preheat the oven to 200°C/400°F/Gas 6. Bake for 30–35 minutes, or until the bread sounds hollow when tapped on the base. Cool on a wire rack.

VARIATION
Alternatively, shape the dough into a loaf, roll in cornmeal and place in an oiled loaf tin. Leave to rise well above the rim of the tin, as in step 8. Bake for 35–40 minutes, or until the loaf sounds hollow when tapped.

GARLIC AND HERB BREAD

EXCELLENT WITH SOUPS OR VEGETABLE FIRST COURSES, GARLIC BREAD IS ALSO IRRESISTIBLE JUST ON ITS OWN. THE BETTER THE BREAD, THE BETTER THE FINAL, GARLICKY VERSION WILL BE.

SERVES THREE TO FOUR

INGREDIENTS
1 baguette or bloomer loaf
For the garlic and herb butter
115g/4oz/½ cup unsalted
butter, softened
5–6 large garlic cloves, finely
chopped or crushed
30–45ml/2–3 tbsp chopped fresh
herbs (such as parsley, chervil and
a little tarragon)
15ml/1 tbsp snipped fresh chives
sea salt and ground black pepper

1 Preheat the oven to 200°C/400°F/
Gas 6. Make the garlic and herb butter
by beating the butter with the garlic,
herbs, chives and seasoning.

2 Cut the bread into 1cm/½in thick
diagonal slices, but leave them attached
at the base so that the loaf stays intact.

3 Spread the butter between the slices,
being careful not to detach them, and
spread any remaining butter over the
top of the loaf.

4 Wrap the loaf in foil and bake for
20–25 minutes, until the garlic and
herb butter is melted and the crust is
crisp. Cut into slices to serve.

VARIATIONS
• Use 105ml/7 tbsp extra virgin olive oil
instead of butter.
• Flavour the butter with garlic, chopped
fresh chilli, grated lime rind and
chopped fresh coriander.

• Add chopped, stoned black olives or
sun-dried tomatoes to the butter with a
little grated lemon rind.
• To make bruschetta, take thick slices
of good country bread. Grill on a ridged
cast-iron grill pan, then rub with garlic
and drizzle with extra virgin olive oil. For
a stronger garlic taste, grill one side of
the bread, then spread some finely
chopped garlic on the untoasted side,
drizzle oil over, then toast until golden.

SPRING ONION, CHIVE AND RICOTTA BREAD

RICOTTA CHEESE AND CHIVES MAKE A MOIST, WELL-FLAVOURED LOAF THAT IS EXCELLENT FOR SANDWICHES. SHAPE THE DOUGH INTO ROLLS, LOAVES, A COTTAGE LOAF, OR EVEN A PLAIT.

MAKES ONE LOAF OR SIXTEEN ROLLS

INGREDIENTS
- 15g/½oz fresh yeast or 10ml/2 tsp active dried yeast
- 5ml/1 tsp caster sugar
- 270ml/9fl oz/generous 1 cup lukewarm water
- 450g/1lb unbleached strong white flour, plus a little extra
- 7.5ml/1½ tsp salt
- 1 large egg, beaten
- 115g/4oz/½ cup ricotta cheese
- 1 bunch spring onions, thinly sliced
- 30ml/2 tbsp extra virgin olive oil
- 45ml/3 tbsp snipped fresh chives
- 15ml/1 tbsp milk
- 10ml/2 tsp poppy seeds (optional)
- coarse sea salt

1 Cream the fresh yeast with the sugar and gradually stir in 120ml/4fl oz/½ cup of the water. If using dried yeast, stir the sugar into the water, then sprinkle it over the surface. Leave in a warm place for 10 minutes.

2 Sift the flour and salt into a warmed bowl. Make a well in the centre and pour in the yeast liquid and the remaining water. Save a little beaten egg, then put the rest in the bowl. Add the ricotta and mix to form a dough, adding a little more flour if the mixture is very sticky.

3 Knead the dough on a floured work surface until smooth and elastic. Set aside in a greased bowl, inside a polythene bag, in a warm place for 1–2 hours, until doubled in size.

4 Meanwhile, cook the spring onions in the oil for 3–4 minutes, until soft but not browned. Set aside to cool.

5 Punch down the risen dough and knead in the onions, with their oil from cooking, and the chives. Shape the dough into rolls, a large or small loaf, cottage loaf, or a plait.

6 Grease a baking sheet or loaf tin and place the rolls or bread on it. Cover with greased polythene or oiled clear film and leave in a warm place to rise for about 1 hour. Preheat the oven to 200°C/400°F/Gas 6.

7 Beat the milk into the reserved beaten egg and use to glaze the rolls or loaf. Sprinkle with poppy seeds, if using, and a little coarse sea salt, then bake rolls for about 15 minutes or a loaf for 30–40 minutes or until golden and well risen. When tapped firmly on the base, the bread should feel and sound firm. Cool on a wire rack

COOK'S TIP
To make a plait, divide the dough into three equal sausage-shaped pieces about 40cm/16in long. Press them together at one end and then plait, pressing the ends together when completed.

RED ONION ᴬᴺᴰ ROSEMARY FOCACCIA

THIS BREAD IS RICH IN OLIVE OIL AND IT HAS AN AROMATIC TOPPING OF RED ONION, FRESH ROSEMARY (DRIED ROSEMARY IS NOT SUITABLE) AND CRUNCHY SEA SALT. IT IS GOOD WITH TOMATO OR PEPPER SALADS, OR AS AN ACCOMPANIMENT TO ALL KINDS OF MEDITERRANEAN DISHES.

SERVES FOUR TO FIVE

450g/1lb/4 cups unbleached strong
  plain flour, plus a little extra
5ml/1 tsp salt
10g/¼oz fresh yeast or generous
  5ml/1 tsp active dried yeast
2.5ml/½ tsp light muscovado sugar
250ml/8fl oz/1 cup lukewarm water
60ml/4 tbsp extra virgin olive oil
5ml/1 tsp very finely chopped fresh
  rosemary, plus 6–8 small sprigs
1 small red onion, halved and
  thinly sliced
coarse sea salt

1 Sift the flour and salt into a bowl. Cream the fresh yeast with the sugar and slowly stir in half the water. If using dried yeast, stir the sugar into the water and then sprinkle the dried yeast over the surface. Set aside in a warm, not hot, place for 10 minutes, until frothy.

2 Add the yeast, the remaining water, 15ml/1 tbsp of the oil and the chopped rosemary to the flour. Mix to form a dough, then gather it into a ball and knead on a floured work surface for about 5 minutes, until smooth and elastic. You may need a little extra flour if the dough is very sticky.

3 Place the dough in a lightly oiled bowl, slip it into a polythene bag or cover with oiled clear film and leave to rise. Leave it all day in a cool place, overnight in the fridge, or for 1–2 hours in a warm, but not hot, place.

4 Lightly oil a baking sheet. Knead the dough to form a flat loaf about 30cm/12in round or square. Place on the baking sheet, cover with greased polythene or clear film and leave to rise in a warm place for 40–60 minutes.

5 Preheat the oven to 220°C/425°F/Gas 7. Toss the onion in 15ml/1 tbsp of the oil and scatter over the loaf with the rosemary sprigs.

6 Drizzle the remaining oil over the loaf, then sprinkle with sea salt. Bake the focaccia for 15 minutes, then reduce the heat to 190°C/375°F/Gas 5 and cook for a further 10–15 minutes. Cool on a wire rack.

VARIATION

To make garlic and thyme focaccia, peel 1–2 heads of garlic but leave the cloves whole. Fry gently in 15–30ml/1–2 tbsp olive oil until lightly coloured, then cook in the oven at 180°C/350°F/Gas 4 for about 30 minutes, until soft, browned, but not at all burned. Stir once or twice during cooking, then leave to cool. When shaping the focaccia, gently knead in the caramelized garlic with about 5ml/1 tsp chopped fresh thyme. Omit the onion topping, but brush with more olive oil and scatter with fresh thyme sprigs and coarse sea salt. Bake as above.

CARAMELIZED ONION AND WALNUT SCONES

THESE SCONES ARE VERY GOOD BUTTERED AND SERVED WITH MATURE CHEDDAR OR LANCASHIRE CHEESE. THEY ARE ALSO EXCELLENT WITH SOUP OR A ROBUST VEGETABLE STEW. MAKE SMALL SCONES TO USE AS A BASE FOR COCKTAIL SAVOURIES, SERVED TOPPED WITH A LITTLE SOFT GOAT'S CHEESE.

4 Add the cooked onion, walnuts and fresh thyme, then bind to make a soft, but not sticky, dough with the buttermilk or smetana.

5 Roll or pat out the mixture to just over 1cm/½in thick. Stamp out scones using a 5–6cm/2–2½in round cutter.

MAKES TEN TO TWELVE

90g/3½oz/7 tbsp butter
15ml/1 tbsp olive oil
1 Spanish onion, chopped
2.5ml/½ tsp cumin seeds, lightly crushed, plus a few extra
200g/7oz/1¾ cups self-raising flour
5ml/1 tsp baking powder
25g/1oz/¼ cup oatmeal
5ml/1 tsp light muscovado sugar
90g/3½oz/scant 1 cup chopped walnuts
5ml/1 tsp chopped fresh thyme
120–150ml/4–5fl oz/½–⅔ cup buttermilk or smetana
a little milk
salt and ground black pepper
coarse sea salt

1 Melt 15g/½oz/1 tbsp of the butter with the oil in a small saucepan and cook the onion gently, covered, for 10–12 minutes, until soft but not browned. Uncover, then continue to cook gently until it begins to brown.

2 Add the crushed cumin seeds and increase the temperature slightly. Cook, stirring occasionally, until the onion browns and begins to caramelize around the edges. Cool. Preheat the oven to 200°C/400°F/Gas 6.

3 Sift the flour, baking powder and oatmeal into a large bowl and add 2.5ml/½tsp salt, a generous grinding of black pepper and the muscovado sugar. Add the remaining butter and rub in with the fingertips until the mixture resembles breadcrumbs.

6 Place the scones on a floured baking tray, glaze with milk and scatter with a little salt and a few extra cumin seeds. Bake for 12–15 minutes, until well-risen and golden brown. Cool for a few minutes on a wire rack and serve warm.

So many sauces, from the classic bases of haute cuisine, to the lively flavoured salsas of modern cooking rely on the alliums. Shallots are wonderful in sauces and pickles, adding a strength of flavour without the bulk of an onion. Strong-flavoured onions, shallots and garlic are favourites for pickling across the globe, from English Pickled Onions, to Hot Thai Pickled Shallots. They are also essential in many sauces and pastes — Italian Salsa Verde, Indonesian Peanut Sauce or Indian spice pastes.

Sauces, Pickles and Pastes

OLD ENGLISH BREAD SAUCE

A CLASSIC SAUCE FOR ROAST GAME, CHICKEN OR TURKEY, BREAD SAUCE IS NOW RESERVED ALMOST EXCLUSIVELY TO ACCOMPANY THE CHRISTMAS TURKEY. HOWEVER, IT IS ALSO GOOD WITH SAUSAGES.

SERVES SIX TO EIGHT

INGREDIENTS

475ml/16fl oz/2 cups milk
1 small onion, stuck with 4 cloves
1 celery stick, chopped
1 fresh bay leaf, torn in half
6 allspice berries
1 blade of mace
90g/3½oz/1¾ cups day-old
 breadcrumbs, from a good-quality
 white loaf
freshly grated nutmeg
30ml/2 tbsp double cream
15g/½oz/1 tbsp butter
salt and ground black pepper

1 Place the milk, onion, celery, bay leaf, allspice and mace in a saucepan and bring to the boil. Take off the heat, half-cover, and set aside for 30–60 minutes.

2 Strain the milk and place in a blender or food processor. Remove and discard the cloves from the onion and add the onion to the milk with the celery. Process until smooth, then strain the liquid back into the clean saucepan.

3 Bring back to the boil and stir in the breadcrumbs. Simmer gently, whisking with a small whisk, until the sauce thickens and becomes smooth. Add a little extra milk if the sauce is too thick.

4 Season to taste with salt, pepper and freshly grated nutmeg. Just before serving, whisk in the cream and butter. Serve warm rather than piping hot.

VARIATION
Muhammara, Middle-Eastern bread sauce with peppers and garlic This sauce is good with grilled fish or chicken or served as a dip with crudités. Crush 2–3 cloves of garlic and place in a food processor or blender with 3 large red peppers, grilled, skinned and seeded; 1 hot red chilli, grilled, skinned and seeded; 90g/3½oz/ scant 1 cup walnuts; and 50g/2oz bread, crusts removed. Process to make a paste, then blend in the juice of half a lemon and 2.5ml/½ tsp each of salt, pepper and muscovado sugar. With the motor running, gradually trickle in about 150ml/5fl oz/ generous ⅔ cup extra virgin olive oil. Season with more lemon juice, salt, sugar and a little toasted ground cumin, then stir in 30ml/2 tbsp chopped parsley. If necessary, thin the sauce with more oil or a little warm water or stock.

ONION GRAVY

THIS MAKES A DELICIOUS, DARK ONION SAUCE TO GO WITH SAUSAGES, LIVER, PORK CHOPS OR TOAD IN THE HOLE. IT IS ALSO GOOD WITH A MOUND OF CREAMY MASHED POTATOES.

2 Add the sugar, increase the heat slightly and cook for another 20–30 minutes, until the onions are dark brown.

3 Stir in the flour, cook for a few minutes, stirring all the time, then gradually stir in 400ml/14fl oz/1⅔ cups of the hot stock. Simmer, stirring, to make a thickened gravy, adding a little more stock if the gravy is too thick.

4 Add the thyme, season with a little salt and pepper, then cook very slowly, stirring frequently, for 10–15 minutes.

5 Stir in the soy sauce, Worcestershire sauce, if using, and more seasoning, if necessary. Add a little more stock if the gravy is too thick, remove the thyme, and serve immediately.

SERVES FOUR

INGREDIENTS
40g/1½oz/3 tbsp butter or
   beef dripping
450g/1lb onions, halved and
   thinly sliced
2.5ml/½ tsp brown sugar
45ml/3 tbsp plain flour
400–500ml/14–17fl oz/1⅔–2 cups
   hot beef or vegetable stock
1 fresh thyme sprig
10ml/2 tsp dark soy sauce
5ml/1 tsp Worcestershire
   sauce (optional)
salt and ground black pepper

1 Melt the butter or dripping over a gentle heat. Add the onions and fry, stirring occasionally, for 15–20 minutes, until soft and beginning to brown.

VARIATIONS
• The onions can be browned in the oven. This is best done in vegetable oil rather than butter or dripping. Place the sliced onions in an ovenproof dish and toss with 45ml/3 tbsp oil. Cook at 190°C/375°F/Gas 5 for 20 minutes, stirring once or twice. Stir in the sugar, then cook at 220°C/425°F/Gas 7 for a further 15–25 minutes, until the onions are dark brown and caramelized.
• Part of the beef or vegetable stock may be replaced with red wine or dark beer. You may need to add a little extra sugar to balance the acidity of the wine or beer.

SAUCE SOUBISE

THIS IS THE CLASSIC FRENCH WHITE ONION SAUCE. IT IS EXCELLENT WITH VEAL, CHICKEN, PORK OR LAMB. IT IS ALSO GOOD POURED OVER SLICED HARD-BOILED EGGS OR POACHED EGGS AND THEN GRATINÉED UNDER A HOT GRILL. IT CAN BE LEFT CHUNKY WITH ONION, OR PURÉED.

SERVES FOUR

INGREDIENTS

40g/1½oz/3 tbsp butter
350g/12oz onions, chopped
25g/1oz/¼ cup plain flour
500ml/17fl oz/generous 2 cups hot
  milk or stock, or a mixture of both
1 fresh bay leaf
a few parsley stalks
120ml/4fl oz/½ cup double cream
freshly grated nutmeg
salt and ground black pepper

1 Melt the butter in a large heavy-based saucepan. Add the onions and fry gently over a low heat, stirring occasionally, for 10–12 minutes, until they are soft and golden yellow, but not at all browned.

2 Stir in the flour and cook gently, stirring constantly, for 2–3 minutes.

3 Gradually stir in the hot milk, stock, or milk and stock mixture and bring to the boil. Add the bay leaf and parsley. Part-cover the pan and cook very gently, stirring frequently, for 15–20 minutes.

4 Remove and discard the bay leaf and parsley, then process the sauce in a blender or food processor if you want a smooth sauce.

5 Stir in the cream and reheat the sauce gently, then season to taste with salt and pepper. Add a little more milk or stock if the sauce is very thick. Season with grated nutmeg to taste just before serving.

VARIATIONS
• For leek sauce, substitute leeks for onions, using the white part of the leeks. Cook for just 4–5 minutes in the butter before adding the flour. Omit the nutmeg and stir in 15ml/1 tbsp Dijon mustard just before serving.
• Season the sauce with about 30ml/ 2 tbsp Dijon mustard at the end of cooking to make *sauce Robert* – a classic French sauce traditionally served with pork chops. It also goes very well with ham or rabbit.

COOK'S TIP
The sauce should be cooked for this length of time to cook out the raw flour flavour. A heat diffuser mat is very useful to keep the heat as low as possible when cooking delicate foods on the hob.

OLIVE OIL, TOMATO AND HERB SAUCE WITH GARLIC AND SHALLOT

THIS SAUCE IS BASED ON SAUCE VIERGE, A CLASSIC DRESSING USED IN NOUVELLE CUISINE, AND INVENTED BY FRENCH CHEF MICHEL GUÉRARD. IT IS DELICIOUS SERVED WARM, RATHER THAN HOT, WITH GRILLED OR POACHED FISH. SERVE GOOD BREAD OR BOILED NEW POTATOES TO MOP UP THE OIL.

SERVES FOUR TO SIX

INGREDIENTS

225g/8oz tomatoes
15ml/1 tbsp finely chopped shallot
2 garlic cloves, finely sliced
  or chopped
120ml/4fl oz/½ cup extra virgin
  olive oil
about 15ml/1 tbsp lemon juice
caster sugar
15ml/1 tbsp chopped fresh chervil
15ml/1 tbsp snipped fresh chives
30ml/2 tbsp torn fresh basil leaves
salt and ground black pepper

VARIATION
Use diced red pepper in place of the tomatoes. Grill, peel, seed and finely dice the pepper. Use balsamic vinegar instead of lemon juice and red onion or spring onion instead of shallot. Omit the chervil and use all basil or a mixture of marjoram and basil. A pinch of ground toasted cumin seeds is good in this.

1 Peel and seed the tomatoes, then cut them into fine dice.

2 Place the shallot, garlic and oil in a small saucepan over a very gentle heat and allow to infuse for a few minutes. The ingredients should warm through, but definitely not fry or cook.

COOK'S TIP
It is essential to the flavour of this sauce that you use the best quality extra virgin olive oil.

3 Whisk in 30ml/2 tbsp cold water and 10ml/2 tsp lemon juice. Remove from the heat and stir in the tomatoes. Add a pinch of salt, pepper and caster sugar, then whisk in the chervil and chives.

4 Leave the sauce to stand for about 10–15 minutes. Adjust the seasoning, adding more lemon juice, salt and black pepper as required.

5 Reheat gently until just warm, then stir in the basil just before serving.

WALNUT AND GARLIC SAUCE

THIS SAUCE, SEVERAL VERSIONS OF WHICH CAN BE FOUND AROUND THE MEDITERRANEAN, IS EXCELLENT WITH ROAST OR POACHED CHICKEN OR STEAMED CAULIFLOWER OR POTATOES.

SERVES FOUR

INGREDIENTS

2 × 1cm/½in slices good white bread,
  crusts removed
60ml/4 tbsp milk
150g/5oz/1¼ cups shelled walnuts
4 garlic cloves, chopped
120ml/4fl oz/½ cup mild olive oil
15–30ml/1–2 tbsp walnut oil (optional)
juice of 1 lemon
salt and ground black pepper
walnut or olive oil, for drizzling
paprika, for dusting (optional)

VARIATION

For an Italian *salsa di noci* for pasta,
process 90g/3½oz/scant 1 cup walnuts
with 2 garlic cloves and 15g/½oz flat leaf
parsley. Blend in 1 slice white bread
(crusts removed), soaked in milk, and
120ml/4fl oz/½ cup fruity olive oil as
above. Season with salt, pepper and
lemon juice. Thin with more milk or
single cream if very thick.

1 Soak the slices of white bread in the
milk for about 5 minutes, then process
with the walnuts and chopped garlic in
a food processor or blender, to make a
rough paste.

2 Gradually add the olive oil to the
paste with the motor still running, until
the mixture forms a smooth thick sauce.
Blend in the walnut oil, if using.

3 Scoop the sauce into a bowl and
squeeze in lemon juice to taste, season
with salt and pepper and beat well.

4 Transfer to a serving bowl, drizzle
over a little more walnut or olive oil,
then dust lightly with paprika, if using.

COOK'S TIP

Once opened, walnut oil has a fairly
short shelf life. Buy it in small bottles
and keep it in a cool, dark place. It is
delicious in many salad dressings.

SALSA VERDE

THIS SIMPLE ITALIAN SAUCE IS A PURÉE OF FRESH HERBS WITH OLIVE OIL AND FLAVOURINGS. IT IS GOOD WITH POACHED OR ROAST BEEF AND CHICKEN, GRILLED STEAK OR GRILLED POLENTA.

SERVES FOUR

INGREDIENTS

1–2 garlic cloves, finely chopped
25g/1oz flat leaf parsley leaves
15g/½oz fresh basil, mint or
  coriander or a mixture of herbs
15ml/1 tbsp snipped chives
15ml/1 tbsp salted capers, rinsed
5 anchovy fillets in olive oil, drained
  and rinsed
10ml/2 tsp French mustard
  (tarragon or *fines herbes* mustard
  are both good)
120ml/4fl oz/½ cup extra virgin
  olive oil
a little grated lemon rind and
  juice (optional)
ground black pepper

1 Process the garlic, parsley, basil,
mint or coriander, chives, capers,
anchovies, mustard and 15ml/1 tbsp of
the oil in a blender or food processor.

2 Gradually add the remaining oil in a
thin stream with the motor running.

3 Transfer to a bowl and adjust the
seasoning to taste – there should be
enough salt from the capers and
anchovies. Add a little lemon juice and
rind if you like (especially if serving with
fish). Serve immediately.

VARIATIONS

• Whisk in 30–45ml/2–3 tbsp crème
fraîche to make a mild sauce that goes
well with grilled polenta, cauliflower
and potatoes.
• Substitute fresh chervil, tarragon, dill
or fennel – or a mixture of aniseed-
flavoured herbs – for the basil, mint or
coriander to make a sauce that goes
particularly well with poached or baked
fish, such as hake or sea bass. It is also
good with prawns and langoustines.

YOGURT WITH GARLIC, CUCUMBER AND MINT

VERSIONS OF THIS COOL, MINTY RELISH ARE FOUND IN GREECE (TZATZIKI), TURKEY (CACIK) AND THROUGHOUT THE MIDDLE EAST. IN INDIA, THE EQUIVALENT IS CALLED RAITA.

SERVES FOUR

INGREDIENTS

15cm/6in piece cucumber
5ml/1 tsp sea salt
300ml/½ pint/1¼ cups Greek yogurt
3–4 garlic cloves, crushed
15ml/1 tbsp dried mint or 45ml/
 3 tbsp chopped fresh mint
ground black pepper
chopped fresh mint and/or ground
 toasted cumin seeds, to garnish

1 Slice, chop or grate the cucumber, place in a sieve and sprinkle with half the salt. Leave on a deep plate for 30 minutes to drip.

2 Rinse the cucumber in cold water, pat dry and mix with the yogurt, garlic and mint. Season with salt and pepper. Leave for 30 minutes, then stir and sprinkle with fresh mint and/or toasted cumin to garnish.

VARIATION

To make a yogurt and garlic salad dressing, omit the cucumber and use 150ml/¼ pint/⅔ cup Greek yogurt instead. Beat in 1 very finely chopped garlic clove, 5ml/1 tsp French mustard, salt and freshly ground black pepper to taste and a pinch of sugar. Finally, beat in 15–30ml/1–2 tbsp extra virgin olive oil and 15–30ml/1–2 tbsp chopped fresh herbs, such as mint, tarragon and chives, to taste.

GARLIC MAYONNAISE

THIS CAN BE AS EASY TO MAKE AS STIRRING CRUSHED GARLIC INTO GOOD QUALITY, READY-MADE MAYONNAISE. BUT A PROPER HOME-MADE MAYONNAISE, WITH GARLIC STIRRED IN, REALLY REVEALS JUST HOW GOOD THIS DELICIOUS DRESSING CAN BE.

SERVES FOUR TO SIX

INGREDIENTS
  2 large egg yolks
  pinch of dried mustard
  up to 300ml/½ pint/1¼ cups mild
    olive oil or olive oil and grapeseed
    oil, mixed
  15–30ml/1–2 tbsp lemon juice,
    white wine vinegar or warm water
  2–4 garlic cloves
  salt and ground black pepper

1 Make sure the egg yolks and oil have come to room temperature before you start. Place the yolks in a bowl with the mustard and a pinch of salt, and whisk.

2 Gradually whisk in the oil, one drop at a time. When almost half the oil has been fully incorporated, add it in a steady stream.

3 As the mayonnaise starts to thicken, thin it down with a few drops of lemon juice or vinegar, or a few teaspoons of warm water.

4 When the mayonnaise is as thick as soft butter, stop adding oil. Season the mayonnaise to taste and add more lemon juice or vinegar as required.

WATCHPOINT
The very young, the elderly, pregnant women and those in ill-health or with a compromised immune system are advised against consuming raw eggs or dishes containing raw eggs.

5 Crush the garlic with the blade of a knife and stir it into the mayonnaise. For a slightly milder flavour, blanch the garlic twice in plenty of boiling water, then purée the cloves before beating them into the mayonnaise.

VARIATIONS
• To make Provençal aioli, crush 3–5 garlic cloves with a pinch of salt in a bowl, then whisk in the egg yolks. Omit the mustard but continue as above, using all olive oil.
• For spicy garlic mayonnaise, omit the mustard and stir in 2.5ml/½ tsp harissa or red chilli paste and 5ml/1 tsp sun-dried tomato paste with the garlic.
• Use roasted garlic purée or puréed smoked garlic to create a different flavour.
• Beat in about 15g/½oz mixed fresh herbs such as tarragon, parsley, chervil and chives. Blanch the herbs in boiling water for 20–30 seconds, then drain and pat them dry on kitchen paper before finely chopping them.

PEANUT SAUCE

THIS IS BASED ON THE FAMOUS INDONESIAN SAUCE THAT ACCOMPANIES GRILLED PORK, CHICKEN OR SEAFOOD SATAY. SLIGHTLY THINNED DOWN WITH WATER, IT IS ALSO USED TO DRESS GADO-GADO, A WONDERFUL SALAD OF MIXED RAW OR COOKED VEGETABLES AND FRUIT.

SERVES FOUR TO SIX

INGREDIENTS
30ml/2 tbsp peanut oil
75g/3oz/¾ cup unsalted
  peanuts, blanched
2 shallots, chopped
2 garlic cloves, chopped
15ml/1 tbsp chopped fresh
  root ginger
1–2 green chillies, seeded and
  thinly sliced
5ml/1 tsp ground coriander
1 lemon grass stalk, tender base
  only, chopped
5–10ml/1–2 tsp light
  muscovado sugar
15ml/1 tbsp dark soy sauce
105–120ml/3–4 fl oz/scant ½ cup
  canned coconut milk
15–30ml/1–2 tbsp Thai fish sauce
  (*nam pla*)
15–30ml/1–2 tbsp tamarind purée
lime juice
salt and ground black pepper

3 Transfer the spice mixture to a food processor or blender and add the peanuts, lemon grass, 5ml/1 tsp of the sugar, the soy sauce and 105ml/3fl oz of coconut milk and the fish sauce. Blend to form a fairly smooth sauce.

4 Taste and add more fish sauce, tamarind purée, seasoning, lime juice and/or more sugar to taste.

COOK'S TIP
To make tamarind purée, soak 25g/1oz tamarind pulp in 120ml/4fl oz/½ cup boiling water in a non-metallic bowl for about 30 minutes, mashing the pulp occasionally with a fork. Then press the pulp through a stainless steel sieve. This purée will keep for several days in a covered container in the fridge.

5 Stir in the extra coconut milk and a little water if the sauce seems very thick, but do not let it become runny.

6 Serve cool or reheat the sauce gently, stirring all the time to prevent it from spitting. Garnish with the remaining sliced chilli before serving.

1 Heat the oil in a small, heavy-based frying pan and gently fry the peanuts, stirring frequently, until lightly browned. Use a draining spoon to remove the nuts from the pan and drain thoroughly on kitchen paper. Set aside to cool.

2 Add the shallots, garlic, ginger, most of the sliced chillies and the ground coriander to the pan and cook over a low heat, stirring occasionally, for 4–5 minutes, until the shallots are softened but not at all browned.

ROASTED PEPPER AND GARLIC DRESSING

THIS DRESSING IS DELICIOUS ON CHICKEN SALAD OR TOSSED WITH HOT OR COLD PASTA. IT IS ALSO GOOD WITH SALADS OF CHARGRILLED VEGETABLES, PARTICULARLY AUBERGINES AND ONIONS.

SERVES FOUR

INGREDIENTS

2 large heads of garlic, outer skin removed but left whole
3 fresh thyme sprigs or 2 fresh rosemary sprigs
150ml/¼ pint/⅔ cup olive oil
2 red peppers, halved and seeded
juice of ½ lemon or 15ml/1 tbsp balsamic vinegar
pinch of caster sugar (optional)
15ml/1 tbsp snipped fresh chives or basil
salt and ground black pepper

COOK'S TIP

If the dressing starts to separate after standing for any length of time, whisk in 15–30ml/1–2 tbsp crème fraîche. This is especially good on hot pasta.

1 Preheat the oven to 190°C/375°F/ Gas 5. Place the garlic on a piece of foil with the herb sprigs and add 15ml/ 1 tbsp of the oil. Close the foil around them and bake for 45–60 minutes, or until the garlic is soft when squeezed. Place the peppers, cut sides down, on a baking sheet and bake at the same time as the garlic, until their skin is blistered.

2 Place the peppers in a bowl, cover and set aside to steam for 10 minutes. Then peel off the skins and place the flesh in a blender or food processor.

3 Set the garlic aside until cool enough to handle, then squeeze the soft pulp out of the skins and into the blender or food processor with the peppers. Add any cooking juices from the foil, but discard the herb sprigs and papery garlic skin, then process the mixture until smooth.

4 Gradually blend in the remaining olive oil while the motor is still running. Gradually add lemon juice or balsamic vinegar to taste. Then season with salt and pepper to taste and add a pinch of sugar, if using. Stir in the snipped chives or basil and use immediately.

THAI GREEN CURRY PASTE

A FASHIONABLE, FAVOURITE INGREDIENT IN RECENT YEARS, THIS PASTE CAN BE MADE AUTHENTICALLY HOT, OR THE NUMBER OF CHILLIES CAN BE REDUCED FOR A MILDER TASTE.

MAKES ABOUT 120ML/4FL OZ/½ CUP

INGREDIENTS

3 Thai shallots, chopped
3–4 garlic cloves, chopped
4 hot green chillies, seeded, if liked, and chopped
2 lemon grass stalks, tender inner parts only, chopped
2.5cm/1in piece fresh galangal root or fresh root ginger, chopped
15g/½oz fresh coriander, with root if possible, chopped
2 kaffir lime leaves
5ml/1 tsp ground toasted coriander seeds
2.5ml/½ tsp ground toasted cumin seeds
15–25ml/3–5 tsp Thai fish sauce (*nam pla*)
15–30ml/1–2 tbsp peanut oil
pinch of light muscovado sugar
salt and ground black pepper

1 Put the shallots, garlic, chillies, lemon grass, galangal or ginger, fresh coriander, lime leaves, ground coriander and ground cumin in a small food processor or clean coffee grinder. Add fish sauce to taste. Briefly process.

2 Add sufficient peanut oil to make a paste. Season with salt, pepper and a pinch of sugar. This will keep for 2–3 days in an air-tight jar in the fridge.

VARIATION

To make red curry paste, process 3 thinly sliced shallots, 3–4 chopped garlic cloves, 6–10 seeded bird's eye chillies, 2 chopped lemon grass stalks, 15ml/ 1 tbsp chopped galangal or fresh root ginger, 30ml/2 tbsp chopped coriander root or stalk, 2 kaffir lime leaves and 5ml/1 tsp each toasted coriander seeds, cumin seeds, and paprika, 2.5ml/½ tsp black peppercorns and 5ml/1 tsp dried shrimp paste (*trassi*). Add the peanut oil and sugar as for the green curry paste. Season to taste with salt. For an authentically hot paste, use a small amount of hot chilli powder in place of the paprika.

Above right: (clockwise from top left) Roasted Red Pepper and Garlic Dressing, Garlic and Rosemary Vinegar, and Thai Green Curry Paste.

GARLIC <u>AND</u> ROSEMARY VINEGAR

VINEGAR SCENTED WITH GARLIC IS USEFUL FOR FLAVOURING SALAD DRESSINGS INSTEAD OF ADDING RAW GARLIC. IT IS ALSO GOOD FOR DEGLAZING THE PAN AFTER FRYING POULTRY OR MEAT.

MAKES 475ML/16FL OZ/2 CUPS

INGREDIENTS
  8–9 large garlic cloves, peeled
  2–3 fresh rosemary sprigs
  1 long fresh rosemary sprig or long
    thin wooden skewer (see method)
  475ml/16fl oz/2 cups good white
    wine vinegar

1 Blanch the garlic and rosemary in boiling water for 30–60 seconds. Drain and pat dry. Strip the leaves from the long rosemary sprig, if using, leaving a few leaves on top. Blanch the stripped sprig or wooden skewer.

2 Thread the garlic cloves on to the stripped sprig or skewer. (This is easier if you sharpen the end of the branch into a point.)

3 Place the threaded garlic and small rosemary sprigs into a sterilized wide-necked bottle of about 550ml/18fl oz/ 2½ cup capacity. Heat the vinegar to just below boiling, then carefully pour it into the bottle and cool before sealing. Allow to mature for 3–4 weeks before use.

VARIATION
You can use other strongly flavoured herbs instead of rosemary, threading the garlic cloves on a thin wooden skewer. Try marjoram, basil or tarragon, for example, or a mixture of fresh herbs. You could also use red wine vinegar instead of white for a variation in flavour.

QUICK-PICKLED RED ONIONS WITH DILL, CORIANDER AND JUNIPER

MILD RED ONIONS ARE BEST FOR THIS QUICK PICKLE, WHICH IS BASED ON A TRADITIONAL MEXICAN METHOD OF PICKLING ONIONS THAT WAS POPULARIZED BY AMERICAN COOK DEBORAH MADDISON.

MAKES ONE JAR

INGREDIENTS

500g/1¼lb red onions, thinly sliced
250ml/8fl oz/1 cup rice wine vinegar
  or tarragon vinegar
5ml/1 tsp salt
15ml/1 tbsp caster sugar
6 juniper berries, lightly crushed
30ml/2 tbsp chopped fresh dill
15ml/1 tbsp coriander seeds, bruised

VARIATION

To make quick Mexican red onions, blanch 1 large sliced red onion, then toss with 5ml/1 tsp sugar and 105ml/ 7 tbsp lime juice or rice wine vinegar and a little finely chopped red or green chilli. Leave for 2–3 hours before draining, then season and serve. These onions are very good drained, then tossed with thinly sliced salted cucumber.

1 Place the onions in a large bowl and pour over sufficient boiling water to cover. Immediately tip them into a colander, then set aside and allow to drain completely. Then return the onions to the dried bowl.

2 In another bowl, mix together the vinegar, salt, sugar, juniper berries and chopped dill.

3 Heat the coriander seeds in a dry frying pan until they give off their aroma. Add the the toasted seeds to the vinegar mixture and stir. Pour the spiced vinegar over the onions, toss to mix, then leave to stand at room temperature for 1 hour. The onions are now ready for use, and will keep in a covered jar in the fridge for up to 1 week. Drain to use.

ENGLISH PICKLED ONIONS

PICKLED ONIONS ARE A TRADITIONAL FEATURE OF PUB FOOD ACROSS THE BRITISH ISLES. THEY ARE
SERVED WITH COLD MEATS, PIES AND, MOST FAMOUSLY, BREAD AND CHEESE. THEY SHOULD BE MADE
WITH DARK MALT VINEGAR AND STORED FOR AT LEAST 6 WEEKS BEFORE EATING.

MAKES THREE TO FOUR 450G/1LB JARS

INGREDIENTS

1kg/2¼lb pickling onions
115g/4oz/½ cup salt
750ml/1¼ pints/3 cups
   malt vinegar
15ml/1 tbsp sugar
2–3 dried red chillies
5ml/1 tsp brown mustard seeds
15ml/1 tbsp coriander seeds
5ml/1 tsp allspice berries
5ml/1 tsp black peppercorns
5cm/2in piece fresh root
   ginger, sliced
2–3 blades of mace
2–3 fresh bay leaves

1 To peel the onions, trim off the root end, but leave the onion layers attached. Cut a thin slice off the top (neck) end of the onion. Place the onions in a bowl, then cover with boiling water. Leave to stand for about 4 minutes, then drain. The skin should then be easier to peel with a small, sharp knife.

2 Place the peeled onions in a bowl and cover with cold water, then drain the water off and pour it into a large saucepan. Add the salt and heat slightly to dissolve it, then cool before pouring the brine over the onions.

3 Cover the bowl with a plate and weigh it down slightly so that it keeps all the onions submerged in the brine. Leave the onions to stand in the salted water for 24 hours.

4 Place the vinegar in a large pan. Wrap all the remaining ingredients, except the bay leaves, in a piece of muslin or sew them into a coffee filter paper and add to the vinegar with the bay leaves. Bring to the boil, simmer for 5 minutes, then remove from the heat. Set aside to cool and infuse overnight.

5 Drain the onions, rinse and pat dry. Pack them into sterilized jars. Add some or all of the spice from the vinegar, but not the ginger slices. The pickle will get hotter if you add the chillies. Pour the vinegar over the onions to cover and add the bay leaves. Store any leftover vinegar in a bottle for your next batch of pickles. Cover the jars with non-metallic lids and store in a cool dark place for at least 6 weeks before eating

COOK'S TIP
For sterilizing, stand clean, rinsed jars upside down on a rack on a baking sheet and place in the oven at 180°C/350°F/Gas 4 for 20 minutes.

VARIATIONS
• The recipe above produces a crisp pickle. For softer onions, simmer the rinsed, salted onions in the malt vinegar for 2–3 minutes before packing them into sterilized jars, then pour over the hot vinegar. Cool the pickles, then seal with non-metallic lids.
• To make sweet pickled onions, follow the same method, but add 50g/2oz/4 tbsp light muscovado sugar to the vinegar. A couple of pieces of cinnamon stick and 5ml/1 tsp cloves are good additions to this version.

HOT THAI PICKLED SHALLOTS

THAI PINK SHALLOTS REQUIRE LENGTHY PREPARATION, BUT THEY LOOK EXQUISITE IN THIS SPICED PICKLE. THE SHALLOTS ARE GOOD, FINELY SLICED, AS A CONDIMENT TO SOUTH-EAST ASIAN MEALS.

MAKES TWO TO THREE JARS

INGREDIENTS
5–6 small red or green bird's eye
   chillies, halved and seeded, if liked
500g/1¼lb Thai pink shallots, peeled
2 large garlic cloves, peeled, halved
   and green shoot removed
For the vinegar
600ml/1 pint/2½ cups cider vinegar
40g/1½oz/3 tbsp granulated sugar
10ml/2 tsp salt
5cm/2in piece fresh root
   ginger, sliced
15ml/1 tbsp coriander seeds
2 lemon grass stalks, cut in
   half lengthways
4 kaffir lime leaves or strips of
   lime rind
15ml/1 tbsp chopped fresh coriander

1 If leaving the chillies whole (they will be hotter if you leave the seeds in), prick them several times with a cocktail stick. Bring a large pan of water to the boil. Blanch the chillies, shallots and garlic for 1–2 minutes, then drain. Rinse all the vegetables under cold water, then leave to drain.

2 To prepare the vinegar, put the cider vinegar, sugar, salt, ginger, coriander seeds, lemon grass and lime leaves or lime rind in a saucepan and bring to the boil. Simmer over a low heat for 3–4 minutes, then leave to cool.

3 Discard the ginger, then bring the vinegar back to the boil. Add the fresh coriander, garlic and chillies, and cook for 1 minute.

4 Pack the shallots into sterilized jars, distributing the lemon grass, lime leaves, chillies and garlic between them. Pour over the hot vinegar. Cool, then seal and leave in a dark place for 2 months before eating.

COOK'S TIPS
• Always be careful when making pickles to ensure that bowls and saucepans used for vinegar are non-reactive, that is, they are not chemically affected by the acid of the vinegar. China and glass bowls and stainless steel pans are suitable.
• When packing pickles, ensure that metal lids will not come in contact with the pickle. The acid in the vinegar will corrode the metal. Use plastic-coated or glass lids with rubber rings. Alternatively, cover the top of the jar with a circle of cellophane or waxed paper to prevent direct contact when using metal lids.
• Take care when handling hot jars. Let them cool slightly after sterilizing and before filling to avoid burning yourself. However, do not let them cool completely, as they may then crack when the hot vinegar is poured in.

PICKLED MUSHROOMS <u>WITH</u> GARLIC <u>AND</u> RED ONION

THIS IS A POPULAR METHOD OF PRESERVING MUSHROOMS THROUGHOUT EUROPE. IT IS GOOD MADE WITH ONLY CULTIVATED MUSHROOMS, BUT TRY TO INCLUDE 1–2 SLICED CEPS FOR THEIR FLAVOUR.

3 Add the mushrooms and simmer for 3–4 minutes, then drain through a sieve. Retain all the herbs and spices.

4 Fill 1 large or 2 small sterilized, cooled jars with the mushrooms. Distribute the garlic, onion, herbs and spices evenly between the layers of mushrooms. Then pour in sufficient olive oil to cover by at least 1cm/½in. You may need extra oil if you use 2 jars.

5 Leave the pickle to settle, then tap the jars on the work surface to dispel any air bubbles. Seal with lids, then leave to stand for at least 2 weeks in a cool, dark place before using.

COOK'S TIP
To keep the mushrooms underneath the oil, wedge 2 wooden cocktail sticks or lengths off a wooden skewer crossways in the neck of the jar.

MAKES 600ML/1 PINT/2½ CUPS

INGREDIENTS
500g/1¼lb mixed mushrooms such as small ceps, chestnut mushrooms, shiitake and girolles
300ml/½ pint/1¼ cups white wine vinegar or cider vinegar
15ml/1 tbsp sea salt
5ml/1 tsp caster sugar
300ml/½ pint/1¼ cups water
4–5 fresh bay leaves
8 large fresh thyme sprigs
15 garlic cloves, peeled and halved, any green shoots removed
1 small red onion, halved and thinly sliced
2–3 small dried red chillies
5ml/1 tsp coriander seeds, lightly crushed
5ml/1 tsp black peppercorns
few strips of lemon rind
250–350ml/8–12fl oz/1–1½ cups extra virgin olive oil

1 Trim and wipe all the mushrooms. (It is better not to wash them, as they absorb water easily and can become waterlogged. Simply wipe them with a damp cloth or kitchen paper.) Cut large mushrooms in half.

2 Put the vinegar, salt, sugar and water in a saucepan and bring to the boil. Add all the remaining ingredients, apart from the mushrooms and oil. Simmer for 2 minutes.

COCONUT CHUTNEY <u>WITH</u> ONION <u>AND</u> CHILLI

SERVE THIS REFRESHING FRESH CHUTNEY AS AN ACCOMPANIMENT FOR INDIAN-STYLE DISHES OR WITH A RAITA AND OTHER CHUTNEYS AND POPPADUMS AT THE START OF A MEAL.

SERVES FOUR TO SIX

INGREDIENTS
   200g/7oz fresh coconut, grated
   3–4 green chillies, seeded
      and chopped
   20g/¾oz fresh coriander, chopped
   30ml/2 tbsp chopped fresh mint
   30–45ml/2–3 tbsp lime juice
   about 2.5ml/½ tsp salt
   about 2.5ml/½ tsp caster sugar
   15–30ml/1–2 tbsp coconut
      milk (optional)
   30ml/2 tbsp groundnut oil
   5ml/1 tsp kalonji
   1 small onion, very finely chopped
   fresh coriander sprigs, to garnish

COOK'S TIP
Add more chillies if you prefer a chutney
with a hotter flavour.

1 Place the coconut, chillies, coriander
and mint in a food processor. Add
30ml/2 tbsp of the lime juice, then
process until thoroughly chopped.

2 Scrape the mixture into a bowl and
add more lime juice to taste. Add salt
and sugar to taste. If the mixture is dry,
stir in 15–30ml/1–2 tbsp coconut milk.

3 Heat the oil in a small pan and fry
the kalonji until they begin to pop, then
reduce the heat and add the onion. Fry,
stirring frequently, for 4–5 minutes, until
the onion softens but does not brown.

4 Stir the onion mixture into the
coconut mixture and leave to cool.
Garnish with coriander before serving.

ONION, MANGO <u>AND</u> PEANUT CHAAT

CHAATS ARE SPICED RELISHES OF VEGETABLES AND NUTS SERVED WITH INDIAN MEALS. AMCHOOR
(MANGO POWDER) ADDS A DELICIOUSLY FRUITY SOURNESS TO THIS MIXTURE OF ONIONS AND MANGO.

SERVES FOUR

INGREDIENTS
   90g/3½oz/scant 1 cup
      unsalted peanuts
   15ml/1 tbsp peanut oil
   1 onion, chopped
   10cm/4in piece cucumber, seeded
      and cut into 5mm/¼in dice
   1 mango, peeled, stoned and diced
   1 green chilli, seeded and chopped
   30ml/2 tbsp chopped fresh coriander
   15ml/1 tbsp chopped fresh mint
   15ml/1 tbsp lime juice
   pinch of light muscovado sugar
For the chaat masala
   10ml/2 tsp ground toasted
      cumin seeds
   2.5ml/½ tsp cayenne pepper
   5ml/1 tsp mango powder (amchoor)
   2.5ml/½ tsp garam masala
   pinch ground asafoetida
   salt and ground black pepper

1 To make the chaat masala, grind all
the spices together, then season with
2.5ml/½ tsp each of salt and pepper.

2 Fry the peanuts in the oil until lightly
browned, then drain on kitchen paper
until cool.

COOK'S TIP
Any remaining chaat masala will keep in
a sealed jar for 4–6 weeks.

3 Mix the onion, cucumber, mango,
chilli, fresh coriander and mint. Sprinkle
in 5ml/1 tsp of the chaat masala. Stir in
the peanuts and then add lime juice
and/or sugar to taste. Set the mixture
aside for 20–30 minutes for the flavours
to mature.

4 Turn the mixture into a serving bowl,
sprinkle another 5ml/1 tsp of the chaat
masala over and serve.

CONFIT OF SLOW-COOKED ONIONS

THIS JAM OF SLOW-COOKED, CARAMELIZED ONIONS IN SWEET-SOUR BALSAMIC VINEGAR WILL KEEP FOR SEVERAL DAYS IN A SEALED JAR IN THE FRIDGE. YOU CAN USE RED, WHITE OR YELLOW ONIONS, BUT YELLOW ONIONS WILL GIVE THE SWEETEST RESULT. SHALLOTS ALSO MAKE AN EXCELLENT CONFIT.

SERVES SIX TO EIGHT

INGREDIENTS
    30ml/2 tbsp olive oil
    15g/½oz/1 tbsp butter
    500g/1¼lb onions, sliced
    3–5 fresh thyme sprigs
    1 fresh bay leaf
    30ml/2 tbsp light muscovado sugar,
      plus a little extra
    50g/2oz/¼ cup ready-to-eat
      prunes, chopped
    30ml/2 tbsp balsamic vinegar, plus
      a little extra
    120ml/4fl oz/½ cup red wine
    salt and ground black pepper

1 Reserve 5ml/1 tsp of the oil, then heat the rest with the butter. Add the onions, cover and cook gently for 15 minutes, stirring occasionally.

2 Season well with salt and pepper, then add the thyme, bay leaf and sugar. Cook slowly, uncovered, for another 15–20 minutes, until the onions are very soft and dark.

3 Add the prunes, vinegar and wine with 60ml/4 tbsp water and cook over a low heat, stirring frequently, for a further 20 minutes, or until most of the liquid has evaporated. Add a little water and reduce the heat if the mixture dries too quickly.

4 Adjust the seasoning, adding more sugar and/or vinegar to taste. Leave the confit to cool, then stir in the remaining 5ml/1 tsp oil. The confit is best stored for 24 hours before eating. Serve either cold or warm.

VARIATION
Baby onions with tomato & orange Gently fry 500g/1¼lb peeled pickling onions or small *cipolline* in 60ml/4 tbsp olive oil until lightly browned, then sprinkle in 45ml/3 tbsp of brown sugar. Let the onions caramelize a little, then add 7.5ml/1½ tsp crushed coriander seeds, 250ml/8fl oz/1 cup red wine, 2 bay leaves, a few thyme sprigs, 3 strips orange zest and 45ml/3 tbsp tomato purée and the juice of 1 orange. Cook very gently, covered, for 1 hour, stirring occasionally until the sauce is thick and reduced. Uncover for the last 20 minutes of cooking time. Sharpen with 15–30ml/1–2 tbsp sherry vinegar and serve cold, sprinkled with chopped parsley.

RED ONION, GARLIC AND LEMON RELISH

THIS POWERFUL RELISH IS FLAVOURED WITH NORTH-AFRICAN SPICES AND PUNCHY PRESERVED LEMONS, AVAILABLE FROM DELICATESSENS AND LARGER SUPERMARKETS OR FROM MIDDLE-EASTERN FOOD STORES.

3 Add a pinch of salt, lots of pepper and the sugar, and cook, uncovered, for 5 minutes. Soak the saffron in about 45ml/3 tbsp warm water for 5 minutes, then add to the onions, with the soaking water. Add the cinnamon stick, dried chillies, if using, and bay leaves. Stir in 30ml/2 tbsp of the sherry vinegar and the orange juice.

4 Cook over a low heat, uncovered, until the onions are very soft and most of the liquid has evaporated. Stir in the preserved lemon and cook gently for a further 5 minutes. Taste and adjust the seasoning, adding more salt, sugar and/or vinegar to taste.

5 Serve warm or cold, but not hot or chilled. The relish tastes best if it is allowed to stand for 24 hours.

VARIATION
To make a quick Lebanese onion relish, chop 500g/1¼lb ripe tomatoes and combine with 1 bunch of sliced spring onions (or 4–6 small grelots). Crush 2 cloves of garlic with a large pinch of salt and gradually work in 15ml/1 tbsp lemon juice and 45–60ml/3–4 tbsp extra virgin olive oil. Toss the tomatoes and onions with the dressing and stir in a small bunch of chopped purslane or 30ml/2 tbsp of chopped marjoram or lemon thyme, then adjust the seasoning with salt, pepper, a pinch or two of sugar and maybe more lemon juice. Serve with grilled lamb or chicken or a grain salad made with bulgur wheat or couscous.

SERVES SIX

INGREDIENTS
 45ml/3 tbsp olive oil
 3 large red onions, sliced
 2 heads of garlic, separated into
  cloves and peeled
 10ml/2 tsp coriander seeds, crushed
  but not finely ground
 10ml/2 tsp light muscovado sugar,
  plus a little extra
 pinch of saffron strands
 5cm/2in piece cinnamon stick
 2–3 small whole dried red
  chillies (optional)
 2 fresh bay leaves
 30–45ml/2–3 tbsp sherry vinegar
 juice of ½ small orange
 30ml/2 tbsp chopped
  preserved lemon
 salt and ground black pepper

1 Heat the oil in a heavy saucepan. Add the onions and stir, then cover and reduce the heat to the lowest setting. Cook for 10–15 minutes, stirring occasionally, until the onions are soft.

2 Add the garlic cloves and coriander seeds. Cover and cook for 5–8 minutes until they are soft.

INDEX

ACKNOWLEDGEMENTS

Photographs are all by William Lingwood except those on the following pages: p6, p7b, p18 The Anthony Blake Photo Library; p7t, p19b Cephas; p8, p13tr, p14t, p17b, p20 The Bridgeman Art Library; p9t, p10t, p10b The Ancient Egypt Picture Library; p9b, p10b, p11t, p11b, p13tl, p14b, p16t, p16b, p21t, p21b, p22b, p23t Mary Evans Picture Library; p12, p14b, p15 e.t. archive; p13b, p22t, p23b AKG Photographic Library; p17t Hulton Getty Picture Library; p19t Food Features; p24,

p28b John Freeman; p28r, p36l, A–Z Botanical Collection Ltd; p37tl Michelle Garrett.
    The author would like to acknowledge the following for their inspiration and information: John Ayto, *A Gourmet's Guide* (Oxford, 1994); Lindsey Bareham, *Onions Without Tears* (London, 1995); Barbara Ciletti, *The Onion Harvest Cookbook* (Newtown, CT, 1998); Bruce Cost, *Foods from the Far East* (London, 1990); William J. Darby and Paul Ghalioungui, *Food: The Gift of Osiris*, 2 volumes (London, 1977); Alan Davidson, *The*

Oxford Companion to Food (Oxford, 1999); John Edwards, *The Roman Cookery of Apicius* (London, 1984); John Evelyn, *Acetaria: A Discourse of Sallets* (1699), edited by Christopher Driver and Tom Jaine (Totnes, 1996); *Four Seasons of the House of Cerruti*, edited and translated by Judith Spencer (New York, NY, 1983); M. Grieve, *A Modern Herbal*, edited by C. F. Leyel (London, 1931, 1998); Dorothy Hartley, *Food in England* (1954, 1996); Katy Holder and Gail Duff, *A Clove of Garlic* (London, 1996);

C. F. Leyel and Hartley, Olga *The Gentle Art of Cookery* (London, 1925, 1974); Harold McGee, *On Food and Cooking: The Science and Lore of the Kitchen* (London, 1991); Charmaine Solomon, *The Encyclopedia of Asian Food* (London, 1998); Colin Spencer, *Vegetable Book* (London, 1995); Tom Stobart, *The Cook's Encyclopaedia* (London, 1998); Waverley Root, *Food* (New York, NY, 1980); J. G. Vaughan and C. A. Geissler, *The New Oxford Book of Food Plants* (Oxford, 1997).

NOTES

NOTES

NOTES

NOTES

NOTES

NOTES

NOTES

NOTES